Kids Can Program Too!

Second Java Edition

By Ely Eshel

ISBN: 1463764014
ISBN-13: 978-1463764012

*To my wife Batia, without whose encouragement and patience
this book would have never been written or published*

*To my children Eynat and Ben, without whose inspiration
this book would not have been conceived*

Table of Contents

PREFACE

This section is like the "orientation" for this book – it sketches the book's overall picture. We will explain why this book was written and why it's useful, describe how it teaches (this is mostly for parents and educators), preview the other sections in the book, and (very important!) explain the special symbols and typefaces used in the book.

What you will learn in this section:

➢ *Why this book was written and what you can get out of it*
➢ *How this book will teach you*
➢ *How this book is structured*
➢ *What do the different symbols and types of letters mean*

Who Needs Another Book About Programming?

Another book about programming? Who needs it? A very good question, considering the following: just go to any book store (real or online), find the "Computers" section and look for a book on programming – and you'll find dozens.

So why not pick one of them? When you look through any of these books, you'll soon see that they are not for you. They are all for grown-ups – either professionals with years of experience in the Computer Industry, or college students studying towards a degree in Computer Sciences or related subject. Even those for "Dummies" are for grown-up dummies…

Some of these books assume a lot of math knowledge. Many expect programming experience. Others are just so boring that one can fall asleep by Chapter 2… None of them was designed to teach programming to children. The text is hard to read and the examples difficult to understand since they don't come from your world, but from the worlds of the adults who wrote them.

This book is different! It uses everyday language and words you are used to (no profanity, though!). The examples are taken, as much as possible, from your life at home or at school and from activities you have with your friends. It is easy to read and understand, and should be fun to study.

It's Not Only *WHAT* You Learn, It's Also *HOW* You Learn!

Programming is not an easy subject to master, but it's not terribly complicated either. There are rules you have to learn, techniques and procedures to accomplish various tasks, and "tricks of the trade" for making things easy. Mostly, programming is a way to think about problem solving. Very similar to solving math problem, programming is a collection of methods that allow you, the programmer, to tell the computer how to solve a problem. But before telling the computer, you have to know what steps have to be taken – if you don't know how the problem can be solved, you cannot write a program to solve it!

It may sound a bit "unexciting," but there is one major reason why programming is much more interesting than plain math – the results are practical. When you solve a math problem, you get some numbers or formulas; when you write a program, you get the computer to *do* something and show you the results. There is an immediate sense of accomplishment in seeing your computer program work and produce the desired result.

This is also the main reason why learning to program is enjoyable – it's based not only on memorizing rules (even though it is a necessary part of the learning process), but mostly on actually writing and running programs. Teachers will call it "Teaching by Example," but we call it "Learning by Doing." This book is a chockfull of examples. For every subject you learn, there are "snippet" of programs or full programs that demonstrate how to apply it. And you can take these examples and change them to your heart's content, experimenting as much as you want. At worst, your program wouldn't work and you'll have to figure out why; at best, you'll immediately see the results of your experiments!

You will Get There, Step By Step…

Almost every time you started a new subject in school, the beginning seemed slow. You had to learn "the basics" of the new topic – terms, definitions, rules etc. – and it wasn't much fun… Only later, where all the pieces of the puzzle started falling in place, the pace picked up and it became more interesting. Unfortunately, there is no way around it: you have to learn to crawl before you can learn to walk.

Part One of the book, "*Who's Who in Hardware and Software,*" does not really talk about programming at all, even though it discusses programs. It describes the pieces that make up a computer, and will provide you with some necessary terminology and perspective. You may think you know much of the stuff described there (and you may be right), but even if you feel that way – please *do* read this section anyway. If you don't know much about the insides of a computer, this section will be a great introduction. It's also quite entertaining: I bet you've never visited an amusement park which is the inside of a computer!

Part Two, "*Programming Boot Camp,*" is the central part of the book. This is where you'll learn all the important stuff about programming. The section start slow (as you were warned…) but it the pace quickly picks up. As a matter of fact, you'll already be writing real program in the first few minutes! The rest of the section will take you step-by-step through all the details of the building blocks you need in order to put together useful programs.

Part Three, "*Object Oriented Programming,*" goes into the latest technology in programming. It builds on what you learned in Part Two, and shows you how all that can be applied to an amazing technique for developing programs that are easier to write and understand.

Part Four, "*The Nitty-Gritty Details,*" is a special section which addresses the practical aspects of writing and testing programs. It will tell you how to set up the environment for using the examples in this book; how to write, edit, and run a program; and how to deal with problems. It is highly recommend that you read this section *first* if you intend to set up a development environment and try out the examples. There you will also find how to download the examples in case you have the hard-copy version of the book (they come packaged together with the eBook version).

This Is What The Symbols Mean…

This book, like most technical and scientific books, is using a set of **notations** ("a system of symbols used in a specialized field to represent numbers, quantities or values") so certain words are written in different visual ways to tell you that they have specific meanings. We use different typefaces (sometimes called fonts when talking about computers) to show you that a particular word or a group of words is special.

The commonly used typeface is used almost everywhere. The `Courier` typeface is used for examples and excerpts (a group of words) from examples.

TEXT

Words in *italics* are used only for emphasis. For example, in the sentence, "do this *before* you do anything else," the word "before" is emphasized.

Words in **bold** are new terms. The text surrounding these words defines and explains them, and you will also find them defined in the Glossary at the end of the book. Often, the new word will be completely new to you, and this will be the first time it is explained. Sometimes you may already know the word itself, but here it is considered a new term because it has a special meaning when discussed in the context of computers and programming.

Words in **_bold italics_** are also new terms, but the precise definition and full explanation are to appear later in the book – at this point you are expected to understand the meaning intuitively. Do not worry if you feel your understanding of these words is incomplete – it will be taken care of later in the book.

Words and symbols in the `Courier` typeface are taken from programs. They may be taken from complete code examples, or are words that have particular meaning for the computer, and are not used as ordinary words in a text but as special words in a program.

Words and symbols in the `Courier` typeface between angel brackets (< and >) describe a piece of code, and in a program will be replaced by actual code. You will see these mostly in Parts Two and Three of this book.

EXAMPLES

Complete examples of programs are in the `Courier` typeface, and are also `shaded`. The lines are numbered:

```
01   // This is an example line
02   // followed by another
```

The output (results) of a program, which are usually displayed on the screen, is also `shaded`, but the lines are not numbered:

```
This is the output
of a program
```

If the output includes some input as well (what you may be typing at the keyboard), it will be in the shaded area but also in **_bold italic_**:

```
The following number is input: 12345
```

You will see these mostly in Parts Two and Three of this book.

PART ONE – WHERE DO HARDWARE AND SOFTWARE LIVE?

In order to understand what programming does, you have to understand the environment in which it is used. First, let us take a "virtual tour" of the inside of a computer, visiting the hardware components. Then, the software will be thrown in to show what it is supposed to do with the hardware.

What you will learn in this section:

> *What is the difference between hardware and software*
> *What are the main parts of the computer's hardware*
> *How does the software make the hardware work*

You may have heard a technician, trying to fix a "misbehaving" computer, mumbling, "This is a software problem, not a hardware problem." What does it mean? Which "part" of the computer was the technician referring to?

In that particular case, he was "blaming" an invisible part of the computer – its software. But his mention of the visible part – the hardware – is significant too. Just as you learned in school that a person has both physical (skeleton, muscles) and mental (mind, behavior) parts, a computer has a hardware part and a software part. And just like a

person, for a computer to function properly both parts must work together. The division of responsibilities between software and hardware is also somewhat similar to that between the physical and the mental – the hardware is where the software "lives," but it's the software that tells the hardware what to do.

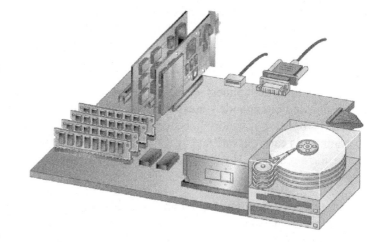

Programming is the skill of creating software. But the software depends on the hardware for its existence, so you need to understand what the hardware is and how it relates to the software. To achieve that, let's take a look inside a computer and identify where exactly the software resides and how it accomplishes its tasks of controlling the hardware.

Hardware: Adventures in the Park

> *What are all these chips and boards? Why do you need them? You will "walk through" a typical Personal Computer (PC), and get to know the major components that make it a computer. As part of this tour, you will also find out how these components need to work together in order for the PC to function, and understand what are the relationships among them – who is leading and who is following.*
>
> *What you will learn in this chapter:*
> - *What is the computer's Central Processing Unit (CPU)*
> - *How are memory and disks used*
> - *What other devices can be hooked up to the computer*

Welcome to "Computer Park," where the inside of the computer is open for your amusement!

You are entering one of many parks – there is one for each individual computer. Please keep in mind that most of the parks are similar, but not identical, because each computer may have a slightly different configuration – which means that not all parks have exactly the same set of "attractions."

Before you embark on your virtual tour, let's look at a park's map. As you look at it for the first time, you'll notice that part of the park is situated on a bunch of islands, while other "attractions" are on the periphery, around the lake. The lake is the computer itself, while the other "attractions" are rightly called **peripherals**. You must go through the peripherals in order to get to the main area – the islands in the middle.

All the attractions are connected by a **bus**. There are no direct connections between the attractions: all "passengers" – information and commands – must travel on the bus from one attraction to the next. The term "bus" is somewhat misleading, because it's more like a central "highway" on which everyone travels; it's named so because information and commands can "get on" and "get off" at any stop – which is a path or a bridge to the attraction itself – just like when using a real bus. This bus, however, travels at an extremely high speed – you can barely see it flashing in front of your eyes…

Another thing worth noting, although the park's map does not show it, is that some of the paths and bridges are wide, while others are narrow. Naturally, more people can walk between the islands (or any other attraction) and the bus, using wide bridges and paths than narrow ones. For examples, a class of students may walk 8 side-by-side across a wide bridge, but have to go single file on a narrow bridge. This characteristic is called **bandwidth**. That means that the wide paths serve heavier traffic, where volume or speed are important. The bus itself also changes its size (width) – it is much larger (wider) in some areas, allowing for more passengers to travel there.

It does not appear on the map, but it's worth mentioning that information moves across the park in pre-defined units. Unlike people, who are all different (tall and short, fat and skinny), information comes in one size – a byte. But a byte is not an indivisible unit – it is actually made up of 8 bits; each bit is so small that it can either be a zero or a one, nothing else.

Each byte represents a number or a character. If you need to say more, use more bytes. For example, if a number is too large to fit in one byte, 2 or more bytes have be used; a sentence will not fit in one byte (unless it is a one-letter sentence…), so you need a string of bytes tied together to hold this sentence. Going back to the issue of bandwidth, the wide bridges can carry several bytes in **parallel** (one *alongside* the other), while the narrow bridges must carry them **serially** (one *after* the other). The really narrow bridges, "Tightrope bridges," can carry only one bit at a time – a process called bit-serial communications or just a serial connection for short. The most common serial interface is USB, which means Universal Serial Bus. It used today for many devices, including printers, scanners, keyboards, mice, disk drives, cell phones, cameras, etc. Another serial interface is SATA, which we will briefly discuss later.

CPU – THE REAL BRAIN

Even though a visitor must take the long way, from the outside in, let us start in the middle – the central island, called *CPU Island* (marked ❶ on the map). The word **CPU** stands for Central Processing Unit, another name for the processor – the "chip" that is the central part of the computer. The chips that most people are familiar with are the Intel® Pentium® chips, but there are quite a few other types.

CPU Island is the control center, or the brains of the whole operation. The CPU is the component that runs the show – this is where the programs run that tell the peripherals what to do. You might look at it as the "event coordinator" – it has a plan (like a script), and based on information reported to it, it decides what to do and sends instructions and information to the other members of the team. You will soon see (in *"The 'Essence' of Programming"*) that the scripts are the programs you are learning to write. You will also find out who the other members of the team are and what they do.

In real life, the CPU is a chip – that is, a highly condensed collection of transistors (and it doesn't really matter what these are…), packaged in a small container with many tiny metal feet sticking out to connect it to the rest of the electronics in the computer.

MEMORY – THE BRAIN'S IMMEDIATE STORAGE

A short walk across the wide bridge takes us from CPU Island to *Memory City* (marked ❷ on the map). It turns out that the CPU has hardly any room for storage – everything it needs is stored in Memory City. Every scrap of information the CPU needs has to be swiftly brought over from memory; every result of the CPU's operations must be quickly stored in memory too. The CPU can hold only very few pieces of information, those on which it is actually working at the moment (and it holds them in **registers**), as well as a very small part of the program which it is running (and this is held in **cache**). We will discuss that later, in *"Stored Programs."*

In order to find things quickly, the memory is organized as a grid of cells, each one with its own number. It may look like a map of a well-organized city, where all the houses are of equal size, all the blocks are perfect squares and all the streets are straight (even though such cities exists only in science fiction). But that would not be enough: in order to get to a house you would still need to drive through the streets, and the further the house is from the edge of town, the longer the drive. So Memory City has a really neat transportation system – transporter beams; every house has a transporter pod and you can get in and out of each house directly. Transporter beams can take you from any of the city's entrances to the house of your choice, but they only work within the city; you must use a bridge to get in or out of the city.

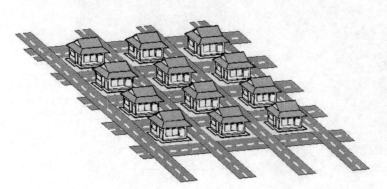

One of the problems with Memory City is that whatever is remembered is good for the moment only. When the park closes, and electricity is turned off, all is forgotten. So you have to be very careful not to use it for stuff that you may need the next day – you must have another place to store that stuff, and it will be shown to you shortly.

The faster the CPU can work, the faster information has to move back and forth between CPU Island and Memory City. That's why we need a very high bandwidth (remember the width of the bridge?) as well as the shortest possible distance between the two. This is why the bus connecting CPU Island and Memory City is also very wide.

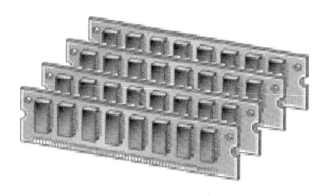

Real memory is also made out of chips, but they are usually smaller and have a different packaging than the CPU. There are so many different types of memory that it is difficult to discuss this subject here, particularly since it is not relevant to learning how to program.

Computer memory is using the **binary** method to store information. Binary means that each unit of information can have only one of *two* values: zero or one. We mentioned earlier that traffic on the bridges is in units of bytes, each one made up of 8 bits. Information in memory is stored exactly the same way – in bytes, each of which has 8 bits. Without going into the math of the binary method (you may have learned that in school), let us just state that a single byte can hold any number between 0 and 255. Larger numbers require more bytes to hold them. Characters (like letters, digits, spaces, question marks, etc.) are usually represented by a byte each, where the value stored in the byte (0 to 255) represent the character – each character has a unique value.

DISKS – FOR LONG-TERM AND LARGE QUANTITIES

The cost of building a place like Memory City is very high, with all the transporters and those special storehouses. What can we do if we need to store much more information, but cannot afford more memory? We need another storage facility, one that can hold more information at a lower cost, and also save it permanently (remember – memory can forget…), or at least until you decide to get rid of it on your own (as if that ever happens…) This is why *Storage Towers* were built (marked ❸ on the map).

Storage Towers are made up of vast cylinders, each holding a stack of spinning platters. Special moving ramps (called **heads**) float above each platter, and from the ramps you can put information on the platter or pick it up.

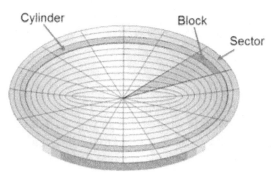

The platters are divided into concentric – one within the other – circles (each one called a **cylinder**) which are identified by their distance from the center of the platter. Each cylinder is divided into **sectors**, just like slices of a pie. In order to get a specific piece of information, you need to know what platter it's on (so that you can pick the right head), which cylinder it's on (so that you know how far from the edge the head has to move) and which sector it's in. You then move the head over the cylinder and wait for the sector to pass below you – this is the **block** you're after –and grab the information (or drop it) at the exact moment the sector shows up. It takes a lot of practice…

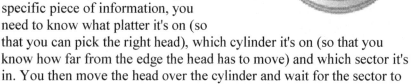

It's amazing that anything can stick to the platters, considering the high speed at which they are rotating. The explanation (even though inaccurate) is that the platters are usually magnetic, and that's how they hold on to the information. There's nothing physical that has to stick – it's only changes in magnetic fields.

How does the information in Storage Towers gets to CPU Island? Via bridge to the bus, of course, and through Memory City. A wide bridge connects Storage Towers to the bus, because the amount of traffic between the two is very large and it has to move fast. The script that the CPU is running includes instructions to Storage Towers to send information down to Memory City, or to take information from there and store it in the towers. These instructions go through a narrow bridge (instructions are very short, and do not need high bandwidth) directly from CPU Island to Storage Towers.

A storage tower is called a **disk drive**. There are many types of drives, varying in size (how much information they can hold), speed (how fast the platters spin and how fast the heads move), and media type (what are the platters made of and whether they are fixed or can be removed), but they all operate in a similar manner.

CD-ROM and DVD drives work substantially the same, but instead of using magnetic technology to read and write they use optical (laser) technology.

Sometimes disk storage is considered a peripheral device, because it is not part of the close relationship between the CPU and memory. But for the purpose of this discussion, we consider disks as part of the "inner circle", and this is why they deserve to have their own island. CD-ROM and DVD drives are truly peripherals, and that's where you'll find them – in the peripherals section of the park (see below).

Disk drives communicate with the CPU and memory in several ways. Just to mention a few that you might encounter when discussing Personal Computers: the most common interface for PCs is ATA or IDE, which are practically identical and are acronyms for AT Attachment and Integrated Drive Electronics, respectively. Newer PCs use SATA, or Serial ATA, which is faster. Very rarely you may find a PC with a SCSI interface and disks; an acronym for Small Computer System Interface, this interface and the disk drives that use it are much faster and more reliable, but also more expensive.

If you are wondering about the flash drives and the various memory cards used in digital cameras and cell phones, here is the scoop: they are actually memory, but they pretend to behave like disk drives in the way they communicate with the computer's CPU and real memory. So are SSD (Solid State Drives) devices, which provide disk-like interfaces at memory speed.

PERIPHERAL DEVICES – MONITORS, KEYBOARDS AND MICE, OH MY!

The peripheral "attractions" in Computer Park are only peripheral in the sense that they are not "the main attraction"; they are nevertheless very important, and without them it would be impossible to enjoy the park – the islands would be inaccessible, so what good will they be?

The peripherals section has four theme areas – _User Interface Square_ (map area ❹), _The Comm Arcade_ (map area ❺), _The Input Pavilion_ (map area ❻) and _The Output Zone_ (map area ❼).

User Interface

There are several attractions around User Interface Square, also known as UI Square. The main one is _Monitor Amphitheatre_ (map location A). This is where you can watch all the action on the islands without being there. The amphitheater is connected to the bus, and thus to Memory City, via two one-way paths: a wide path and a narrow one. Why one-way? Because information goes only from memory to the monitor, never the other way! Why the narrow path? To send instructions to the crew at the amphitheater. And the wide path? There is a lot of information (besides the instructions) that needs to get to the amphitheater very fast – the scenery can change 50 times a second!

The way it works is like this: the CPU puts in Memory City the information to be displayed, and sends the instructions on how to display it over the narrow path; the crew of Monitor Amphitheatre gets the instructions, and then the information itself over the wide path as fast as possible, and performs the acts and stunts they are directed to accomplish – called the **video** presentation.

Monitor Amphitheatre is an output venue. The other two booths in UI Square are for input. One is _Keyboard Korner_ (map location B) and the other is _Mouse Hole_ location C). At Keyboard Korner, you can hop and skip all over the keyboard – every key you step on will send its symbol to the CPU via the bus, over the special narrow path. At Mouse Hole, you chase the mouse, and every one of its movements is sent to the CPU; when you tap the mouse on the head, this too is sent to the CPU, as a "click". Mouse Hole, just like Keyboard Korner, is using its own narrow path.

What the CPU does with the information it gets from the keyboard and the mouse depends on the script it is running. It would usually send the information back to the monitor, showing the characters that were typed in or moving the mouse cursor, in addition to perhaps storing the keystrokes or making decisions on its next action based on mouse movements and clicks.

Communications

The Comm Arcade is where you can find all kinds of options to communicate with other parks. Sadly, in most cases your park admission ticket will only get you into the arcade, but you will have to pay in order to use any of the booths. Only if you are communicating with a park to which you already have a season pass or has another "affiliation" (such as your school network, a sibling's park, etc.) will you be exempt from additional fees.

Each booth provides a different method of communication, and not all booths are always available at all parks. You may be able to connect to another park via any of several booths, and the difference may be in the cost and the speed of this connection.

The slowest booth, and least expensive one, is _Modem Peak_ (map location D). It uses regular telephone lines, and you have to dial up a specific number for your destination. Modems provide the slowest connections because they operate like very long tightrope bridges, moving one bit a time, and the bits are assembled into bytes at the other end. Modem Peak is connected to the bus via a tightrope bridge, but the CPU is only responsible for sending and receiving the information one byte at a time – there is a small staging area just off CPU Island that takes the bytes and disassembles them into bits, and vice versa. Modems are rarely used anymore because of their slowness. If you want to use a modem to connect to the Internet, you would dial-up into another park (called an **ISP – Internet Service Provider**) that has a much faster connection to the Internet.

The fastest connection can be found in _LAN Lane_ (map location E) – LAN stands for Local Area Network. This particular booth has a wide path connecting to the bus, and its hookup to other parks is also fast. It is, however, usually limited in connectivity to nearby parks only (that's the "local" part of the name). The CPU, using a narrow path, sends instructions to LAN Lane to send or receive information from Memory City.

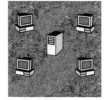

Speaking about the Internet – there is a booth called _WAN Ways_; WAN means "Wide Area Network". In this booth, you will find three stalls: back-to-back are standing the _Broadband Boys'_ stalls: Fiber Optics and Cable; opposite these stalls stands the _Wireless_ stall. All provide high-speed access to the Internet at a relatively low cost, without the need to dial anywhere. If you decide to use any one of these, and assuming that they are available in your particular park, their connection is always on to the ISP which provides them. The only downsides (why is there always a downside?!) are that there is no direct path from CPU Island to any of the Broadband Boys – the CPU must go through LAN Lane to get there, and LAN Lane treats each one as another park; and to get from the Wireless stall requires a special gizmo that uses a cellular phone for the connection. However, if you want to communicate with the Internet while your Computer Park is travelling, this is the booth you want to use!

A new addition to the Comm Arcade is the _Wireless Wing_. This area should not be confused with the Wireless stall in WAN Ways, although they have some very similar attractions. At present, there are two gaming boots: _Bluetooth Blast_ and _Wi-Fi Wheel_. At Bluetooth Blast you can communicate with peripheral devices that are close to the park, or even in the park, but have no direct roadway (namely wires) to connect to directly from Wireless Wing. These can be input and output peripherals (of which you'll read below), or more fun devices such as earphones. Wi-Fi Wheel is different – it is another way of connecting to other parks, much like from LAN Lane, but without any wired connection. This allows for communication to the Internet when your Computer Park is itself travelling.

The difference between Wi-Fi Wheel and Wan Way's Wireless stall is that Wi-Fi is usually limited in range so you need a "hot spot" to let your communication jump from Wi-Fi Wheel to the internet, while the Wireless stall only requires a cellular phone connection but is usually slower. So as you see, each good thing comes with a little bad thing…

Input

Input Palace is where you actually enter the park. Keyboard Cluster and Mouse Hole are in a sense part of the Input Zone too. What options do you have in getting into the park? Quite a few. _CD Corral_ (map location F) is where input comes from a CD-ROM or DVD drive. _The Scanner Picture Show_ (map location G) is where pictures are scanned in. _Mic's Place_ (map location H) is the place for audio input, using (you guessed it!) a microphone. These booths are not always available in all parks.

An obvious question at this point would be how do all these input devices work? The answer can be quite complex, and depends on the device. We will oversimplify the answers, because these details are not terribly important to learning how to program. So here goes…

CD-ROMs and DVDs work like disk drives (see section _"Disks – For Long-Term And Large Quantities"_ above).

Scanners and microphones use narrow oaths to go to the bus, and through it to CPU Island, where the CPU will take the information and send it to Memory City for temporary storage. Depending on the source, the CPU interprets the information differently – sounds (from the microphone) are vastly different than pictures (from the scanner), but they all show up as a pile of bytes for the CPU to handle. In most cases, after storing the information in memory, the CPU will direct Storage Towers to take it from Memory City and safely store it in one of the towers.

There are other booths in Input Palace, but for now, we have covered the important ones.

Output

You must leave the park through The Output Zone, and your choices are also quite extensive. For example, _Printer Palace_ (map location I) is where the printers are (Duh!) and

at _Audio Hut_ (map location J) you can listen to the speakers; in both cases, the CPU will send bytes of information to the device over the bus and then the narrow path, and the device will do what it has to do… _Burner Barn_ (map location K) is where you can burn your own CDs; in this case, only instructions travel over the narrow path, while the actual information to be written on the CD will come from Storage Towers through Memory City using the wide paths (after traveling on the bus, of course) – speed is very important when you burn a CD.

Just like at Input Palace, a few more booths may be available at The Output Zone (such as Video View, Speakers Stage, etc.), but we will not describe them now.

What you learned in this chapter:

↖ _The CPU controls the operation of the computer_

↖ _Memory is used for short-term storage of small quantities_

↖ _Disks are used for long-term and large-quantities storage_

↖ _Peripheral devices are used to get information in and out of the computer_

Software: Listen to the Man Behind the Curtain

You can see the hardware, but what makes it do anything? It's the software. But software is invisible – it's somewhere "in" the hardware! We will explain this mystery and uncover the secrets of how software makes hardware work.

What you will learn in this chapter:

- ➢ *What is a computer program*
- ➢ *What are the types of computer languages used to write programs*
- ➢ *How does the computer handle programs*
- ➢ *What is the computer's Operating System*

We hope you had fun in Computer Park. After you rest a little, it's time to continue on our road to learning how to program. But you still do not know what a program is, even though you may have an idea by now from you visit to the park. Let us remind you that when we described the CPU in "*CPU – The Real Brain*," we said that it has scripts to follow. These scripts are called **programs** in "computerese."

In the next few sections, we will investigate these scripts and find out what they are and how they are used.

THE 'ESSENCE' OF PROGRAMMING

Scripts are used to direct actors in a play or a movie – the script has every word they are supposed say, every move they are expected to make; the actors must follow the script *exactly*, or else the director may be very upset… A computer program is very similar: it tells the CPU *exactly* what to do, leaving nothing to its imaginations (not that it has any!), nor allowing any improvisation.

As you might expect, there are some differences between a movie script and a computer program. In a movie, actors have some room to express their interpretation of the scripts in the way they act – after all, this is what distinguishes a good actor from a bad one; in a computer program, however, no personal interpretations are allowed or possible – the computer is not supposed to have a personality anyway (we are talking about today's standard computers, not R2D2…)

Another major difference is a little bit more complicated, and more difficult to understand. We need a big word to describe it: **deterministic**, from the word *determine* – to decide conclusively. We also have to discuss this as a philosophical concept, but do not worry – it is important, and it will not take long...

A movie is deterministic – it can be repeated a hundred times, and it will always end the same way (the good guys always win…); the end was determined even before the movie started. Your life, on the other hand, is completely non-deterministic: you never know what might happen when you do something; you might have a good guess – that is how you are supposed to stay out of trouble! –   But sometimes even when you do the right thing the results can be different from what you wanted, almost unpredictable. Your life's script gives you the ability to make decisions based on the information in front of you, so the end has not been determined before the beginning.

A computer program is closer to a video game – it has the tricky appearance of being non-deterministic, but in reality it is fully deterministic. How can that be? When you play a video game, such as a car racing game, you decide what to do – how fast to drive the car, when and where to turn, which shortcut to take – this is the non-deterministic view – these are all your choices, nothing seems pre-determined. But (hopefully…) you know that the games reaction to every move you make has been determined when it was created – this is the deterministic reality – and the game does not learn anything new and does not change its behavior. Seems impossible? Of course not. The trick is for the program (in case you were wondering, the video game is actually a program running on the game console) to have all the possible actions and reactions in the script, and add to that the ability to make decisions based on your actions.

The way it works, and this is a very over-simplified description, is as follows: the program says that if you press the "left" button, your car will turn left; if there is a wall to your left, your car will be bounced back to the right, but if the road is clear and actually turns to the left, the car will continue to the left. The program must cover *all* the options at every moment of the game. If it does not, the program may crash or freeze! This is called a **bug**, and we will talk about these critters later (in "How to Tackle Errors" in Part Two of the book). So the non-deterministic illusion is that you can do whatever you want; the deterministic reality is that all your actions are expected and responses to them have been pre-programmed.

This is how you have to write your programs! You must expect all possible inputs to the program and decide on the response to each and every one, no exception! The ability to do that is another difference between a movie script and a program: a program has decision points, where it examines the current situation – the input received (the button you pressed) and the current status (where the car, the road and the wall are) – and make a decision as to what to do next (go left or bounce to the right).

The last important difference between the script of a play and a computer program has to do with the human intelligence. Humans are much more intelligent than computers, even though computers create the illusion of intelligence by being much faster than humans in performing their limited tasks. Most people understand the *meaning* of a request, even though the word used are not precise. For example, when you tell a friend, "drop in anytime," you don't expect him to actually drop from the sky. If you told a computer to drop in, assuming that it has these words in its vocabulary and can control its own movements, it might attempt to physically drop itself into your house. Computers are silly this way... Beyond this inability to understand idioms ("drop in" is an idiom) is the bigger inability to understand human thinking. You know that "10 - (3 + 7)" is different than "10 - 3 + 7." But if you tell another person to calculate "ten minus three-plus-seven" (you make a pause between the words "minus" and "there", and say the " three-plus-seven" quickly), the parentheses are likely to be "heard" by that person. But if you don't write the parentheses in a program, you are guaranteed that the computer will calculate without them, getting the wrong result. Computers are dumb this way... The lesson from these examples is: *computers do exactly what they are told, not necessarily what you meant them to do*. Keep this in mind – forgetting this rule is one of the major reasons for buggy programs!

STORED PROGRAMS

When you were visiting CPU Island in Computer Park, we told you that the CPU is following a script, and you now know that this is really a program. We say that the CPU is **running** the program, or **executing** it (the two words mean the same). Where does the CPU hold the program? Think it through: we haven't shown you any place that is dedicated to storing programs, so you have to assume that it is stored like any other information. Correct! Programs are stored in memory, together with the information they process (the **data**). The only way to know which part of memory holds a program and which holds data is by assigning separate memory regions to each. If you didn't know where a byte is in memory, you wouldn't be able to tell if it's a program byte or a data byte. This is called the **stored program** concept – programs are stored like data; as a matter of fact, they *are* data – this is the information the CPU needs to tell it what to do, this is the script it is following.

A computer may have many programs, but only a few running at any moment. For example, you may have several games on your computer, as well as your e-mail program, your instant messenger (IM) and a word processor. You probably have your IM program running all the time, run your e-mail program occasionally, and at the same time you could be working on a school paper using a word processor and playing a shoot'm'up game (not to mention talking on the phone with a friend, listening to music and watching TV – but at least these have nothing to do with the computer...) All the running programs must be in memory for the CPU to execute them, but those that are not in use – where are they? Again, using your detective mind, you should conclude that they are on a disk – the only place where a lot of information (like programs) can be stored indefinitely. When needed, namely when you tell the computer to run a program, it is brought into memory and stays there until you close it.

MACHINE AND ASSEMBLY LANGUAGES

If the programs in memory (and on disk) are stored as just bytes, what does a program look like? How do these bytes tell the CPU what to do? Bytes that represent programs have special meaning – they are not treated like numbers or characters, but as **machine instructions**. Each group of bytes represents one instruction. The size of the group depends on the specific type of CPU as well as on the instruction itself. The CPU picks up the instructions one after the other, in the order they are stored in memory, unless told otherwise. An instruction might be "add the number from this memory location to the number at that memory location," or "check if the number you have is greater than zero, and if so jump to the instruction over there." As you can see, instructions are generally very specific and perform one small action; some CPUs can understand more complex instructions than others. The CPU knows what an instruction is based on the values of the bytes, or, more precisely, the values of specific bits in those bytes – pretty complex, but after all that's what it was built to do…

The collection of machine instructions is frequently called the **machine language** – it's the only "language" the CPU really understands on its own. The machine language is different from one type of CPU to another, and may even be different among different versions of the same CPU type (for example, the Pentium® IV has a few more machine instructions than the Pentium® III).

Machine instructions are not really readable by people – they are just strings of bits (or bytes). In order to make it a little easier for us humans to deal with it, each machine instruction can usually be written in a human-readable form, as a command. This is called **assembly language**. Machine languages are the foundation of programming language, at the basement level; assembly languages are what you will find at the ground-level.

For example, the instructions to add two numbers in memory locations 100 and 110 and store the result in memory location 80 may look like this: "`ADD 100, 110, 80`" (in a completely make-believe machine language!). This is how a programmer would write the instruction, but it has yet to be translated into the machine language itself before the CPU can execute it. If you gave names to the memory locations, the instruction might be '`ADD FIRST, SECOND, RESULT`'.

Obviously, it's not easy writing programs in machine language. First, each instruction does so little, so you need many of them to accomplish even the tiniest task; besides being tedious, this also opens up the way for making more mistakes. Second, it's difficult to understand what a program does because every small task looks so long – as goes the saying that "you cannot see the forest for the trees…" Third, if you write a program in one CPU type's machine language, you would not be able to run it on any other CPU type unless you re-write it completely – this is called **portability**, or actually lack of it.

HIGH-LEVEL LANGUAGES

As you can probably guess from the description above, assembly languages are not that great. As a matter of fact, they are viewed as low-level languages. That is so because they are just a notch "higher on the evolution scale" than machine languages (just like a fish is higher than an amoeba) – but they are still very low on intelligence, ease-of-use and productivity. What the world needs are higher-level languages! And surely enough, there are plenty of those too… You may have heard about C or C++ (pronounced "see-plus-plus"), PERL (pronounced like "pearl"), and certainly Java. There are many many others, some of them tailored for specific applications (such as math or text processing) and some general-purpose. Continuing our climb up the stairs from the basement (machine languages) to the ground floor (assembly languages), we are now getting to the first and second floors (high level languages).

What all high-level languages have in common is that they are designed to be "evolutionally" more advanced – they are to assembly languages as apes are to slugs… What does that suggest? As a computer language, they are closer to what human beings can understand; they are "smarter" – and for a language it means that it would be easier for you to "express" yourself, namely write your program; they do not depend on a specific CPU type and can be used on practically any type, so they are portable.

There are many differences among the various high-level languages, with advantages and disadvantages to each; we are not going to write a "contrast and compare" essay now. Many programmers have their mind set on one, and only one, language, and are willing to defend it to the last drop of ink; we do not want to be caught in the cross-fire here… This book is using the Java language for all its examples, but the skills you learn here can be applied to any other high-level language you may choose to learn and use later.

ASSEMBLERS, COMPILERS AND INTERPRETERS

If we are using assembly languages or high-level languages, but the CPU can only understand the machine instructions as a sequence of bytes – how will the CPU be able to use the high-level or even low-level languages? Let us ask *you* a question: if you only speak English, and you need to talk with someone who knows another language, what would you do? An obvious solution would be to get a translator – someone who knows both languages and can translate what you are saying into the other person's language. In the same way, we have translators for computer programming languages too. The translator starts with the **source program**, a program written in an assembly or high-level language, and translates it into a machine language. The result of its work is called an **executable program**, because the CPU can then execute the program directly.

Assemblers

The simplest translator is called an **assembler**, and is used to translate from assembly language into machine language. It is a program that takes as input a program, written in assembly language (namely a program written and readable by a human), and turns it into a program in machine language (so that the CPU can take it and execute the machine instructions).

The work of an assembler is relatively simple: each line in the program (remember the examples of the `'ADD'` instruction above?) translates directly into a single machine instruction. The assembler may have to deal with names of and locations of storage areas, but not much more. Naturally, there is a different assembler for each machine language.

Compilers

Higher level languages are more of a challenge for the translators, which are now called **compilers**. The effort to translate a high-level language is much higher, and a compiler is tremendously more complex than an assembler. The result, however, is similar – an executable program. Each language must have its own compiler for each type of CPU, and that compiler produces machine language instructions for the specific CPU only, so the executable program generated by the compiler would be good only for that CPU type. Sometimes a compiler may be capable of producing programs in several machine languages (called **cross-compiling**), when you request it to do so, but it's quite rare and in most cases these machine languages would just be variations of the same CPU type. So for each high-level language (and there are quite a few!) we need as many compilers as there are types of CPUs (and there are so many of these too!) It does make life complicated, doesn't it? Unlike assemblers, though, the same source program can be given to different compilers running on different CPUs; the resulting executable programs, even though different in their machine instructions, should perform exactly the same – each on the CPU for which it was compiled.

Interpreters

But compilers are not the only way we can use high-level languages. In our attempts to simplify things, we would like to eliminate the compilation step. We would like to take a source program and run it directly, apparently in contrast to our earlier statement that source code cannot be understood by the CPU. What we need to do is trick the CPU… And here's how we do it: we put an **interpreter** between the source program and the CPU. Exactly like a human interpreter, who translates what one person is saying in one language into another language *even while the person is speaking*, a computer interpreter is a program that reads the source program and does on-the-fly translation to execute the program immediately. Because it is a program run by the CPU, it knows that CPU and therefore knows what machine instructions to produce or execute for each high-level instruction in the program. It must be at least as smart as a compiler, because it has to understand the program in the high-level language, but it does not produce another program, in machine language – it just decides what machine instructions to execute and does it on the spot. We still need an interpreter for each type of CPU, of course, because it has to run on that CPU, but we can skip the compilation step. Still, for each high-level language we need as many compilers as there are types of CPUs – and as we have already said before, there are many of each. Life is still too complicated, isn't it?

The disadvantage of using an interpreter is that because there is no compilation step the program (the one in source format) execute slower than if it were first compiled into machine language and then executed; that is so because when the program is running, the interpreter has to continuously interpret the source program from the high-level language to the machine language, and that takes some effort that would otherwise be done by the compile *before* running the program. If a program were executed only once *ever*, it would make no difference (you have the compile and execute steps done only once each), but a program that needs to run many times would perform better if you compile it (you have the compile step done only once instead of every time the program runs). The bad news is that in most case you don't have a choice – most high-level languages are either compiled or interpreted, rarely both; the good news is that with today's fast computers it may not matter that the program runs slightly slower!

VIRTUAL MACHINES

As you followed carefully our story of the "evolution" of programming languages and the tools necessary to make them useful, one though must have come to your mind: we have a big problem because we have to take care of so many types of CPUs and so many programming languages. If there were only one type of CPU, we would only need one compiler or interpreter; but we have many CPU types, so we need many compilers and interpreters even for the same high-level language. So how about this idea: let's pretend that there is just one CPU! We will call it a **virtual machine**, because it's not an actual machine that exists but an imaginary one. But as long as everyone agrees to pretend together, it can be *almost* real. And then, we can take it one step further and decide that we will have only one high-level programming language for our virtual machine. This way, we do not need to build compilers for all the other languages as well.

From the perspective of compiler builders, suddenly life is beautiful: we need only one compiler, because it runs on the one-and-only virtual machine, compiles source programs in one language only and produces executable programs only for the virtual machine. How wonderful – a single solution! But here's the catch – since the virtual machine does not really exist (that's why it's called virtual, Duh!), we need to "train" every CPU type to behave like the virtual machine so that we can have *actual* virtual machines…

And that is exactly what was done. The only combination of a programming language and its matching virtual machine that exists today is the Java environment. The high-level language is called Java, the machine language is called the Java Byte Code, and the virtual machine is called the JVM (meaning, as you correctly guessed, Java Virtual Machine).

To a linguistic (a scientists who studies languages), a virtual machine is like Esperanto – a universal language that everyone should understand, "to facilitate communication between people of different lands and cultures." And even in its short history, Java has already proven itself to be much more successful than Esperanto ever was.

As enthusiastic as you may become regarding Java (and many people are), it is not a perfect solution. First, the saying that "you can fool some people all the time, all people some of the time, but *not* all people all the time" is still true; no single language, as wonderful as it may be, is likely to be perfect for all applications; there is still room, and need, for other languages to ease the writing of programs where Java as a language or as an environment is less than appropriate. Second, every good invention has a cost; in this case, the cost is in the fact the Java Byte Code is not a true machine language, and therefore when the JVM executes a Java program it looks suspiciously like an interpreter of the Java Byte Code; it's faster than interpreting a high-level language, but slower than executing machine instructions. Nevertheless, Java is quite a good language, particularly for beginners, and this is why we chose it for all the examples in this book.

THE OPERATING SYSTEM

It seems as if there are many things happening in the computer besides the program you want to run. Don't we need someone to manage it? Yes, we do. At school, you have the principal, vice principal, guidance counselor and secretaries (called "administration") to "run" the school (of course, you think they are not doing such a great job – adults never do, right? – but imagine the school without them!) What the administration staff does, among many other things, is scheduling the school activities (such as classrooms and teachers schedules), making sure that everyone is where they are supposed to be (you too!), taking care of supplies, and so on.

In the computer, the administration staff is called the **Operating System**, while all other participants (programs) are called **applications**. It's a heavy responsibility, and without it you wouldn't be able to use the computer. Windows® is an operating system, just as are others you may have heard of: DOS®, Solaris®, Linux, etc. The various operating systems are different in how each one does its job, but the jobs they do are almost identical. We will not go into all the services an operating system has to provide, but a few are important enough to discuss now.

Going In and Out – Input/output Services

Let us take you back to your visit of Computer Park. Surely you remember the large number of different peripheral devices, and that each of them used a combination of narrow and wide paths to move instructions and data between the device and the CPU or memory. At that visit, we told you that the CPU puts information in memory, or that the CPU sends instructions, and so forth. By now you probably realize that in reality the CPU does not do anything that is not part of a program – it has no life of its own, no initiative.

The program that contains the machine instructions for the input/output tasks we mentioned is the operating system. It's the operating system that contains small sub-programs to deal with each and every device (these are called **device drivers**), sub-programs to package series of bits into bytes when a device is using what we called a "tightrope bridge," sub-programs to put in memory the information in such a way that the video presentation will work properly, and so on. These collection of small programs is called **input/output services**, and are a major part of the operating system. As a matter of fact, the functions of the input/output services are much more complex than what we described here, but unless you want to study "operating systems architecture," you do not need to know all the details (only few people do…)

Getting Organized – Files and Folders

One of the input/output services is the one that manages disk storage. There are two challenges we must deal with regarding the organization of disks. The first is finding the information that the CPU is looking for, and the second is handling large chunks of information.

Let's look at how your school library is organized. When you are looking for a book, let's say by its title, you go to the catalog. It might be a card catalog, or it might be on the computer. In the case of a card catalog, you flip through the cards (in alphabetical order) until you find the card for the book you need. On that card, you find the location of the

book in the library – which aisle and may be which shelf the book is at. Then you walk over to that aisle and shelf, and look for the book itself (again, hopefully the books are in some order – perhaps in the order of the special location codes used for libraries). You are not likely to start looking through the cards from the beginning (the first card under the letter 'A') – you are smarter than that! You start with the box that has the cards of the first letter (or letters) of the title, and perhaps use some smart short-cuts like looking in the middle of the box first, to see if the card you need is in the first or second half of the box, and so forth. It's easier if the library's catalog is on the computer: you just type in the title, and – bingo! – the book's location comes up. A good secretary will organize the office files in a similar manner – perhaps first by subject and within the subject by dates or by people or any other key.

When the CPU is executing a program (following a script), it may want to get a specific piece of information, such as a paper you wrote for school that needs some editing now. The program that the CPU is running does not know, and does not even care, where exactly on the disk that paper may be – it only knows its name, "History of Colonialism," for example, or "Why I Like Shopping." Each document, just as in an office, is called a **file**; there can be many files on each disk drive, and each has its own name. The program only needs to know the name of a file, not its physical location. The look-up in the catalog is done behind the scene, and the instructions to fetch the file, with it's physical location, are sent to the storage device.

This look-up is similar to a parent walking into the school building for a meeting with a teacher at Parent/Teacher Conferences Night: The parent knows the name of the teacher, but not the room where the meeting may be. When entering the building, the parent would look for a list of teachers and their rooms posted at the entrance. This list is called a **directory**.

In addition to having files, you should be familiar with the concept of a **folder**. This is just an aid to organizing your files; it has no effect on storing the files themselves, only on storing the information *about* the files. A folder is a group of files that have something in common. They could belong to the same project, or to the same person (if many people are sharing the computer), or containing information of the same type (like pictures or essays) – it's up to you to decide. Folder can be organized in multiple levels; for example, you may decide to have a folder for each subject (history, science, math), and in this folder have sub-folders for each type of file (papers, drawings, photos, spreadsheets, web pages). The folders' information is part of the directory, and the disk service knows how to look for the file you need based on the names of the folders the program uses together with the file's name when a it is looking for that file.

The term "folder" is appropriate because it is used exactly as you would use real-life folders. For example, you may have in your backpack a folder for each subject, with pockets for different type of assignments; or a doctor's office has a folder for each patient, perhaps with sub-divisions for different types of medical information. On a larger scale, however, it becomes a little bit more difficult to imagine a folder the size of a whole filing cabinet if it includes sub-folders for each student in the school… But it is still a useful model, even if we run out of reasonable real-life examples.

Let us recall our discussion in of the structure of a disk drive during your recent visit to Computer Park (in "*Disks – For Long-Term And Large Quantities*"). Each sector on the disk can hold only a limited amount of information, because it is of a fixed size and is only so big. Therefore, a single file may require a large number of sectors in order to store it, just as a paper you write may take more than one page (you wish that was not so, don't you?) Unlike a book, however, which has all its pages bound together and at the same location (unless the dog got it first…), the sectors that make up a file can be scattered all over the disk, on many platters and cylinders. It wouldn't matter, as long as we can pull them all together when we need the whole file and pretend that they are one piece. The information in the directory must somehow point to all the sectors, so that the disk management service can find all of them – another task for the operating system.

Timing is Everything – Scheduling

So many programs, so little time! Apparently, many programs and sub-programs are running at the same time. We have the input/output services, and the disk management in particular; we have other operating system programs; and of course we have the real programs, the applications. It may get extremely complex if you have many windows open at the same time, for example Instant Messenger (probably with a few windows, for all the people you talk with), Word Processor (may be with two windows, one for a History paper and one for Language Arts), Web Page Editor, E-mail (with a few windows open for several e-mails in progress), and it can go on and on… But magically, when you move the mouse and click on one window, it pops to the front and lets you type in; then you click on another, and that one comes to the front as if it was there all along; and your word processor is printing out at the same time that you are downloading a file; and you get two instant message at the same time, even as you are clicking on the 'Send' button in your e-mail program. Something must be taking care of all that switching back and forth, and of all this activity in the background.

Once again, it's your friendly operating system, at your service! It's a service called **scheduling**, and is part of the operating system's ability to do **multi-tasking**. When you do a few things at the same time, such as talking on the phone while cleaning up you room (a rare activity – cleaning – we all know!) or doing your homework while watching TV and fighting with a sibling (this one is not very rare, is it?), you are multi-tasking. We jokingly say of someone who cannot multi-task (cannot do more than one thing at a time) that he or she "cannot walk and chew gum at the same time." You don't even realize it, but your brain actually skips from one activity to another, spending a very short period of time on each. This is why your parents always tell you that you cannot concentrate on your homework while watching TV – you lose your focus every time your eyes (and therefore brain) jump from homework to TV and back.

But it's different for a CPU. First of all, it doesn't have parents… But seriously, unlike a human being, it does not need to concentrate – it only needs to follow instructions in machine language, and it doesn't really care which program they belong to. So it can easily execute a dozen instructions in one program, then jump over and execute a few in a second one, and then a third, and perhaps then go back to the second, and then jump over to a fourth program, and only then go back to the first and continue as if it never left. You would be panting heavily if you had to do all this running around, but for the CPU it's all in a day's work…

You have a brain to control your multi-tasking; it happens sub-consciously. The operating system provides a scheduling service for the computer to manage the CPU's multi-tasking. It's a complex service, but here is how it works in a nutshell: every so often (actually, a very short period of time in human terms) the CPU is interrupted in what it is doing (in between two machine instructions in whichever program it is executing at the moment), and the scheduling service is executed – remember, this is a program too! That program looks at which other programs need attention – need the CPU to execute instructions in them – and jumps there, until the next interruption. In deciding which program to jump to next, the scheduling program uses a complex set of criteria and tries to be fair to every program. Sometimes, when the CPU gets to a point where it must wait (for example, for input from you), it would voluntarily jump to the scheduling program to let it decide who is going to enjoy next a visit by the CPU. From the outside it looks like all the programs are running at the same time, but now you know that this is only an illusion – only one is executed at any point in time, but the switching is so quick and for such short periods of time that no one notices!

Let's look at some examples. It's not simple, so hold on to your hats! You Instant Messenger is waiting for input, either from you or from your friend, so the scheduler is not going to give it the CPU. But as soon as you click on the IM window, the scheduler will give control to the service of the operating system that draws the window on top of the others. For every keystroke, the scheduler passes control from the service that reads the keyboard to the IM program, which then passes it to the service that paints the letter in the window. When you click on the 'Send' button, which is like a "tap on the shoulder" to the scheduler, the mouse service gets control and passes the information about the click to the IM program; the IM program then packages the message from all the characters you typed so far, and passes control to the transmission service, which would shortly lose control itself after sending the message out.

Are you still with us? Good; let's continue. While the IM program was waiting, you opened another document in your word processor. That means that the word processing program receives control from the scheduler in response to the click on the 'Open' button. It then requests the disk service to read the file into memory, and thus loses control – it has nothing to do anyway until the file is in memory. Or may be it does – you may ask to print the document that was already open. So it loses control again to the printing service of the operating system, but not before it gave it the information needed to print your masterpiece.

And you thought the life of a computer is easy…

What you learned in this chapter:

⋏ *A computer program is a sequence of instructions, which the CPU follows like a movie script*

⋏ *The program is stored in the computer's memory*

⋏ *A program can be expressed in machine language, in low-level (assembly) language or in high-level language*

⋏ *Assemblers and compilers translate programs to machine language, so that the CPU can execute them*

⋏ *An interpreter does "compilation on-the-fly," without producing machine instructions*

⋏ *A virtual machine is a make-believe CPU that behaves the same no matter what real CPU it's running on*

⋏ *An operating system is a collection of programs and sub-programs that manage the operation of the computer by providing vital services*

> ### *PART ONE REVIEW:*
>
> Hardware *is the name for all the physical parts of the computer – CPU, memory, disks and peripherals*
>
> Software *is the name for the instructions that direct the hardware in performing its tasks; software is made up of* programs, *which are sequences of instruction for the CPU*
>
> *The computer has no personality, no imagination and no initiative – it can only follow the instructions in the programs*
>
> *Programs are written in programming languages; there are many languages and several different ways for the computer to handle them*
>
> *The operating system is a special collection of programs that manage the computer's operations*

PART TWO – THE ELEMENTS OF PROGRAMMING

It's time to start programming! In this section, we begin exploring the basic concepts. We open with an example of a very simple (and not very useful) program, and then proceed to discuss all the elements that you need in order to write useful programs. You will learn how to describe to the computer the information you want to use, how to get information from outside the computer, how to tell it what to do with this information, and how to present the results.

What you will learn in this section:

> *The "anatomy" of a program*
> *How to describe the data to be used by the program*
> *How to describe processing logic and calculations*
> *How to get data in and out of the program*

Putting a Program Together

Let's analyze a few very simple programs. They may not do much, but they will let you recognize the important elements that make up a program. We will explain the roles of the important elements of the example programs, so that later you will be able to expand each part to be more meaningful.

What you will learn in this chapter:

> *What are the elements of a program*
> *What are the roles of declarations and statements*
> *Some rules for writing declarations and statements*

YOUR VERY FIRST PROGRAM!

Here is a very simple program:

```
01  // Example 1, file 'Wassup.java'
02  // This program displays 'Wassup?'
03  public class Wassup
04  {
05     public static void main(String[] args)
06     {
07        // Declare a string
08        String textWassup;
09        // Store the text in the string
10        textWassup = "Wassup?";
11        // Display "Wassup?"
12        System.out.println(textWassup);
13     }
14  }
```

After compiling and running it, it would simply display:

```
Wassup?
```

At first glance, this program may look like gibberish to you. But don't you worry – later in this book you will learn what each and every line means. For now, the important lines are lines 8, 10 and 12:

- ❑ Line 8 defines an area for the text we want to display and gives it the name `textWassup`,
- ❑ Line 10 stores the text `"Wassup?"` in that area, and
- ❑ Line 12 produces that display; writing `System.out.println` is just a long way of saying "print."

As you can see, there are two different types of instructions: one is a definition (line 8), the other an action (lines 10 and 12). In the next sections we will learn the purpose of each type of instruction and how they work together.

Lines 1 and 2 are just comments for a person reading the program; The *"Comments"* section below talks about them in more detail. Lines 3 and 5 are required by the Java Compiler and the Java Virtual Machine; every program must have these lines, with minor variations; we will not bother discussing them now, but their meaning will be described later.

ANYTHING TO DECLARE? – SETTING UP THE PARTS AND TOOLS

Remember the last time you built something from a construction set? At the beginning of the instructions for each step was a list of the parts you need for that step, and the tools you need in order to assemble this piece. It was very useful to have this list, so that you could gather all parts and tools before beginning the step and didn't have to rummage through the box for a certain part while trying to hold together the incomplete piece that desperately needed just this part to hold it together…

In programming, this is more than a question of convenience. The compiler *must* know of each part and tool you intend to use, before you use it. The parts are the data (information) that your program will use, and the tools are the instruments with which your program is going to handle this information. The compiler needs to know what type of a information is in each piece, so that it can allocate memory to store it and make sure that what your program is trying to do with that piece makes sense. It needs to know what tools you want to use, so it can verify that the right tool is used for each step.

Unlike a construction set, in programming *you* are the one writing the instructions! So it is your responsibility to declare, for each step, what tools and what parts are needed by your program. Without these **declarations**, the compiler would not be able to compile your program.

In *"Variables"* below we will go over the different types of declarations for data items (called "variables"), and *"The Structure of a Function"* will cover the declaration of tools (called "functions").

An important thing to remember is that declarations are really for the compiler. They don't tell the computer to *do* anything, only what parts and tools we are planning for it to use in the program.

In the example above, line 8 is such a declaration. It tells the compiler that we will need a `String` to store a text. This is a declaration for a "variable", which means an area in memory that can have varying (changing) information; this variable is set up to hold only text (strings), so it cannot hold numbers; and its name is `textWassup`. We will talk about the different types of storage and variables in much more details in *"Variables"*.

MAKING A STATEMENT – WRITING DOWN THE DIRECTIONS

We have laid out the parts and tools we need for this program. We now need to give the computer the directions, telling it what to do with these parts and tools. The instructions in a construction set are usually in pictures, showing (with little arrows) how the parts fit together, in which direction to apply tools, and so forth. In programming, the same is done by writing down **statements**, each being a step in the program leading to the final result. The statement is executed by the computer, one after the other.

There are many types of statements – they are the essence of programming. A significant part of this book is devoted to them. How you write these statements, what each one does and how to "string" them together in order to accomplish the desired results is what you will learn in the rest of this book. But there is one thing common to all statement: they are telling the computer exactly what to do. What to calculate, what decision to make, where to get data from, where to store data – all this is expressed using statements.

Unlike declarations, statements are for the computer, to be used when the program runs. They are the steps the computer will execute in order to produce the result you want it to produce.

In the example above, line 10 is such a statement: it tells the computer to store the text `"Hello World!"` in the String which was declared earlier. This statement is called an *assignment*, because it tells the computer to assign a value to a variable. Line 12 is another statement: it tells the computer to display the text stored in the String.

Sometimes declarations are also referred to as statements, but in this book we use the term *statement* only for executable instructions, and not for declarations.

COMMENTS

You may have notices a few lines beginning with `'//'`. These lines are completely ignored by the compiler, and don't make it into the compiled (executable) program at all. These are **comments**. The use of comments is extremely important in programming. They serve two major purposes:

❑ You may be looking at a program you wrote a while ago, and you can't figure out what you did or why you did it that way. If you wrote good comments in the program, they will remind you.

❑ Someone else may be looking at a program you wrote. Unless you are ready and willing to answer questions, it may be very difficult for a stranger to understand your program.

A good programmer knows that the quality of the comments is an indication of the quality of the program – so good programmers write plenty of comments, explaining to themselves and others what the program is doing every step of the way, and why particular choices were made in the programming.

TOKENS AND WHITE SPACES

The program is constructed of words (such as `public`, `args`, `System`) and special symbols (=, [, +, ;). Each one of these is called a **token**. The special thing about tokens is that they cannot be broken down without losing their meaning. The individual letters in the word System have no special meaning to the program – only the complete word has. Obviously, the special symbols in this program cannot be broken down because they are already only single characters, but you will learn later on that there are also combinations of special characters that must be together in order to have a specific meaning.
Examples:

```
ThisIsAToken
another_token
++
+=
>
]
```

What separates one token from another is called **white space**. A white space is any combination of regular spaces, new line markers and tabs. Just like in written English, there must be white space between word tokens, as well as between special-characters tokens, otherwise the compiler wouldn't know where one token ends and the next begins. However, between a word token and a special-characters token you usually would not need any white space. It is good practice, though, to put spaces around special-characters tokens – it makes the program easier to read – except around parentheses and brackets.
Examples:

```
Tokens separated by spaces
no_spaces_needed_here()
a*b/(c-d)
a * b / ( c - d )
```

It is important to remember that line breaks are white spaces, and therefore have no meaning. You can break a line anywhere a white space can appear, and you would usually do it in order to make your program easier to read.
Example:

```
Result =
    (Value1 + Value2) /
    (Value3 - Value4);
```

MORE SIMPLE PROGRAMS

A Plain Calculator

Let's take a look at another program. This one is doing a little more than the last one: it actually performs a calculation. simple

```
01 // Example 2, file 'TwoPlusTwo.java'
02 // This program displays the value of 2+2
03 public class TwoPlusTwo
04 {
05    public static void main(String[] args)
06    {
07       // Declare a numeric variable for the numeric result
08       int numberResult;
09       // Calculate
10       numberResult = 2 + 2;
11       // Declare a string variable for the result text
12       String textResult;
13       // Store the result in the string
14       textResult = "2 + 2 = " + numberResult;
15       // Display the result
16       System.out.println(textResult);
17    }
18 }
```

Running this program produces this output:

```
2 + 2 = 4
```

(Anything else would be a great surprise, wouldn't it?)

Line 8 declares an area for the numeric result, named `numberResult`. Line 12 declares a string area for the result, named `textResult`. These area are called variables, and we will talk more about them in *"Variables"* below. Line 10 is the "heart" of this program: it adds two numbers, and puts the results in the `numberResult` variable we set aside on line 8. Since the result is a number, and humans cannot read numbers stored in the computer the way that the computer can, we need to turn the result into text. We do that on line 14, which creates the text that include the problem (`"2 + 2 = "`) and the result (from `numberResult`), in the variable we set aside for the text result (`textResult`). Now, on line 16, we can display this result text. Throughout this program we wrote comments, to explain what each declaration or statement does.

You will learn more about calculations later in *"Smooth Operators – Manipulating Values and Variables"* and *"When Things Go Wrong – Truncation and Overflow,"* but even now you can experiment with different numbers, to see if the computer calculates correctly… Note, however, that if you change the 2 + 2 on line 12, for example to 3 + 7, but you don't change the `"2 + 2 = "` text on line 14, the displayed result will say 2 + 2 = 10. This is because that text is a constant, and does not depend on the actual calculation.

You might have observed that in this example the declarations and the statements are mixed. That means that you do not have to put all the declarations at the beginning, before the statements. The only rule is that you must have a declaration before you use what was declared. The order of the declarations is not important, either – usually it does not matter if a certain declaration comes before another, or the other way around.

The part of a statement or a declaration that describes some calculation is called an *expression*. For example, the 2 + 2 on line 10 or the `"2 + 2 = "` + `numberResult` on line 14 are both expressions. There are many rules regarding expressions, and you will learn most of them later, mostly in *"Express Yourself – Using Expressions"* below. But it is important to note that expressions are the main building blocks of a program – this is how you tell the computer what calculations or data manipulations to perform.

Sometimes it is possible to combine a declaration with a statement, to create an **initializer**, called so because it calculates an *initial* (first) value. The two initializers we could have used in the example are:

```
int numberResult = 2 + 2; // replacing lines 8 and 10
String textResult = "2 + 2 = " +
  numberResult;            // replacing lines 12 and 14
```

It is important to note, however, that in *this* case the order of the two initializers is very important: it would not make sense to write the second one first, since `numberResult` would not have a value, and would not even be defined, for the initialization of `textResult`. The compiler would have sounded an alarm had we coded the program that way.

An Interactive Calculator

Let's take the primitive calculator we saw in *"A Plain Calculator"* above and improve it a little bit. I am sure it annoyed you that in order to try different values you had to change the program and re-compile it. Let's write a calculator (for addition only!), that can get the numbers to add from the outside, so that they are not a fixed part of the program. This is called an **interactive program**, because it interacts ("to act on each other") with its user. Here is the program:

```
01  // Example 3, file 'Calc.java'
02  // This program adds two input numbers
03
04  import java.io.*;
05
06  public class Calc
07  {
08      public static void main(String[] args) throws IOException
09      {
10          BufferedReader inputReader = new BufferedReader(
11              new InputStreamReader(System.in));
12          String line;
13          double result;
```

```
14
15        System.out.println("I know how to add!");
16
17        System.out.print("Enter 1st number: ");
18        line = inputReader.readLine();
19        double x1 = new Double(line).doublevalue();
20        System.out.print("Enter 2nd number: ");
21        line = inputReader.readLine();
22        double x2 = new Double(line).doubleValue();
23        result = x1 + x2;
24        System.out.println(x1 + " + " + x2 + " = " + result);
25     }
26 }
```

(In this program there are a few more lines that we will treat as "magic" for now. In addition to lines 6 and 8, which are required in every program in one form or another, the other lines that we will not discuss now deal with getting input from the keyboard. Lines 10-11 declare and create the input stream, which is "representing" the keyboard in the program; lines 18-19 and 21-22 read in what you type and turn it into a number; and that's enough for now.)

Putting aside the "technical details", this program reads in two numbers and stores them in two variables, called x1 and x2 (lines 17–19 and then 20–21). It then adds them up (line 23), storing the result in a variable called result (did you expect any other name?!), and then prints it out (line 24). The beauty of this program, compared to the one in *"A Plain Calculator"* above, is that you type in the numbers to add when you *run* the program, not when you *write* it! So the same program can be compiled once and then run as many times as you want to add any two numbers – it's a real data processing program!

When you run the program, one possible result is:

```
I know how to add!
Enter 1st number: 3.14
Enter 2nd number: 1.567
3.14 + 1.567 = 4.707
```

A reminder: the numbers 3.14 and 1.567 appear in *bold italics* to show you that this is what *we* typed, not what the program produced. If you type different numbers, you will get different results. Go ahead, play with it!

One note of caution: if you type in something that is not a good number, you will get a nasty message from the program, telling you how naughty you are! Try it!

What you learned in this chapter:

⋏ *All programs have two elements:* declarations *and* statements

⋏ *Declarations are used to define the tools and parts that the program needs*

⋏ *Statements tell the computer what to do with these parts in order to produce result*

⋏ *The parts of statements and declarations that describe calculations are called* expressions

⋏ *Declarations and statements can be combined to create* initializers

⋏ *Programs can read input from the keyboard and print out results on the screen*

It Takes All Kinds – Types, Values and Variables

The first step in programming is laying out the data that the program will process. This chapter explores the different types of information that a program may need and how they are defined.

What you will learn in this chapter:

> *What are data types and what each one means*
> *How to use literal values and variable storage for each type*
> *How to handle groups of identical data*
> *How to work with strings of characters*
> *What are references and how to use them*

TYPES AND VALUES

In a construction set you have several types of parts: you have rods, wheels, connectors, panels, and perhaps others as well. Each one is different, and usually it is easy to tell them apart. Some of them can be connected to others, but there are rules as to how this can be done. For example, it is likely that a panel cannot connect directly to a wheel – it may need a special connector or a rod. But all parts of a certain type are very similar; they may have different sizes, but long rods and short rods are still rods.

Surprisingly enough, in programming we find a similar situation. The data a program is processing, as well as intermediate results, could be of several types. The differences among the types are primarily in the values that belong to each type. For example, the type *integer* means whole numbers.

To be more specific, the data types fall into three major groups:

❑ **Numeric** – these are generally numbers.
❑ **Boolean** – these are yes/no or true/false values.
❑ **Text** – these are "strings" of characters.

The numeric types are further divided:

❑ **Integers** – whole numbers.
❑ **Floating point** – numbers with decimal fractions.

Text types are more complex, and we will talk about them later in *"Variables"* and *"Multi-Dimensional Arrays."*

Each one of the numeric types is also divided based on the range of values that they represent. The table below summarizes all the numeric types:

Primary Type	Secondary Type	Minimum Value	Maximum Value
Integer	byte	-128	127
	short	-32,768	32,767
	int	-2,147,483,648	2,147,483,647
	long	-9,223,372,036,854,775,808	9,223,372,036,854,775,807
	char	0	65535
Floating point	float	-(1.4 · 10 45) (approximately)	3.4 · 10 38 (approximately)
	double	-(4.9 · 10 324) (approximately)	1.79 · 10 308 (approximately)

As you can see, the floating point types can handle extremely large or small numbers, but they are meant primarily for numbers with fractions or digits to the right of the decimal point – the integer types can only handle whole numbers.

Note also that the further away from zero the floating point number is (in both positive and negative directions), the less precise it becomes – it loses digits after the decimal points; this happens because the number of meaningful digits that can be stored (called the **precision** of the number) is limited, and it's one of the tradeoffs of using floating point numbers.

The integer char type does not really belong there – it is an integer value, but it is used to represent a single character in a universal encoding scheme that is intended to cover all possible character sets used in all languages (such as English, German, Russian, Japanese, Chinese, Hebrew, etc.).

There is one more type, called the *reference* type, about which we will learn later, in *"References."*

LITERALS, VARIABLES AND CONSTANTS

Our interest in the various types is generated by our desire to manipulate and process different types of information. In order to do so, we need to know not only what types they are, but how to tell the computer what their values are or where they are stored. This is where **literals** and **variables** come into the picture.

Literals

Literals are values that are explicitly part of the program. For example, when you wrote 2 + 2 in the example in *"A Plain Calculator"* above, the number 2 is a literal. It "literally" means the value of 'two'. Similarly, the text "2 + 2 = " is also a literal, this time a character string rather than a number. For each type of data, there are specific rules of how to specify literals for that type:

❑ Integer numbers (types `byte`, `short`, `int`, `long`): there are three variations of integer literals: decimal, octal and hexadecimal. (octal is a base-8 number representation, hexadecimal is base-16. If you don't know what this means, don't worry; it is not that important.):

   ○ Decimal literals are just a sequence of decimal digits (0–9).
     Examples: 1   2001   12345

   ○ Octal literals are a zero, followed by sequence of octal digits (0–7).
     Examples: 0123   010   0777

   ○ Hexadecimal literals are a zero, followed by the letter x or X, followed by sequence of hexadecimal digits (0–9, a–f, A–F).
     Examples: 0x123   0xA1A   0xabcde   0xBADBEAD   0xDeadBeef   0xFFFF

You can add the letter l (ell) or L to any integer literal to make it a `long` integer.
Examples: 123456789123456789L   07777L   0xAL
Use of L is preferred to l, because the letter l (ell) looks too much like the digit 1 (one).

❑ Floating-point numbers (types `float`, `double`): a floating-point literal has the following parts: a whole-number part, a decimal point, a fraction part, an optional exponent, and an optional type suffix. Sounds complex? Not really. Let's look at each part separately:

○ The *whole* and the *fraction* parts are actually just sequences of decimal digits.

○ The *decimal point* is the character `.` (period).

○ The *exponent*, is indicated by the letter `e` or `E`, followed by an optionally signed integer. Examples: `E7` `e+10` `e-123` `E-3`.
It means that the value of the literal is the number described by the whole-and-fractional parts, multiplied by 10 to the power of the integer after the `e` or `E`.

○ The *type suffix* is one of the letters `F`, `f`, `D`, `d` and indicates if the number is of a `float` or `double` type. If you don't specify this suffix, the literal is assumed to be of type `double`.

In most cases you would not use the exponent, just the whole and fraction parts, separated by the decimal point. These three together make a normal decimal number, just as you are used to seeing in math.

By the way, the "presentation" of a number using an exponent is also known as the scientific notation, named after the equivalent way that numbers are written in math and science as a fraction and a power of 10 (such as $1.4 \cdot 10~45$), where the letter E stands for the number 10.

Some examples may be useful here:

```
3.14
-74.963124
5.1E2    is (5.1·102) which is (5.1·100) which is 510
123.456E10 is (123.456·1010) which is 1234560000000
2001e-5 is (2001·10-5) which is 0.02001
```

❑ Boolean: a Boolean (type `boolean`) literal can only be one of the two words `true` or `false`.

❑ Characters: a character literal is a single character between a pair of single quotes.
Examples: `'A'` `'+'` `'j'` `'?'`
In addition to a single character between the quotes, you can also specify an **escape sequence**. This is a special combination that represents special characters. It always starts with the character \ (backslash – this is the "escape" character), and is followed either by a single character from among b, t, n, f, r, ", ', \ or by an octal number between 0 and 377.
Examples: `'\t'` `'\\'` `'\''` `'\40'` `'\177'`
The octal numbers specify a character whose internal numerical representation has that value. The single characters represent special characters, as follows:

  \b – Backspace (BS)
  \t – Tab (HT)
  \n – Line Feed (LF)
  \f – Form Feed (FF)
  \r – Carriage Return (CR)
  \" – Double quote
  \' – Single quote
  \\ - Backslash

These characters have special meanings, some of which will be explained later. The backslash serves to tell the compiler that the character following it in the program must have special treatment and taken as is, rather as a token; if we had not used the escape sequence in the literal '\"', the second quote would be matched with the first (creating an "empty" character) and the third quote would be "lonely" and unbalanced – producing a compiler error.

❑ Strings: a string literal is made of zero or more characters, including escape sequences as defined above, between a pair of double quotes.
Examples: `"Hello World!"` `"This is another string"` `"Escape sequence: \n\r."`
You will learn more about the String data type in Part Three.

❑ References: We don't know much about these yet, but let's just note that the only literal value for a reference is the word `null`.

You must keep in mind that literals are like constants in an equation: no matter what happens in your program, the values of the literals will never change!

Variables

If programming dealt only with literals and fixed values, there wouldn't be much to do… Programming is about processing information, and that means that you have to manipulate data that is external to the program and cannot be a fixed part of the program. This data comes from the outside as the program's input, is processed by performing calculations and other manipulations, and the results are finally sent back to the outside as the output of the program.

Where is this data going to be for the program to find it and work with it? You guessed correctly – in variables. They are probably the most important element of programming. The simplest way to describe variables is by saying that they are named storage areas for data. "Storage" – because this is where data in the computer is stored by the program. "Named" – because each variable has its own name, so that it's possible to identify each one individually. Variables are somewhat like variables in a math equation, but you don't have to solve the equation – the program you write calculates and assigns the values to the variables.

Before we can use variables, we have to learn the rules… There are two rules: how to name them, and what can be stored in them.

The name of a variable must begin with a letter (a–z, A–Z) and followed by any number of letters or digits (0–9) or _ (underscore) or $ (dollar sign). The use of the underscore and the dollar sign is discouraged. *No other characters are allowed!*
Examples of valid names: `X  x  abc  ThisIsAVariable  this2isavariable`
`This_One_Uses_Underscores  getValue  Result  DoNotUse$  u2  me3`
Examples of invalid names: `Question?  NoAnswer!  No Space Allowed  Bad-Name`
`__WrongBeginning  0123abcd`

It is important to remember that names are **case-sensitive**. That means that lower-case letters (a–z) are different than upper-case letters (A–Z). Thus, `hello` and `Hello` are two different names!

There is one minor limitation on your choice of names for variables: you cannot use the Boolean literal values (`true` and `false`), the reference literal value (`null`) or any of the set of predefined keywords listed below. Some of these keywords you already know; the others will be explained later throughout the book. The "forbidden" keywords (called **reserved words**) are:

```
abstract   default    if           private        this
boolean    do         implements   protected      throw
break      double     import       public         throws
byte       else       instanceof   return         transient
case       extends    int          short          try
catch      final      interface    static         void
char       finally    long         strictfp       volatile
class      float      native       super          while
const      for        new          switch
continue   goto       package      synchronized
```

Names of variables are often known as **identifiers**, since they identify the variables.

The rules as to what can be stored in a variable are much simpler: anything that matches the data type of that variable. The type is determined when you declare the variable, and cannot be changed. You already saw declarations in the examples: in *"A Plain Calculator"* line 8 declares a variable named `textResult` with a type of `String` and line 10 declares a variable of type `int` named `numberResult`. That means that `textResult` can store any string, but only strings, and `numberResult` can store only integer numbers. Examples:

```
double pi;
float squareRootOf2;
long looooong;
int i;
```

By the way, when declaring a few variables of the same type, you can combine the declarations into one by specifying the type only once and separating the names with commas. Examples:

```
int i, j, k;
boolean yes, no;
byte onePotato, twoPotato, threePotato, four,
     fivePotato, sixPotato, sevenPotato, more;
```

Constants

There is one more "creature" you have to know about, one that lies between literals and variables. It's called a **constant**. It's a way to take a literal and give it a meaningful name. For example, you know the value of *pi* to be "approximately" 3.1415926535897932384626. But if you are writing a program that is heavily involved in calculations requiring this value, you don't really want to write it in each and every formula. So the solution is to declare a constant with this value, and you would do it like this:

```
final double pi = 3.1415926535897932384626;
```

Then you can use pi as you use any variable, but it would always have the value you assigned to it with the declaration; the word final guarantee that. But, you might ask, why shouldn't I just use a variable declaration without the word `final`? When you use this word you force the compiler to make sure that no one ever tries to assign a different value to this variable – that's why we call it a constant! it would cause a compiler error if someone later even tries to write:

```
pi = 3.1415;  // error!!! pi is a constant!
```

You should use constants as much as possible when you have values that you know in advance will not change during program execution. The benefit is not only that you have to specify the value only once, but also that because they have meaningful names (that's very important!) everyone who reads the program would immediately understand their purpose.

Examples:

```
final int courtLength = 94;       // basketball court, feet
final int courtWidth = 50;        // basketball court, feet
final int freezingPoint = -32;    // degrees Fahrenheit
final double moonMass = 7.349e+22;   // kilograms
final double flOz = 0.0078125;    // fluid ounce, in gallons
final double mile = 1.609344;     // kilometers
final long feetPerMile = 5280;    // feet per mile
```

All Together Now: Literals, Variables and Constants

We pulled together all the examples (and then some more) from this section, and created a program that shows how literals, variables and constants appear in real life.

```
01 // Example 4, file 'LitVars.java'
02 // This program demonstrates the use of
03 // variables, literals and constants
04
05 public class LitVars
06 {
07     public static void main(String[] args)
08     {
09
10        ///////////////////////////////////////
11        // Variables
12        ///////////////////////////////////////
13
14        int i, j, k;
15        float squareRootOf2;
16        long looooong;
17        byte onePotato, twoPotato, threePotato, four,
```

```
18          fivePotato, sixPotato, sevenPotato, more;
19
20      ////////////////////////////////////////
21      // Literals (used as initializers)
22      ////////////////////////////////////////
23
24      System.out.println("\nLiterals \n");
25
26      int littleChicken = -123456789;
27      int bigChicken = 123456789;
28      long longSnake = 1234567890123456789L;
29      int octal100 = 0100;
30      int hexABCDEF = 0xABCDEF;
31      long hex1234567890ABCDEF = 0X1234567890abcdefL;
32      boolean OK = true;
33      char theLetterQ = 'Q';
34      char exclamationPoint = '!';
35      char quote = '\'';
36      double pi = 3.14159265358979323846264;
37      float f1 = 5.1e2f;
38      double d1 = 123.456E10;
39      double d2 = 2001E-5;
40      String anythingGoes =
41          "Almost anything ...";
42      String fox = "The quick brown fox";
43      String dog = "jumps over the lazy dog";
44      String escapeChars =
45          "Here are some escape characters: \', \", \\";
46
47      System.out.println("littleChicken = "
48          + littleChicken);
49      System.out.println("bigChicken = " + bigChicken);
50      System.out.println("longSnake = " + longSnake);
51      System.out.println("octal100 = " + octal100);
52      System.out.println("hexABCDEF = " + hexABCDEF);
53      System.out.println("hex1234567890ABCDEF = "
54          + hex1234567890ABCDEF);
55      System.out.println("OK = " + OK);
56      System.out.println("theLetterQ = " + theLetterQ);
57      System.out.println("exclamationPoint = "
58          + exclamationPoint);
59      System.out.println("quote = " + quote);
60      System.out.println("pi = " + pi);
61      System.out.println("f1 = " + f1);
62      System.out.println("d1 = " + d1);
63      System.out.println("d2 = " + d2);
64      System.out.println("What can you put in a string? "
65          + anythingGoes);
66      System.out.println("fox and dog = " + fox + " "
67          + dog);
68      System.out.println("escapeChars = " + escapeChars);
69
70      ////////////////////////////////////////
71      // Constants
72      ////////////////////////////////////////
73
74      System.out.println("\nConstants\n");
75
76      final boolean yes = true, no = false;
77      final int CourtLength = 94; // basketball court, ft
78      final int CourtWidth = 50;     // basketball court, ft
79      final int FreezingPoint = -32; // degrees Fahrenheit
80      final double MoonMass = 7.349e+22; // kilograms
81      final double FlOz = 0.0078125; // fluid ounce, in gals
82      final double Mile = 1.609344;  // kilometers
83      final long FeetPerMile = 5280;
84
85      System.out.println("yes = " + yes + ", no = " + no);
```

```
86      System.out.println("CourtLength = " + CourtLength +
87          " ft, CourtWidth = " + CourtWidth + " ft");
88      System.out.println("FreezingPoint = " + FreezingPoint +
89          " degrees");
90      System.out.println("MoonMass = " + MoonMass + " Kgs");
91      System.out.println("One FlOz = " + FlOz + " gallons");
92      System.out.println("One Mile = " + Mile + " Kms");
93      System.out.println("FeetPerMile = " + FeetPerMile);
94    }
95 }
```

When you run this program, you should expect the following output:

```
Literals

littleChicken = -123456789
bigChicken = 123456789
longSnake = 1234567890123456789
octal100 = 64
hexABCDEF = 11259375
hex1234567890ABCDEF = 1311768467294899695
OK = true
theLetterQ = Q
exclamationPoint = !
quote = '
pi = 3.141592653589793
f1 = 510.0
d1 = 1.23456E12
d2 = 0.02001
What can you put in a string? Almost anything ...
fox and dog = The quick brown fox jumps over the lazy dog
escapeChars = Here are some escape characters: ', ", \

Constants
s
yes = true, no = false
CourtLength = 94 ft, CourtWidth = 50 ft
FreezingPoint = -32 degrees
MoonMass = 7.349E22 Kgs
One FlOz = 0.0078125 gallons
One Mile = 1.609344 Kms
FeetPerMile = 5280
```

There are a few things we would like to point out about this program and its output:

❑ Using `System.out.println()` for printing does not allow you to tell the computer exactly how to print the results. For example, `pi` is not printed with all its digits, `d1` and `d2` are displayed with one digit before the decimal point but `f1` with three, etc. There are other ways to print out information, where you can determine exactly how you want the results displayed, but for now this is a "quick and dirty" way to get things printed.

❑ When escape characters are printed (`quote` and `escapeChars`), the backslash character (\) is *not* printed. This is the way it should be – it is not part of the value of the literal.

Try changing some of the declarations or initializers in this program, and see what happens!

ARRAYS

Computers are good at working with lots of information, such as lists of game scores, sequences of phone numbers, piles of job applications, and so on. Sometimes the processing they do is just repeated for each item (for example, making sure that each form has all the fields filled out); sometimes the work involves the whole list (such as averaging the ages of people in a survey). In both cases, the information is repeating itself in structure, but with different values (take for example a list of the ages of all players in a team – each age is a number, but the ages vary from one player to another). We have to find a way to organized the data so that the program can go from one item to the next and do what it has to do without having to repeat writing the same code for each item individually. If we want to find the average of the ages of all players in a team, we don't want to say, "add the first age and the second age and the third age and the fourth age and…" for two reasons: first, it's tedious and can turn out to be very long; second, we may not know in advance how many ages there are – not all teams have the same number of players. We'd rather say, "add the first through the last ages."

One-Dimensional Arrays

You will learn later (in *"While You Can – Repetitive Execution"* below) how to tell the computer to go through a list, repeating the same action on each item. For now, we are concerned about how to declare such a list. The answer is called an **array**. In its simplest form, it is a way to take a certain data type and have it repeated. The array gets a name just like any variable, but we use the square brackets ([and]) to show that we want an array, not a single variable. For example, you would declare an array of ages like this:

```
int[] age;
```

It is also permissible to declare an array this way:

```
int age[];
```

We prefer the first method because it puts the array indication([]) immediately next to the data type (int), making it obvious that we mean "an array of type int."

If you want to also create the **elements** of that array, you should use a special initializer (sometimes called an "allocator") and write:

```
int[] age = new int[5];
```

This will create an array with 5 elements, as the number between the brackets says; the dimension of this array is therefore 5. Later (in Part Three), we will talk a lot about the meaning of the word new; for now, let's just say that it directs the program to **allocate** (which means to reserve) the memory for the elements of the array.

It is important to note that *all elements of an array must be of the same type*. The individual elements of the array in this example are of type int and are called age[0], age[1], age[2], age[3] and age[4]. *Note that the first element is numbered zero, not one!* Each of the numbers 0 through 4 is called an **array index** of the array, and the square brackets show that each number is an index value. Any of the elements can appear wherever a variable can appear. Assigning value to the last element would be done this way:

age[4] = 47;

A statement adding up the first three ages would look like this:

```
first3Ages = age[0] + age[1] + age[2];
```

To calculate the odd-numbered ages, you could write:

```
oddAges = age[1] + age[3];
```

The indexes of an array (actually we should say "indices", but most people use the word "indexes") do not have to be literals; they can be variables or constants, or even expressions; the following code fragment

```
double[] distance = new double[7];
int midIndex = 3;
sumMidDistances =
    distance[midIndex - 1] +
    distance[midIndex] +
    distance[midIndex + 1];
```

will add the distances at indexes 2, 3 and 4 – the middle portion of the range 0 through 6.

Remember the initializers we discussed earlier (in *"A Plain Calculator"* above)? In order to combine the declaration of an array with the initialization of its values, one can use curly braces ({ and }) instead of the word new, and write:

```
int[] familyAges = {47, 43, 17, 12, 10, 5};
```

The size of the array is obvious from the number of values in the initializer, 6 in the example above. When using initializers, you cannot write a value between the square brackets – the size of the array is automatically calculated.

The values of array elements do not have to be in any particular order, such as increasing or decreasing; the values depend completely on what information the array is used for. In addition, the value assigned to an element of an array has nothing to do with its index (as demonstrated by the example of familyAges[] above), unless you *want* it to have a relationship; in the following declaration-with-initialization

```
double[] squareRoot = {0.0, 1.0, 1.4142, 1.7320, 2.0};
```

the value of squareRoot[i] would be the square root of the value of i.

```
int number = 3;
squareRoorOfnumber = squareRoot[number];
```

The value of an array's index must be between zero and the size of the array less 1; if you try any other value, you will cause an error! That means that if the array was declared with an allocator of int[100], the value of an index can be between 0 and 99 only, no more, no less.

Multi-Dimensional Arrays

The arrays we discussed so far are called one-dimensional arrays, obviously because they have only one **dimension** – it's as if they are spread along a single line (much like in geometry, where a line is a single-dimension entity made up of individual points). They are nice and useful if your information is actually **linear** (resembling a straight line) in its organization. But what if it is not? It's enough to look at a multiplication table, and you immediately know that you are out of luck with one-dimensional arrays: the table has two dimensions – the two numbers you multiply. To solve this problem, we present you with multi-dimensional arrays.

Let's start simple – with two dimensions. The declaration

```
int[][] multiplicationTable = new int[4][4];
```

gives you a four-by-four multiplication table. One way to load it up with values would be:

```
multiplicationTable[0][0] = 0;
multiplicationTable[0][1] = 0;
multiplicationTable[0][2] = 0;
multiplicationTable[0][3] = 0;
multiplicationTable[1][0] = 0;
multiplicationTable[1][1] = 1;
multiplicationTable[1][2] = 2;
multiplicationTable[1][3] = 3;
multiplicationTable[2][0] = 0;
multiplicationTable[2][1] = 2;
multiplicationTable[2][2] = 4;
multiplicationTable[2][3] = 6;
multiplicationTable[3][0] = 0;
multiplicationTable[3][1] = 3;
multiplicationTable[3][2] = 6;
multiplicationTable[3][3] = 9;
```

Now it's easy to get the value of a multiplication: the value of two-times-three can be found at multiplicationTable[2][3]. Of course, multiplicationTable[3][2] would contain the same number, but it's the value of three-times-two.

The dimensions of an array do not need to be equal. You can define an array for game scores like this:

```
int[][] score = new int[24][2];
```

The first dimension is the game number; each index value is the number of one of the 24 games in the season, starting with game number 0, not 1 – it's weird, but that's how arrays work. The second dimension is the team number (0 for our team, 1 for the other). With this array, score[10][0] is the number of points our team scored in the eleventh game, and score[6][1] is the score of our opponents in the seventh game. You can visualize this array as a table:

Game Number	Us (0)	Them (1)
0	7	5
1	3	2
2	11	4
...	...	...
22	2	13
23	8	8

The array's values are in the table's shaded area; the top row with the legend and the left column with the game numbers are for human readability only. Notice that the second dimension is not used as a normal number to be used in calculations, but as a team identification.

Here is another table: classroom scheduling. We have two periods to schedule (AM block and PM block), four classes (numbered 0, 1, 2, 3) and six classrooms (103, 104, 105, 106, 205, 206). The table might look like this:

Period	Class 1	Class 2	Class 3	Class 4
AM (0)	104	106	103	205
PM (1)	104	205	105	206

You can declare and initialize the array like this:

```
final int AM = 0, PM = 1;
int[][] schedule =
{
  {104, 106, 103, 205},    // AM block
  {104, 205, 105, 206}     // PM block
};
```

Notice how the curly braces are used at two levels? At the first level they enclose the whole initializer, at the second level they enclose each row. Using this declaration, you can easily find that class 3's PM block assignment is room 105: it's schedule[2][PM]. In case you are wondering why the index of the first dimension is 2 and not 3 (as you would expect for class 3), let us remind you that indexes begin with 0, not 1, and therefore class 1's index is 0, class 2's is 1, and so on. Note also that we are using a constant for the AM and PM index values; it's easier to remember than zero and one, isn't it?

The number of dimensions is not limited. Assuming that the classroom schedule array we just played with is for only one day of the week, we can declare a five-day schedule array:

```
int[][][] weekSchedule = new int[5][2][4];
```

In that array the first dimension indicates the day of the week (0 for Monday, 4 for Friday), and the initializer will use three levels of curly braces.

```
int[][][] weekSchedule =
{
  { // Monday
    {104, 106, 103, 205},    // AM block
    {104, 205, 105, 206}     // PM block
  },
  { // Tuesday
    {206, 106, 103, 205},    // AM block
    {205, 104, 105, 103}     // PM block
  },
  // ... The other days
};
```

Arraying It All For Review

The program below includes some of the examples of arrays we saw in the last few sections.

```
01 // Example 5, file 'Arrays.java'
02 // This program demonstrates the use of
03 // arrays
04
05 public class Arrays
06 {
07    public static void main(String[] args)
08    {
09
10       ///////////////////////////////////////
11       // The 'ages' and 'familyAges' arrays
12       ///////////////////////////////////////
13
14       System.out.println("\nThe 'ages' and " +
15          "'familyAges' arrays\n");
16
17       int[] age = new int[6];
18       age[0] = 47;
19       age[1] = 43;
20       age[2] = 17;
21       age[3] = 12;
22       age[4] = 10;
23       age[5] = 5;
24       int[] familyAges = {47, 43, 17, 12, 10, 5};
25
26       System.out.println("Family ages are " +
27          familyAges[0] + ", " +
28          familyAges[1] + ", " +
29          familyAges[2] + ", " +
30          familyAges[3] + ", " +
31          familyAges[4] + ", " +
32          familyAges[5]);
33
34       ///////////////////////////////////////
35       // The 'squareRoot' array
36       ///////////////////////////////////////
37
38       System.out.println("\nThe 'squareRoot' array\n");
39
40       double[] squareRoot = {0.0, 1.0, 1.4142, 1.7320, 2.0};
41       int Number = 3;
42
43       System.out.println("Square root of " + Number +
44          " is " + squareRoot[Number]);
45
46       ///////////////////////////////////////
```

```
47        // The Game Scores Table
48        /////////////////////////////////////
49
50        System.out.println("\nThe Game Scores Table\n");
51
52        int[][] GameScore =
53        {
54            {7, 5}, {3, 2}, {11, 4}, {2, 23}, {11, 0}, {4, 4},
55            {4, 3}, {7, 8}, {1, 3}, {9, 3}, {21, 1}, {0, 5},
56            {5, 5}, {6, 1}, {9, 14}, {3, 13}, {10, 9}, {2, 4},
57            {5, 7}, {6, 2}, {15, 12}, {12, 27}, {2, 13}, {8, 8}
58        };
59
60        System.out.println("\"Our\" score in the 11th game: "
61            + GameScore[10][0]);
62        System.out.println("\"Their\" score in the 7th game: "
63            + GameScore[6][1]);
64
65        /////////////////////////////////////
66        // The Multiplication Table
67        /////////////////////////////////////
68
69        System.out.println("\nThe Multiplication Table\n");
70
71        int[][] multiplicationTable = new int[4][4];
72            multiplicationTable[0][0] = 0;
73            multiplicationTable[0][1] = 0;
74            multiplicationTable[0][2] = 0;
75            multiplicationTable[0][3] = 0;
76            multiplicationTable[1][0] = 0;
77            multiplicationTable[1][1] = 1;
78            multiplicationTable[1][2] = 2;
79            multiplicationTable[1][3] = 3;
80            multiplicationTable[2][0] = 0;
81            multiplicationTable[2][1] = 2;
82            multiplicationTable[2][2] = 4;
83            multiplicationTable[2][3] = 6;
84            multiplicationTable[3][0] = 0;
85            multiplicationTable[3][1] = 3;
86            multiplicationTable[3][2] = 6;
87            multiplicationTable[3][3] = 9;
88
89        System.out.println("3 times 2 = " +
90            multiplicationTable[3][2]);
91        System.out.println("2 times 3 = " +
92            multiplicationTable[2][3]);
93
94        /////////////////////////////////////
95        // The Classroom Schedule Table
96        /////////////////////////////////////
97
98        System.out.println("\nThe Classroom Schedule Table\n");
99
100       final int AM = 0, PM = 1;
101       final int Monday = 0, Tuesday = 1, Wednesday = 2,
102           Thursday = 3, Friday = 4;
103       int[][][] weekSchedule =
104       {
105         { // Monday
106           {104, 106, 103, 205}, // AM block
107           {104, 205, 105, 206}  // PM block
108         },
109         { // Tuesday
110           {206, 106, 103, 205}, // AM block
111           {205, 104, 105, 103}  // PM block
112         },
113         { // wednesday
114           {205, 206, 105, 104}, // AM block
```

```
115                 {104, 106, 103, 205}   // PM block
116            },
117            {  // Thursday
118                 {104, 106, 206, 205},  // AM block
119                 {105, 206, 103, 106}   // PM block
120            },
121            {  // Friday
122                 {206, 106, 103, 104},  // AM block
123                 {205, 104, 105, 103}   // PM block
124            }
125         };
126         System.out.println("Schedule for Wednesday:");
127         System.out.println("Block    " +
128            "Class1  Class2  Class3  Class4");
129         System.out.println(" AM        " +
130            weekSchedule[wednesday][AM][0] + "      " +
131            weekSchedule[wednesday][AM][1] + "      " +
132            weekSchedule[wednesday][AM][2] + "      " +
133            weekSchedule[wednesday][AM][3]);
134         System.out.println(" PM        " +
135            weekSchedule[wednesday][PM][0] + "      " +
136            weekSchedule[wednesday][PM][1] + "      " +
137            weekSchedule[wednesday][PM][2] + "      " +
138            weekSchedule[wednesday][PM][3]);
139      }
140  }
```

This program produces the following output:

```
The 'ages' and 'familyAges' arrays

Family ages are 47, 43, 17, 12, 10, 5

The 'squareRoot' array

Square root of 3 is 1.732

The Game Scores Table

"Our" score in the 11th game: 21
"Their" score in the 7th game: 3

The Multiplication Table

3 times 2 = 6
2 times 3 = 6

The Classroom Schedule Table

Schedule for Wednesday:
Block  Class1  Class2  Class3  Class4
 AM      205     206     105     104
 PM      104     106     103     205
```

Some notes, as usual:

- We used constants for the names of the days – better than remembering that Monday is day 0…
- We broke long statements into several lines, and tried to arrange them so that the program looks nice and neat – it's easier to read.
- We used strings with spaces to arrange the output of the schedule to look like a table. That section of the program looks a little long, but the output is nice!
- We used an escape sequence to print the double quote in the scores output. That's the only way we could print out double quotes, because they are used to enclosed the string itself and without the backslash the compiler would think the string ends right at the beginning.

STRINGS

In the discussions up till now, we were focusing on data that is of numeric nature, and on calculations that involve these types of data. We used non-numeric – text data – only for creating output that people can understand by providing some text that describes the numbers we were printing. The way we have used strings were very simple: we just put them where we wanted text to appear. Sometimes we connected a few strings together (called *concatenation*) to create a single string out of several pieces of information from other strings. We also turned numeric values into strings (called **conversion**) when we concatenated strings and numbers. We did not really "peek" into any string, did not try to "chop" strings into pieces or do any other "surgery" on them.

But we have not done them justice… Text strings are very important to data processing, because much of the processing of information is not numeric. For example, names of people, addresses, subjects of classes, titles of books, whole essays – all these are not numbers, but texts. And the data type that allows us to take good care of texts is the string.

Unlike the **primitive data types** you learned about in *"Types and Values"* below (such as integer and floating point numbers, characters, etc.), strings are a complex data type, and are actually *objects* (a concept about which you will learn in Part Three). In a sense they are similar to arrays: they can be viewed as a one-dimensional array of characters. As a matter of fact, each character has an index, which is its position in the string (beginning, of course, with an index value of 0 for the first character). But because they are *not really* arrays of characters, the index value cannot be used between square brackets to access individual characters; we need different methods to deal with strings, and we will learn all about it in section Part Three.

For now, there are two things we know how to do with strings: concatenation and conversion. The rules for both are very simple:

❑ Concatenation – use the + sign between two strings to create a new one.
❑ Conversion – use any primitive data type where a string should be used, and it's value will be converted to a string.

Examples of how these rules are used can be found in many of the examples we already saw. Look at lines 89–92 in the program in *"Arraying It All For Review"*: we use both conversion (`multiplicationTable[3][2]` and `multiplicationTable[2][3]` are of type `int`, and are converted to a string because of the concatenation with the string to their left), and concatenation (using the + sign between a string and any other data type). Lines 94–95 use plain concatenation between two strings, and we use it there only to break a long line into two – we really want only one string with both parts together.

REFERENCES

Most variables, whether of a primitive or a complex data type, are expected to be homes for some data. A variable of type `int` is housing integers, a string variable is home for a text string. But variables of type **reference** are not like that; the only information they have is where the data actually is – they point, or refer, to the data; they do not have the data itself. That is also the reason that they are also called **pointers**.

You already used variables of type reference without knowing (yes, we tricked you…): when you declared (in *"One-Dimensional Arrays"* above) the array `int[] age` you actually declared a reference to an array of type `int`, not the array itself. If you recall, in order to allocate the array itself, namely all its elements, you needed to use the initializer `new int[5]`. The reference you declared without the initializer was pointing nowhere (actually, its value was the reference literal null – remember that one from *"Literals"* above?). Only when you added the initializer was it pointing to the data. Let's break it into steps:

```
float[] testScores;    // declare a reference to an array
            // of type float
testScores = new float[30];// allocates 30 elements for the array,
            // and set the reference to the first one
```

Between the first and the second lines, the value of the testScores is null. If you tried to use an element at that point, such as testScore[14], you would get an error because there are no elements yet, just a reference pointing into never-never land… After the second line is executed, the reference has a real value – it points to the actual elements of the array.

It gets even more interesting when we look into multi-dimensional arrays. A two-dimensional array, declared using [] [], is actually an array of references to a reference. Confused? Don't worry – let's break it down into steps.

Assume we want to have an arrays of test grades in four subjects, but we do not have the same number of tests in each subject: 12 for Math, 8 for Science, 3 for Health and 5 for Social Studies. The table might look like this:

Test Number	0	1	2	3	4	5	...	10	11
Math (0)	A-	B+	B	C-	A-	B-		A+	B
Science (1)	B-	A-	B+	B+	A	A-		---	---
Health (2)	C-	B-	C+	---	---	---		---	---
Social (3)	D	D+	C-	C+	D-	---		---	---

We need all 12 columns for Math, but only 3 columns for Health. If we create an array of size 12 by 4, we will be wasting a lot of memory for all the "slots" that do not have a grade to be stored in. So it would be wasteful to declare:

```
String[][] testGrades = new String[4][12];
```

We are allocating 48 elements (12 times 4) when we actually need only 28 (12+8+3+5). In order to avoid that waste, we can allocate each row separately, using references to arrays:

```
final int subjectMath = 0, subjectScience = 1,
subjectHealth = 2, subjectSocial = 3;
String[][] testGrades;     // an array of references to
                // arrays of type String
testGrades = new String[4][]; // allocate an array
                // of 4 references
testGrades[subjectMath] = new String[12];   // allocate 12 Strings
testGrades[subjectScience] = new String[8]; // allocate 8 Strings
testGrades[subjectHealth] = new String[3];  // allocate 3 Strings
testGrades[subjectSocial] = new String[5];  // allocate 5 Strings
```

We could use initializers for the rows, accomplishing the same allocation but also assigning values to the array's elements:

```
testGrades[subjectMath] = new String[]
   {"A-", "B+", "B", "C-", "A-", "B-",
   "A-", "B", "B-", "A", "A+", "B"};
testGrades[subjectScience] = new String[]
   {"B-", "A-", "B+", "B+", "A", "A-", "C+", "A"};
testGrades[subjectHealth] = new String[]
   {"C+", "B-", "C-"};
testGrades[subjectSocial] = new String[]
   {"D", "D+", "C-", "C+", "D-"};
```

Reference variables have some other interesting behavior: when you assign from one variable to another, you are not creating a copy of the data – just another reference to it.

To demonstrate this behavior, let's look at another example of an array: this time, we will collect information about students' fund-raising activities. Each of the 20 students is selling candy to raise money for the school trip; there are three types of candy: chocolate, taffy and cookies. A table summarizing the quantities that each student sold would look like this:

Student Number	Chocolate (0)	Taffy (1)	Cookies (2)
0	3	4	4
1	5	1	0
2	12	23	17
3	2	0	1
...			
18	7	0	5
19	0	2	4

The declaration of this array and its associated constants would be this:

```
final int chocolate = 0, taffy = 1, cookies = 2;
int[][] candySales = new int[20][3];
```

Let's pick one student, number 2, whose amazing taffy sales are stored in `candySales[taffy][2]`. If we get a report that one more taffy package was sold by this student, making his total 24, we would write

```
candySales[2][taffy] = 24;
```

It so happens that students 6 and 7 are twins, and usually do everything together and in the same way. So their sales are the same, and we would like to record this information in the following way:

```
candySales[6][chocolate] = 6;
candySales[6][taffy] = 3;
candySales[6][cookies] = 8;
candySales[7] = candySales[6];
```

Note that the last line intends to copy the information about one twin's sales to the other twin's row, but we will soon see that there is a problem with that operation.

Now the second twin, younger by only 10 minutes and tired of always being a copy of his "older" sibling, sneaks out and sells 5 more chocolate packages to a neighbor, making his total sales 11 packages. We update his record by writing

```
candySales[7][chocolate] = 11;
```

If we print out `candySales[6][chocolate]` and `candySales[7][chocolate]`, we would expect them to be 6 and 11. But here's the surprise: they will *both* be 11! Why??? Simple enough: when you thought you were copying the information from row 6 to row 7, you were not; you only copied the reference, so both `candySales[6]` and `candySales[7]`, which are only references to the arrays, are now pointing to the *same* row in memory. It's like two people watching a car through two windows: if the car's door is opened, both watchers will see it, not only the one who was there first. The correct way to make the copy of the whole row is to copy each element individually, by writing:

```
candySales[7][chocolate] = candySales[6][chocolate];
candySales[7][taffy] = candySales[6][taffy];
candySales[7][cookies] = candySales[6][cookies];
```

(There are also other, simpler, ways – we would learn them later.)

You must remember this trap – *references are not the data itself, only pointers to it*, and there can be many pointers pointing to the same data.

There is another secret we would like to share with you: variables of type String are also references. They point to a String object which holds the actual text. But unlike arrays, strings are **immutable** (unchangeable) – you cannot use the reference to get to the text and change it; the contents of the string is "read-only". Since strings are references, the two statements

```
String s1 = "abc";
String s2 = "abc";
```

cause both strings variables s1 and s2 to point to the same literal string "abc". Adding

```
String s3 = s1;
```

will cause s3 also to point to the same place, but because strings are immutable you do not have to worry about the multi-reference trap – you will never be able to change the contents of any of the strings anyway.

To summarize the subject of references, here is a program that uses them heavily:

```
01  // Example 6, file 'Ref.java'
02  // This program demonstrates the use of
03  // references
04
05  public class Ref
06  {
07      public static void main(String[] args)
08      {
09
10          /////////////////////////////////////////
11          // The Test Grades Table
12          /////////////////////////////////////////
13
14          System.out.println("\nThe Test Grades Table\n");
15
16          final int subjectMath = 0, subjectScience = 1,
17              subjectHealth = 2, subjectSocial = 3;
18          // Make sure that the order of values
19          // in the initializer is the same as
20          // the order of the subjects
21          final String[] subjects =
22              {"Math", "Science", "Health", "Social Studies"};
23          int testNumber, subjectNumber;
24
25          // Initialize table
26          String[][] testGrades = new String[4][];
27          testGrades[subjectMath] = new String[]
28              {"A-", "B+", "B", "C-", "A-", "B-",
29              "A-", "B", "B-", "A", "A+", "B"};
30          testGrades[subjectScience] = new String[]
31              {"B-", "A-", "B+", "B+", "A", "A-", "C+", "A"};
32          testGrades[subjectHealth] = new String[]
33              {"C-", "B-", "C+"};
34          testGrades[subjectSocial] = new String[]
35              {"D", "D+", "C-", "C+", "D-"};
36
37          // Print out specific grades
38          subjectNumber = subjectScience;
39          testNumber = 5;
40          System.out.println("Grade in " +
```

```
41          subjects[subjectNumber] +
42          " test #" + testNumber +
43          " is " + testGrades[subjectNumber][testNumber]);
44      subjectNumber = subjectHealth;
45      testNumber = 2;
46      System.out.println("Grade in " +
47          subjects[subjectNumber] +
48          " test #" + testNumber +
49          " is " + testGrades[subjectNumber][testNumber]);
50      subjectNumber = subjectMath;
51      testNumber = 11;
52      System.out.println("Grade in " +
53          subjects[subjectNumber] +
54          " test #" + testNumber +
55          " is " + testGrades[subjectNumber][testNumber]);
56
57      ///////////////////////////////////////
58      // The Fundraising Table
59      ///////////////////////////////////////
60
61      System.out.println("\nThe Fundraising Table\n");
62
63      final int chocolate = 0, taffy = 1, cookies = 2;
64      // Make sure that the order of values
65      // in the initializer is the same as
66      // the order of the candyTypes
67      final String[] candyTypes =
68          {"Chocolate", "Taffy", "Cookies"};
69      int[][] candySales = new int[20][3];
70      int studentNumber, candyNumber;
71
72      // Initialize a student row
73      candySales[6][chocolate] = 6;
74      candySales[6][taffy] = 3;
75      candySales[6][cookies] = 8;
76
77      // Copy a row (or perhaps not...)
78      candySales[7] = candySales[6];
79
80      // Print out students' sales information
81      candyNumber = chocolate;
82      studentNumber = 6;
83      System.out.println("Student #" + studentNumber +
84          "'s " + candyTypes[candyNumber] +
85          " sales are " +
86          candySales[studentNumber][candyNumber] +
87          " packages");
88      studentNumber = 7;
89      System.out.println("Student #" + studentNumber +
90          "'s " + candyTypes[candyNumber] +
91          " sales are " +
92          candySales[studentNumber][candyNumber] +
93          " packages");
94
95      // Update a single student's sales quantity
96      // (or may be more than only a single student's...)
97      candySales[7][chocolate] = 11;
98      System.out.println("Updated student #7's" +
99          " chocolate sales quantity");
100
101     // Print out students' sales information, again
102     studentNumber = 6;
103     System.out.println("Student #" + studentNumber +
104         "'s " + candyTypes[candyNumber] +
105         " sales are " +
106         candySales[studentNumber][candyNumber] +
107         " packages");
108     studentNumber = 7;
```

```
109        System.out.println("Student #" + studentNumber +
110            "'s " + candyTypes[candyNumber] +
111            " sales are " +
112            candySales[studentNumber][candyNumber] +
113            " packages");
114    }
115 }
```

Once you run this program, here is what you should expect:

```
The Test Grades Table

Grade in Science test #5 is A-
Grade in Health test #2 is C+
Grade in Math test #11 is B

The Fundraising Table

Student #6's Chocolate sales are 6 packages
Student #7's Chocolate sales are 6 packages
Updated student #7's chocolate sales quantity
Student #6's Chocolate sales are 11 packages
Student #7's Chocolate sales are 11 packages
```

What you learned in this chapter:

⋏ *Programs work with different* data types: *numeric(integers and floating-point), Boolean and text (characters and strings)*

⋏ *Specific values in a program are expressed as* literals

⋏ *Changing values are stored in named* variables

⋏ *Fixed values can be stored in* constants

⋏ *Repeating data is stored in* arrays; *each array is made up of elements, all of which are of the same type; each element can be accessed directly using an* index

⋏ *Arrays have one or more* dimensions; *to access an element in a multi-dimensional array, index values for each dimension are needed*

⋏ *Text data is stored in* strings; *unlike arrays, strings cannot be changed*

⋏ Reference *variables point to other variables, literal or constants*

Smooth Operators – Manipulating Values and Variables

> *Once we know what data we are going to process, we have to learn how to "phrase"*
> *the instructions for performing this processing. We will show you what operators do,*
> *very much like in math, to produce new values from a combination of existing values.*
> *Starting with math-like operators (like addition and subtraction), and progress to*
> *more complex and interesting operators, such as those that allow you to test the*
> *relationship between two values (for example, which one is greater).*
>
> *What you will learn in this chapter:*
> - *How to specify calculations using operators*
> - *How to compare values*
> - *How to use logical operators*
> - *About other "special" operators*

"COMMENCE OPERATIONS" – INTRODUCTIONS TO OPERATORS

The "heart" of programming is performing calculations and other types of data manipulations. You know for sure what calculation are; this is what you learned in math – using the four basic arithmetic operators (addition, subtraction, multiplication and division), together with a few more "sophisticated" ones (such as roots, powers, etc.), you know how to calculate results of equations. For example, you know how to calculate the volume of a geometric shape; you know how to figure out the mean, median and average of a set of numbers; and you know many other formulas as well. But what do we mean when we talk about "data manipulation?" This term includes calculations but has much more to it. It describes all the actions that you can program the computer to do with your data: numerical calculation, data organization (like re-arrangement of a table by changing rows into columns as if rotating it 90 degrees), string manipulations (such as extracting the first name of a person from a full name – getting the "George" from "George Washington"), sorting (for example, by last name, first name and age), and so on. Many of these activities do not involve mathematical operations, but they work with the data and change – that's why we call it "data manipulation."

In order to tell the program what data manipulation it has to perform, we use **operators**. An operator is a symbol that has a special meaning for the compiler which makes it produce the machine code to perform a specific actions. The addition operator is a simple one – it only produces code to add two numbers. Other operators may produce much more complex code to perform a more complex operation.

In the following sections we will go over many of the operations you can put in a program. There many categories of operators, based on the type of operation they perform. We will begin with the simple ones, and move on to the more complex ones. We will start with some things that apply to all categories.

Operands and Values

Operators perform operations (Duh!); their "victims" are called **operands**, and the result of performing the operation, namely applying the operator to the operands, is the **value** of the operation. A combination of operators and operands (following certain rules, which you will learn shortly) is called an **expression**; performing the operations on the operands is called **evaluation** of the expression.

For example, in the expression

```
pi * radius
```

pi and radius are the operands of the multiplication (*) operator, and the value of this operation is the multiplication of the value in pi by the value in the variable radius.

Operands can be values of other operations. Look, for example, at the following expression:

```
(pi * radius) * 2
```

We start by multiplying pi by radius, and then the resulting value is multiplied by 2 – the two operands of the second multiplication are the value of the first one and the literal 2. There is no end to the complexity of an operand – it can be any valid variable, literal, constant or value of another operation.

Unary and Binary Operators

Besides the different actions that an operator may perform, there is another distinction separating the operators into two major types. Look at the statement

```
int b = 11, c = 7;
int a = b - c;
```

It means: take the value stored in variable c and subtract it from the value in variable b, and then store the result in variable a. The value of a will be 11 - 7 which is 4. The minus sign (-) operator was applied to *two* operands, b and c; it's a **binary operator**. But in the statement

```
double minusPi = -pi;
```

there is no literal value; the expression -pi means "the negative value of the variable named pi." The minus sign operates on only *one* operand. It's a **unary operator**.

But be careful: not all minus signs are operators! If you take the minus sign in front of -7 in the statement

```
negSeven = -7;
```

it serves to tell us that we are using the value "negative seven;" it's not an operator, but part of the literal value.

NUMERICAL OPERATORS

Basic Arithmetic Operators

We all know the basic numerical operators – these are the same as the arithmetic operators we always use. The well-known binary operators are addition (+), subtraction (-), multiplication(*) and division(/). Usually, they behave as you might expect, except for the situations described in *"When Things Go Wrong – Truncation and Overflow"* above. The unary plus (+) and minus (-) operators are also pretty dull…

The Remainder Operator

There are few more operators, though, which are quite interesting. Let's introduce a valuable member of the numeric binary operators group – the **remainder** operator (%). It does exactly as it name says – calculates the remainder of a division. And it works for both integers and floating-point numbers, even though there are some differences in the results.

```
int remainderInteger = 27 % 4;
System.out.println("remainderInteger = " +
  remainderInteger);
The expected result is remainderInteger = 3. However,
double remainderDouble = 24.6 % 3.5;
System.out.println("remainderDouble = " +
  remainderDouble);
```

prints out remainderDouble = 0.1999999999999993, which is not the 0.2 that we expected; it's close, though, and this happens because of the way floating-point numbers are stored internally and how floating-point operations are calculated – they sometimes lose precision, when they cannot hold all the digits of a number, as we discussed in *"Types and Values"* above.

The Increment and Decrement Operators

Another group of interesting unary operators is the **increment** and **decrement** operators. Increment is "the process of increasing in number", and decrement is, well, the opposite. These operators apply only to variables, and they add (or subtract) the value of 1 to (or from) the variable to which they are applied. After

```
int numInc = 12;
int numDec = 12;
++numInc;
--numDev;
```

the value of `numInc` is 13, and `numDec` is 11. Perfectly reasonable: the increment and decrement operations worked fine. But these operators appear to have **side-effects**, which are things that happen in addition to the expected behavior of the operation: let's assume we have two variables, `oldNum` and `newNum`, both of type `int`; after executing the statements

```
oldNum = 12;
newNum = 100 + ++oldNum;
```

the value of `newNum` will be 113: we started with 12, the `++` added 1, and then we added 100 with the regular addition (+) operator. But `newNum` is not the only variable that changed: `oldNum` has changed too (this is the side-effect!), and is now 13 – the `++` does not only add 1, it stores the new value back in the variable. The decrement operator works the same way:

```
oldNum = 12;
newNum = 100 + --oldNum;
newNum will be 111, oldNum will be 11.
```

The `++` or `--` in these examples appear before the variable; they **prefix** it. But you can also put these operator after the variable, so that they **postfix** it. When you do that, the value of the variable will change as before (up or down by 1), but the value used in the expression will be the value *before* the change. In

```
oldNum = 12;
newNum = 100 + oldNum++;
```

`newNum` will be only 112, because the value of `oldNum` *before* applying the `++` is used; `oldNum` will be incremented *after* its value is used, and will become 13 as before.

The increment and decrement operators work exactly the same way with floating-point variables. They do not, however work with *any* type of constant (a variable declared using the word `final` – we talked about this in *"Constants"* above), because you are not allowed to change such a variable after the first time it was assigned a value.

Let's Operate Numerically Together

The following program combines the examples in the previous sections:

```
01  // Example 7, file 'NumOp.java'
02  // This program demonstrates use of
03  // numeric operators
04
05  public class NumOp
06  {
07      public static void main(String[] args)
08      {
09          //////////////////////////////////////
10          // Remainder operator
11          //////////////////////////////////////
12
```

```
13          System.out.println("\nRemainder operator\n");
14
15          int remainderInteger = 27 % 4;
16          System.out.println(
17            "Remainder of 27 divided by 4 = "
18            + remainderInteger);
19
20          double remainderDouble = 24.7 % 3.5;
21          System.out.println(
22            "Remainder of 24.7 divided by 3.5 = "
23            + remainderDouble);
24
25          ///////////////////////////////////////
26          // Increment/decrement operators
27          ///////////////////////////////////////
28
29          System.out.println("\nIncrement/decrement " +
30            "operators\n");
31
32          int numInc = 12;
33          int numDec = 12;
34          ++numInc;
35          --numDec;
36          System.out.println("numInc = " + numInc +
37            ", numDec = " + numDec + "\n");
38
39          int oldNum, newNum;
40          oldNum = 12;
41          newNum = 100 + ++oldNum;
42          System.out.println("newNum = " + newNum +
43            ", oldNum = " + oldNum);
44          oldNum = 12;
45          newNum = 100 + --oldNum;
46          System.out.println("newNum = " + newNum +
47            ", oldNum = " + oldNum);
48          oldNum = 12;
49          newNum = 100 + oldNum++;
50          System.out.println("newNum = " + newNum +
51            ", oldNum = " + oldNum);
52          oldNum = 12;
53          newNum = 100 + oldNum--;
54          System.out.println("newNum = " + newNum +
55            ", oldNum = " + oldNum);
56      }
57 }
```

When running, this is its output:

```
Remainder operator

Remainder of 27 divided by 4 = 3
Remainder of 24.7 divided by 3.5 = 0.1999999999999993

Increment/decrement operators

numInc = 13, numDec = 11

newNum = 113, oldNum = 13
newNum = 111, oldNum = 11
newNum = 112, oldNum = 13
newNum = 112, oldNum = 11
```

RELATIONAL OPERATORS

Here is a group of binary operators which are extremely useful: they allow you to compare values and make decisions based on the result of the comparison. There are six operators in this group, called **relational operators**:

Operator Symbol	Operator Name
==	Equal
!=	Not Equal
<	Less Than
<=	Less Than or Equal
>	Greater Than
>=	Greater Than or Equal

The result of applying a relational operator to two values is always Boolean, namely either `true` or `false`, and it tells you what were the results of comparing those two values.
Examples:

```
11 == 7          is false
11 == 11         is true
7 != 7           is false
11 > 7           is true
11 >= 7          is true
11 < 7           is false
11 <= 7          is false
7 <= 7           is true
3.14 > 3.15      is false
12.34E2 <= 1233  is false
true != true     is false
```

You can use these operators to compare between any combination of variables and literals, or even expressions:

```
pi > 3.2        is false (assuming a correct value for pi)
zero == 0       is true (assuming that the variable zero contains 0)
zero > one      is false (assuming the variable one contains 1)
a >= b              would depend on the values of a and b
time + 5 < time             is false if time is positive
(pi * r * 2) <= (pi * r * r)  would depend on the values of pi and r
(x + y) != (p / q)          who knows…
```

When comparing variables or literals of type `boolean`, only the equal (==) or not-equal (!=) relational operators can be used – it doesn't make sense to check if `true` is larger or smaller than `false`!

You can also use the equal and not-equal operators to compare references. As with `boolean` values, it only makes sense to check if two references point to the same place, not if one is larger than the other. For example, in the case of:

```
int[][] candySales = new int[20][3];
candySales[7] = candySales[6];
int[] row5 = candySales[5];
int[] row6 = candySales[6];
int[] row7 = candySales[7];
boolean areTheyEqual = (candySales[6] == candySales[7]);
boolean is5Equal6 = (row5 == row6);
boolean is6Equal7 = (row6 == row7);
```

the value of `areTheyEqual` will be `true`, `is5Equal6` will be `false` and `is6Equal7` will be `true`.

A relational operator (with its two variables) can appear anywhere a Boolean value can appear. We will see later (in *"Logical Operators"*, *"The Concatenation Operator"* and *"What if – Conditional Execution"*) how this is useful.

Here is a program with examples of relational operators:

```
01  // Example 8, file 'RelOp.java'
02  // This program demonstrates the use of
03  // relational operators
04
05  public class RelOp
06  {
07      public static void main(String[] args)
08      {
09
10          /////////////////////////////////////
11          // Relational operators - numeric values
12          /////////////////////////////////////
13
14          System.out.println("\nRelational operators - " +
15              "numeric values\n");
16
17          int one = 1, zero = 0;
18          double pi = 3.1415;
19
20          System.out.println("11 ==  7 is " + (11 == 7));
21          System.out.println("11 == 11 is " + (11 == 11));
22          System.out.println(" 7 != 7  is " + (7 != 7));
23          System.out.println("11 >  7  is " + (11 > 7));
24          System.out.println("11 >= 7  is " + (11 >= 7));
25          System.out.println(" 7 <= 7  is " + (7 <= 7));
26          System.out.println("3.14 > 3.15 is " +
27              (3.14 > 3.15));
28          System.out.println("12.34E2 <= 1233 is " +
29              (12.34E2 <= 1233));
30          System.out.println("true != true is " +
31              (true != true));
32          System.out.println("pi > 3.2 is " + (pi > 3.2));
33          System.out.println("zero == 0 is " + (zero == 0));
34          System.out.println("zero > one is " + (zero > one));
35
36          /////////////////////////////////////
37          // Relational operators - reference values
38          /////////////////////////////////////
39
40          System.out.println("\nRelational operators - " +
41              "reference values\n");
42
43          int[][] candySales = new int[20][3];
44          candySales[7] = candySales[6];
45          int[] row5 = candySales[5];
46          int[] row6 = candySales[6];
47          int[] row7 = candySales[7];
48          boolean areTheyEqual =
49              (candySales[6] == candySales[7]);
50          boolean is5Equal6 = (row5 == row6);
51          boolean is6Equal7 = (row6 == row7);
52
53          System.out.println("Are They Equal? " +
54              areTheyEqual);
55          System.out.println("Is row 5 equal to row 6? " +
56              is5Equal6);
57          System.out.println("Is row 6 equal to row 7? " +
58              is6Equal7);
59      }
60  }
```

And its output is:

```
Relational operators - numeric values

11 ==  7 is false
11 == 11 is true
 7 != 7  is false
11 >  7  is true
11 >= 7  is true
 7 <= 7  is true
3.14 > 3.15 is false
12.34E2 <= 1233 is false
true != true is false
pi > 3.2 is false
zero == 0 is true
zero > one is false

Relational operators - reference values

Are They Equal? true
Is row 5 equal to row 6? false
Is row 6 equal to row 7? True
```

In case you were wondering why we used parentheses around all relational expressions that were part of the `System.out.println()` statement, such as the (`zero == 0`) – we did that to make sure the compiler understands that the relational expression has to be evaluated first, before using its value to print the result. The use of parentheses is discussed at length later in *"Express Yourself – Using Expressions"* below.

LOGICAL OPERATORS

Logical operators, sometimes called Boolean operators, deal only with values of `true` and `false`. There are one unary and three binary operators in this group.

The unary operator is called logical **complement**, but most people call it the **"not" operator**. Don't confuse the word *complement*, which the dictionary defines as "something that completes or brings to perfection" and usually means "saying the opposite," with the word *compliment*, which is defined as "an expression or act of courtesy or praise" and usually means "saying something nice."

The symbol for this operator is the exclamation point (`!`). When applied to a Boolean value, it produces the opposite: `!true` (pronounced "not true") is obviously `false`, and `!false` is `true`. (It's impolite to say that "not true" is a lie… We just call it false…)

The binary logical operators are a little more powerful and complex. They are called the **and, or** and **xor** (**exclusive or**) operators. Their symbols are `&`, `|` and `^`. For `&`, the result value is `true` if both operand values are `true`; otherwise, the result is `false`. For `|`, the result value is `false` if both operand values are `false`; otherwise, the result is `true`. For `^`, the result value is `true` if the operand values are different; otherwise, the result is `false`. Complex? Not really. Just think about it "logically."

When you say, "That building is tall and brown," it is true only if the building is *both* tall and brown – if both things you said are true; if it is not tall or it is not brown – if any of the things you said is false – everything you said is false; if it is not tall and not brown (let's say it's short an black) – if both parts are false – the statement you made is false too. So both parts of an "and" statement must be true in order for the statement to be true. If we look at all the combinations – there are four altogether – this is what we see:

a	b	a & b
True	True	True
True	False	False
False	True	False
False	False	False

An "or" statement is working the same way, with a different rule. "This car won the race because it's fast or because it's driver is good" is true if *any* of its parts is true – it could be that the car is not fast, but the driver is good, or that the driver is not that good but the car is really fast, or it could be that *both* parts are true. However, if the car is not fast and the driver is not good, the statement will be false (the car may still have won the race, but for a different reason – may be all its competitors crashed…) In a table, it would look like this:

a	b	a | b
True	True	True
True	False	True
False	True	True
False	False	False

The "xor" operator determines if the two values are different, but is much less useful. It is difficult to describe in words, so we will just use its table:

a	b	a ^ b
True	True	False
True	False	True
False	True	True
False	False	False

At this point, you are probably wondering how does all this apply to programming? We need the logical operators to test complex conditions. It is not enough to be able to only compare two numbers (using a relational operator as described in *"Relational Operators"* above) – we may want to make decisions based on more complex situations.

For example, we may want to find out if someone is in middle school by checking if the student is in a grade between 6 and 8 – greater or equal to 6, less or equal to 8; the complete expression for this test is

```
(grade >= 6) & (grade <= 8)
```

It will be `true` only if both conditions are `true` – only grades 6, 7 and 8 are greater-or-equal to 6 and less-or-equal to 8.

Or you might want to check if a person's name is *either* John *or* Jane; you would write

```
(name = "John") | (name = "Jane")
```

This expression will be `false` unless the name is one of those two (it will also be `true` if the person's name is *both* John and Jane, but that's unlikely...) If you want to select people who are *not* John or Jane, there are two ways to say it:

```
!((name = "John") | (name = "Jane"))
(name != "John") & (name != "Jane")
```

The first is saying, "I want all those who are not John-*or*-Jane." The second is asking for "all those who are not John *and* are not Jane." These are two ways to the say the same thing.

Here is a different example: your local police department asked you to make a list of all families in your town which have two or more cars, but their garage is not large enough for all their cars (so they have to park at least one car outside). Of course, they promised to provide you with the information about each family – you only have to help them write the program. A Boolean expression for testing this condition for each family would be:

```
(numberOfCars >= 2) & (garageSize < numberOfCars)
```

If you were also required to list those families which have a boat (most likely also parked outside), the more complex expression would be:

```
((numberOfCars >= 2) & (garageSize < numberOfCars)) | hasBoat
```

Note two interesting things about this expression: First, we used a boolean variable named `hasBoat`, which we expect to be `true` if the family has a boat and `false` if they don't. Second, we used parentheses to make sure that it is clear what the two operands of the "or" operator are – one is the test for "enough garage spaces for all cars", the other "do they have a boat." To get on your list, a family must have more cars that garage spaces, or have a boat, *or have both*.

There are still two things about which you may be wondering: how are you supposed to read in the information from the police department, and how are you going to use this expression in the program you promised to write for them. Not to worry – you will learn this later; you have no reason to be afraid of the police… yet…

BIT AND SHIFT OPERATORS

The bit operators are not very important at this point. You can skip this section, and come back to it later when its subject is more relevant.

The bit operators are the unary "complement" (~) and the binary "and" (&), "or" (|) and "exclusive or" (^).

The shift operators are "left shift" (<<), "right-shift" (>>) and "right-shift-with-zero-fill" (>>>).

THE CONCATENATION OPERATOR

So far, we have discussed operators that perform calculations, comparisons and logic; but we have not discussed operators that work with texts. There are many ways you might want to operate on texts, and we will put off discussing most until we know more about the `string` object (in Part Three).

But at least one operation is important enough, and simple enough, that we want to cover it now. This operation is called **concatenation**, which means "to connect in a series or chain." This is a computer term for taking small pieces and connecting them into a larger piece. Like in a construction set, where you can fit the piece sticking out of one part to the hole in another part and create a chain. The symbol for this operation is the plus sign (+), and when it appears between two string operands it tells the computer to concatenate, or connect, the two strings together into a new, large, one. For example,

```
"This is" + " a string"
```

will create one string: `"This is a string"`. Note the space before the `"a"`: it must be there, otherwise we will have `"This isa string"`! The operands can be string literals or string variables, in any order. Look at this:

```
String part1 = "Welcome to ";
String part2 = "Our Home";
String welcomeMessage = part1 + part2 + "!";
```

This would create the string variable `welcomeMessage`, containing the string `"Welcome to Our Home!"`, made out of three parts: two coming from the string variables `part1` and `part2`, and the last one coming from a string literal `"!"`. It is important to remember also that the original strings that "contributed" to the new one are not changed – they stay exactly as they are and can be used again with the same value.

You probably think, "Big deal! Just take a few strings and slap them together!" But the concatenation operator is smarter than that. You have seen in previous examples that it can also deal with operands that are *not* strings. When we wrote (in the example of *"All Together Now: Literals, Variables and Constants"* above):

```
System.out.println("yes = " + yes + ", no = " + no);
System.out.println("MoonMass = " + MoonMass + " Kgs");
System.out.println("One Mile = " + Mile + " Kms");
System.out.println("FeetPerMile = " + FeetPerMile);
```

We were mixing strings with variables of type `boolean`, `int`, `long` and `double`. The concatenation did not complain – it just silently did the needed "conversion" from the various non-string types into strings, and created new strings from the combination of string literals, string variables and other values converted into strings. Pretty smart, isn't it? You can generally trust the concatenation operator to reliably do these conversions; the only down side is that you have no control on how the result will look: for example, you cannot decide if a floating-point number will be converted into normal decimal or the scientific notation. There are more powerful ways to control the formatting of numbers, but will put off discussing them until later.

THE CONDITIONAL OPERATOR

We talked about unary and binary operators, and they all seemed natural to you because they are based on the operators you know from math. So here's a strange one – a **ternary operator**! Ternary comes from a Latin variation of the word "three," so you can expect this peculiar operator to have three operands. It is called the **conditional operator**.

Let's start by looking at an example in words: do you remember the definition of the absolute value of a number? It is the number itself if it is positive, or its negative value if it is negative. So the absolute value of 5 is 5, and the absolute value of -7 is $-(-7)$ which is 7. If we try to put it in a formula, it would look like this: the absolute value of x (written as $|x|$) is x if $x \geq 0$, and $-x$ otherwise (that is if $x < 0$). Notice that there are three elements to this formula: the condition ($x \geq 0$), the value in case the condition is `true` (x) and the value if it is `false` ($-x$).

And here is how the conditional operator, which knows how to handle three operands, will do the job:

```
int absX = (x >= 0 ? x : -x);
```

The first operand, between the (and the ?, is the condition; the "if true" operand comes next, between the ? and the :; and last comes the "otherwise" operand, between the : and the).

(Don't tell anybody, but the parentheses around the three parts are not really required; we use them just for clarity – without them, it's not always clear where the first operands starts and the last one ends.)

Here is a program using the conditional operator:

```
01 // Example 9.1, file 'CondOpAbs.java'
02 // This program demonstrates the use of
03 // the conditional operator by calculating
04 // absolute values
05
06 import java.io.*;
07
08 public class CondOpAbs
09 {
10    public static void main(String[] args)
11       throws IOException
12    {
13
14       BufferedReader inputReader = new BufferedReader(
15          new InputStreamReader(System.in));
16       String line;
17
18       ////////////////////////////////////////
19       // The conditional operator
20       ////////////////////////////////////////
21
22       System.out.println("\nThe conditional operator - " +
23          "absolute value\n");
24
25       double x, absX;
26
27       System.out.print("Enter a number: ");
28       line = inputReader.readLine();
29       x = new Double(line).doubleValue();
30       absX = (x >= 0 ? x : -x);
31       System.out.println("|" + x + "|" + " = " + absX);
32    }
33 }
```

Lines 1–4 are the usual comment; lines 6, 8 and 10–11 are those required lines that we never explained (yet…), and lines 14–16 set up reading from the keyboard. Then come lines 27–29, which read in a number you type. The conditional operator is used on line 31 to calculate the absolute value of the number you entered, and line 30 prints out the results on your screen. It would look like this:

```
The conditional operator - absolute value

Enter a number: 9.5
|9.5| = 9.5
```

Or, if you run it again and type another number:

```
The conditional operator - absolute value

Enter a number: -0.0031415e3
|-3.1415| = 3.1415
```

(Note that the program prints out the floating point (type double) numbers any way it sees fit. You have no control over it when you use System.out.println()).

The condition operand (the first operand) of the conditional operator can be any Boolean value or expression. The second and third operands must be both of the same type, which can be numeric, Boolean or reference.

Of course, the conditional operator can be used in more complex situations. Here is a program that classifies people according to their age (telling you which age group a person belongs to):

```
01  // Example 9.2, file 'CondOpAge.java'
02  // This program demonstrates the use of
03  // the conditional operator by determining
04  // a person's age group
05
06  import java.io.*;
07
08  public class CondOpAge
09  {
10     public static void main(String[] args)
11        throws IOException
12     {
13
14        BufferedReader inputReader = new BufferedReader(
15           new InputStreamReader(System.in));
16        String line;
17
18        /////////////////////////////////////////
19        // The conditional operator - age groups
20        /////////////////////////////////////////
21
22        System.out.println("\nThe conditional operator - " +
23           "age groups\n");
24
25        int senior = 55, youth = 18;
26        int age;
27
28        System.out.print("Enter person's age: ");
29        line = inputReader.readLine();
30        age = new Integer(line).intValue();
31        System.out.println("A person of age " + age +
32           "\n belongs to the age group of\n 'older than " +
33           (age >= senior ? senior :
34              (age >= youth ? youth : 0))
35           + " and\n younger than " +
36           (age < youth ? youth :
37              (age < senior ? senior : 150))
38           + "'");
39     }
40  }
```

Ignoring all the "as yet unexplained" lines, let's focus on lines 33–34 and 36–37. Each one is using the conditional operator *twice*. Hang on to your hats – we are "diving" into an explanation that is quite long…

We have three age groups: youth (0–18), adult (18–55) and senior (55–150 – may you live that long!), so the "boundary" ages are 18 and 55. We have to compare the age that was entered with at least two of these limits (and if it is not in the two groups we check for, we assume it is in the third group by **default**).

On lines 33–34, we check for the lower boundary, "older than…" We first determine if the person's age is greater or equal to the "senior" age (as defined on line 25 to be 55) using the condition `age >= senior` (before the first ?); if the result is `true`, the value of the conditional operator will be the value of senior (between the first ? and :) and we are done. If, however, the age is less than the "senior" age, we then have to check if it falls in the adult or youth groups – we use the "otherwise" part of the operator (between the first : and the second)), which we have put between another pair of parentheses for clarity; here we use another conditional operator to check if the age is greater or equal to the age of "youth" (18, as defined on line 25) and the value of the second conditional operator will be either youth or 0 based on this test; this value will be the value of the first conditional operator, because this is the value of its "otherwise" part (after the first :). Lines 36–37 check for the upper boundary, "younger than…", using the same structure.

Here are some of the possible outputs:

```
The conditional operator - age groups

Enter person's age: 17
```

```
A person of age 17
 belongs to the age group of
 'older than 0 and
 younger than 18'
```

```
The conditional operator - age groups

Enter person's age: 45
A person of age 45
 belongs to the age group of
 'older than 18 and
 younger than 55'
```

Try different numbers, and see how it works. Then look very carefully at these lines, because they may not be obvious but are typical of expressions you will be putting together as part of your future programs.

WHEN THINGS GO WRONG – TRUNCATION AND OVERFLOW

Sometimes you need to pay special attention to what some operators are doing. These are situations where the compiler cannot warn you about something about to go wrong, because it cannot know what the actual numbers would be at the time the calculation is performed. Here are a few situations like that.

Integer variables can hold only whole numbers. What would happen if you try to divide 5 by 2? The result should be 2.5, but that's not a whole number; the integer result will be 2, and the 0.5 will fall off – this is called **truncation** ("shortening by cutting off"). We lose information when this happens, but what can one do, except for being careful?

When we discussed types and values (in *"Types and Values"* above), we said that for every type there is a maximum value that the computer can work with. In some cases, you may try to perform a calculation where the result will exceed that value. This is called an **overflow** – it's like a sink overflowing because you poured too much water into it. For example, what will happen if you write:

```
int n = 3;
int i = 1000000000;
int intOverflow = n * i;
System.out.println("intOverflow = " + intOverflow);
```

You would expect a result of 3,000,000,000 (printed without the commas), but that is more than the maximum of 2,147,483,647 allowed for type `int`; what you will get is the unexpected result of `intOverflow = -1294967296`! Obviously, we should not have expected the correct result, because we had an overflow. But why did the number become negative? That is because of the way numbers are stored in memory; the details are not important. Using an `int` variable which contains an overflowed value is allowed, and it's value will be whatever strange number was the result of the overflowed calculation.

When floating-point numbers are used, overflow looks different: instead of getting a strange, unexpected number, you get a value called `Infinity`. This indicate that from the computer's perspective, the number is too big for it to handle and seems infinitely large. The result of the following code:

```
int k = 2;
double s = 1E308;
double doubleOverflow = s * k;
System.out.println("doubleOverflow = " + doubleOverflow);
```

is the text `doubleOverflow = Infinity`. This is so because the maximum value for a `double` is about $1.79 \cdot 10^{308}$, and the result of the calculation would be $2 \cdot 10^{308}$ – overflow!

An overflowed floating-point variable (which has the value of `Infinity`) will cause every expression it is used in to come up as infinity. The only way to "cure" such a variable is to assign it a new, valid, value.

```
double useInfinity = doubleOverflow / 10.0;
System.out.println("useInfinity = " + useInfinity);
```

This will produce `useInfinity = Infinity`.

A similar situation occurs when you divide a number by zero. In math, this gives you a number infinitely large: when you divide 6 by 2 and get 3, it means that 2 fits 3 times in 6; but zero fits an infinite number of time into any number! So the following code:

```
double anyNumber = 1000;
double zero = 0;
double divideByZero = anyNumber / zero;
System.out.println("divideByZero = " + divideByZero);
```

Will produce `divideByZero = Infinity`.

Dividing an integer by zero, however, causes a program error – there is no integer `Infinity`.

The following program contains examples of all the situations described above:

```
01  // Example 10, file 'TruncOflow.java'
02  // This program demonstrates cases of
03  // truncation and overflow
04
05  public class TruncOflow
06  {
07     public static void main(String[] args)
08     {
09        ////////////////////////////////////
10        // Truncation
11        ////////////////////////////////////
12
13        System.out.println("\nTruncation\n");
14
15        int truncatedValue = 5 / 2;
16        System.out.println("truncatedValue = " +
17           truncatedValue);
18
19        ////////////////////////////////////
20        // Overflow
21        ////////////////////////////////////
22
23        System.out.println("\nOverflow\n");
24
25        int n = 3;
26        int i = 1000000000;
27        int intOverflow = n * i;
28        System.out.println("intOverflow = " +
29           intOverflow);
30
31        int k = 2;
32        double s = 1E308;
33        double doubleOverflow = s * k;
34        System.out.println("doubleOverflow = " +
35           doubleOverflow);
36
37        double usedInfinity = doubleOverflow / 10.0;
38        System.out.println("usedInfinity = " +
39           usedInfinity);
40
41        ////////////////////////////////////
42        // Divide by zero
43        ////////////////////////////////////
44
45        System.out.println("\nDivide by zero\n");
46
47        double anyDouble = 1000;
48        double zeroDouble = 0;
49        double divideByZeroDouble = anyDouble / zeroDouble;
50        System.out.println("divideByZeroDouble = " +
```

```
51          divideByZeroDouble);
52
53      int anyInteger = 1000;
54      int zeroInteger = 0;
55      int divideByZeroInteger = anyInteger / zeroInteger;
56      System.out.println("divideByZeroInteger = " +
57          divideByZeroInteger);
58    }
59 }
```

This program will generate this output:

```
Truncation

truncatedValue = 2

Overflow

intOverflow = -1294967296
doubleOverflow = Infinity
usedInfinity = Infinity

Divide by zero

divideByZeroDouble = Infinity
Exception in thread "main" java.lang.ArithmeticException: / by zero
        at ClassTruncOflow.main(ClassTruncOflow.java:52)
```

Notice the error message ("exception") on the last lines? We will talk about errors and how to handle them later, in *"How to Tackle Errors."* But the message gives you a pretty good idea of what went wrong, doesn't it?

What you learned in this chapter:

⋏ Operators *are used to describe calculations and other data manipulations*

⋏ *Operators operate on* operands*:* unary *operators have one operand,* binary *operators have two, and* ternary *operators have three*

⋏ *The result of an operator operating on its operands is its* value

⋏ Numerical *operators are used for* calculations *of numeric values; their values are numbers*

⋏ Relational *operators are used to* compare *values; their own values are "true" or "false"*

⋏ Logical *operators are used to* check *for truth or falsehood; their values are also "true" or "false"*

⋏ *The* Concatenation *operator is used to "attach" strings together; its value is a string*

⋏ *The* Conditional *operator is used to select a value based on a condition; its own value is the selected value*

⋏ Truncation *or* Overflow *can happen when a calculation comes up with a result that the computer cannot handle*

Express Yourself – Using Expressions

> *Knowing what data you work with and what you want to do with it is not enough. We will now show you how to put this into a form that can actually tell the computer to perform calculations or other data-manipulation activities, and then save the results somewhere so that they can be used later.*
>
> *What you will learn in this chapter:*
> - *How to tell the computer to perform calculations*
> - *How to instruct the computer to store result*
> - *How to mix different data types*

To tell you the truth, much of what you will learn in this section you already know – you have read about most of it in the previous sections and saw it in the examples. But we need to make sure that we did not miss anything, so we will summarize some things you already know but define them precisely, and also add a few more details that we have not discussed yet.

We saw many examples of expressions, but have never really defined what they are. So here goes: as we explained in *"Operands and Values,"* an *expression* is a combination of literals, variables and operators that can be evaluated (calculated) and produces a value. This definition is not "mathematically precise," but should give you an idea. Of course, there are rules as to how to put together that combination of elements so that the evaluation works the way we want it to. And this are the rules for expression *evaluation*. We will go over these rules shortly, in *"Expression Evaluation."*

Once we have an expression evaluated, and we have its value in our hands, what can we do with it? Many things. But the most important one is storing it somewhere – usually in a variable. This is called *assignment* of the value to a variable. That will be described later in *"Assignments."* The reason we discuss assignments *before* we finish discussing expressions is that assignments are actually a special type of expressions, so we want to cover that before we close the subject of expressions.

Most of the expressions we saw dealt with only one data type (integers, floating-point, and others). Some situations, however, call for mixing different data types. In these cases we have to force one data type to become another. This is called *casting*, and we will explore these circumstances in *"Mixed-Type Expressions – Promotions, Conversions and Casts."*

EXPRESSION EVALUATION

Not All Operators Are Equal – Precedence and Parentheses

Most likely you learned in math that in an expression using both multiplication/division and addition/subtraction, the multiplication/division has **precedence**, which mean they come first and are evaluated before the addition/subtraction. For example, in the mathematical expression 5 · 3 + 6, you know to multiply 5 by 3 before adding the result to 6. If you want to first add 3 to 6 and then multiply the result by 5, you would write 5 · (3 + 6) – the parentheses changing the order of evaluation. The same rules apply to expressions in your programs.

When you have an expression with only addition and subtraction, they have the same precedence. So the rule is that they are evaluated left-to-right: the first operator to be evaluated is the one on the left, then the next one to its right, and so on. So in 9 + 6 – 3 the addition is evaluated first, while in 8 – 2 + 9 the subtraction is done first, just because of their position in the expression. We say that the addition and subtraction are **left-associative operators**. So are the multiplication and division operators: when you only have those in an expression, they too are evaluated left-to-right. Of course, you *need* parentheses if the order of evaluation *is* important, such as in 8 − (5 + 1) which is different than (8 − 5) + 1. As before, the same rules apply in programming.

Keep in mind that in all the examples we just looked at, you would usually find some variables instead of all literals. For example the next-to-last sentence in the previous paragraph means that a − (b + c) is different than (a − b) + c. (When *will* the two expression give the same result? What should be the values of a, b and c?)

The conditional operator is different: not only is it a ternary operator (the only one!), it is also one of the few **right-associative operators** – evaluation of expressions using this operator goes from right-to-left: first the rightmost expression is evaluated, then the one to its left, and so forth. The expression

```
n < 10 ? n : n < 100 ? n / 10 : n < 1000 ? n / 100 : n / 1000
```

which figures out the leftmost (first) digit in a number (as long as it is smaller than 9999), is equivalent to

```
n < 10 ? n : (n < 100 ? n / 10 : (n < 1000 ? n / 100 : n / 1000))
```

which is also easier to understand because of the parentheses. In words, it says the following: if n is less than 10 (it has only one digit), take it as the value of the expression; otherwise, if it is less than 100 (it has only two digits), divide it by 10 – because we are dealing with integers it has the same effect as "chopping off" the rightmost digit, leaving us with the leftmost; otherwise, if the number is less than 1000 (now we are dealing with 3 digits), divide by 100 to "chop off" the two rightmost digits; finally (assuming we have four digits), divide by 1000 the get rid of the rightmost three. You can see that the operator associates from right to left by the way the parentheses are placed, even though they are not necessary for the compiler to know what to do – only for us humans… Frankly, using left-association with this operator would not make sense anyway…

The following program lets you experiment with the expression we just developed:

```
01  // Example 11, file 'Assoc.java'
02  // This program demonstrates the right-
03  // associativity of the conditional
04  // operator
05
06  import java.io.*;
07
08  public class Assoc
09  {
10
11      public static void main(String[] args)
12          throws IOException
13      {
14          BufferedReader inputReader = new BufferedReader(
15              new InputStreamReader(System.in));
16          String line;
17
18          /////////////////////////////////////////
19          // Right-associative Conditional operator
20          /////////////////////////////////////////
21
22          // Read a number
23
24          System.out.print("Enter a number between 0 and 9999: ");
25          line = inputReader.readLine();
26          int i = new Integer(line).intValue();
27
28          // Figure out first digit and print it
29
30          int f = i < 10 ? i : i < 100 ?
31              i / 10 : i < 1000 ?
32              i / 100 : i / 1000;
33          System.out.println("The first digit of " + i +
34              " is " + f);
```

```
35     }
36 }
```

Here is output from running this program:

```
Enter a number between 0 and 9999: 8765
The first digit of 8765 is 8
```

Another run produced this output:

```
Enter a number between 0 and 9999: 765
The first digit of 765 is 7
```

The rules regarding order of evaluation do not stop with the left- or right-association. We also have to deal with the order of evaluation of the operands themselves (when there are more than one – mostly for binary operators), because each operand might be an expression in its own right. The rule is that the left operand is evaluated first, and then the right operand. This is extremely important because of possible dangerous side-effects. We will show you one such case shortly, in *"Chained and Embedded Assignments."*

Truncation and Overflow Strike Again

Following the rules of math does not always work in programming. Remember truncation (*"When Things Go Wrong – Truncation and Overflow"* above)? In math, $4 \cdot 7 / 2$ is the same as $7 / 2 \cdot 4$. But not in programming! But *why*, you might ask in outrage? Calm down… Here's the explanation: when the expressions are evaluated left-to-right, the first one produces 14 ($4 \cdot 7$ is 28; 28 / 2 is 14), while the second one produces 12 (7 / 2 is 3, *not 3.5*, because of integer truncation; $3 \cdot 4$ is 12). *Beware of truncation! It is hiding where you least expect it!* So the order of the operators in the expression *is* important, if only to avoid truncation. (Another reason is side-effects, which we will discuss shortly.)

Overflow is another trap waiting for you to fall into, and it's trickier than truncation.

```
double d = 8e307;
double e1 = 4.0 * d * 0.5;
double e2 = 2.0 * d;
```

Mathematically, `e1` and `e2` should have the same value: $1.6 \cdot 10^{308}$ (`1.6e308`). But when `e1` is evaluated, multiplying $8 \cdot 10^{307}$ by 4 will cause an overflow, whose value is `Infinity`, and then everything you try to do with `Infinity` will always produce Infinity. So `e2` will have the correct value, but `e1` will have the value of `Infinity`. Too bad…

Your Evaluation, Please...

The program below shows some examples of expression evaluation:

```
01 // Example 12, file 'Eval.java'
02 // This program demonstrates the use of
03 // assignment  operators
04
05 public class Eval
06 {
07    public static void main(String[] args)
08    {
09
10       ////////////////////////////////////////
11       // Expression evaluation
12       ////////////////////////////////////////
13
14       System.out.println("\nExpression evaluation\n");
15
16       boolean same;
17
18       int a = 8, b = 5, c = 1;
```

```
19       same = (a - b + c) == (a - (b + c));
20       System.out.println(
21          "for a=" + a + ", b=" + b + ", c=" + c +
22          "\n (a - b + c) == (a - (b + c)) is " + same);
23
24       double x = 2.5, y = 11.25, z = 7.333;
25       same = (x * y / z) == (x * (y / z));
26       System.out.println(
27          "for x=" + x + ", y=" + y + ", z=" + z +
28          "\n (x * y / z) == (x * (y / z)) is " + same);
29
30       long k = 21, l = 13, m = 74;
31       same = (k * l + m) == (k * (l + m));
32       System.out.println(
33          "for k=" + k + ", l=" + l + ", m=" + m +
34          "\n (k * l + m) == (k * (l + m)) is " + same);
35
36       // Overflow
37
38       double d = 8e307;
39       double e1 = 4.0 * d * 0.5;
40       double e2 = 2.0 * d;
41       System.out.println("e1=" + e1);
42       System.out.println("e2=" + e2);
43    }
44 }
```

You should get this output when you run it:

```
Expression evaluation

for a=8, b=5, c=1
 (a - b + c) == (a - (b + c)) is false
for x=2.5, y=11.25, z=7.333
 (x * y / z) == (x * (y / z)) is false
for k=21, l=13, m=74
 (k * l + m) == (k * (l + m)) is false
e1=Infinity
e2=1.6E308
```

Lines 19, 25 and 31 are where we test the use of parentheses. On each of these lines, we compare an expression without parentheses, where the normal order of evaluation is used, with a similar expression that has parentheses forcing a different order of evaluation. In all cases, of course, you can see that the parentheses actually make a difference in the final result (even though we do not print out the actual numbers, just the result of the comparison). Notice that when the operators belong to the same group (addition/subtraction or multiplication/division) the order of evaluation without parentheses is left-to-right – these are all left-associative; when the two groups are involved, the multiplication/division group has precedence over the addition/subtraction and these operators are evaluated first. Try to modify these expressions using different operators and perhaps more complex expressions. (Note, however, that lines 22, 28 and 34 contain strings, not expressions, so changing the expressions on lines 19, 25 and 31 will have no effect on those lines – you have to change them separately if you want the text printed out to reflect the test!)

A final note about this example: lines 39 and 40 show the effect the order of evaluation can have on generating errors, as we have described in *"Truncation and Overflow Strike Again"* above.

ASSIGNMENTS

We already hinted at the special circumstances surrounding assignments. Let's clarify: **assignment statements** are used to store the value of an expression in a variable, but are themselves expressions. Naturally, the value of the expression is that variable. In most cases this will mean the value of the just-calculated expression, but when references are involved it may get a little more confusing – it would be the pointer to wherever that variable was pointing to. Later, in *"Chained and Embedded Assignments,"* we will discuss the importance of these rules.

Compound Assignments

You are now familiar with the basic assignment operator, where we use the = sign. But this is not the only assignment operator. There is a whole set of assignment operators that combine regular operator with assignment, called **compound assignment operators**. They are *=, /=, %=, +=, -=, <<=, >>=, >>>=, &=, ^=, |=. Let's look at the += operator:

```
int i = 3;
i += 5;
```

Is equivalent to:

```
int i = 3;
i = i + 5;
```

The value of i will be 8 in both cases. Simple enough, isn't it? The other compound assignment operators work exactly the same way. The way you "construct" a compound assignment operator is by taking the symbol of the standard operator and putting a = after it; that's all it takes.

It might occur to you that the compound assignment operators have a lot in common with the increment and decrement operators which we met in *"The Increment and Decrement Operators"* above, and you would be correct: all these operators do more than just calculate – they also store the results back into the operand which is a variable. You might even look at the prefix increment and decrement operators as a compound assignment (+= or -=) with the second operand having the value of 1; the postfix operators, however, are different because they only store the new value back in the variable *after* the operation is done, so they have a "delayed effect" on the variable. The significance of that will become clear shortly.

Chained and Embedded Assignments

Expressions involving assignments have one more thing to consider: we can have **chained assignments**. For example:

```
int a, b, c;
a = b = c = 11;
```

Intuitively, you expect that all variables will get the value 11, and that is what will actually happen. But the steps to get there are less intuitive: first, the expression c = 11 is evaluated; the value 11 is assigned to the variable c, and the value of this expression is c, which is then assigned to b; and so on. To make it perfectly clear, parentheses might help:

```
a = (b = (c = 11));
```

You can see here that the simple assignment operator is right-associative. The compound assignment operators are right-associative too.

Assignments can also appear in the middle of any expression, and are then called **embedded assignments**. Take, for example, the following:

```
int i, j;
i = 5 * (j = 8) + 11;
```

It's like calculating $5 \cdot 8 + 11$ and assigning that value to the variable i, only we also snuck in the assignment of the value 8 to the variable j.

It is worth while remembering that the value of the variable in the left-hand side of an assignment is saved before the expression on the right-hand side is evaluated. Here is an example of the importance of this rule:

```
int m = 3;
m *= (m = 5) * (m - 1);
```

The value of m will be 60, because the evaluation goes in the following sequence: first, the value of m (that is, 3) is saved; then the expression (m = 5) * (m - 1) is evaluated by assigning the value 5 to m, and then multiplying it by m - 1 (now 4) to get 20; then the original value of m (the saved 3) is multiplied by the 20 to give us 60; this value is then assigned to m. This is exactly like writing:

```
m = m * (m = 5) * (m - 1);
```

It can get even worse when we have side-effects. As an example, let's look at what might happen when using compound assignments as embedded assignments:

```
double f1 = 22.5, f2 = 22.5;
f1 /= ((f1 -= 17.5) + (f1 - 2.5));
f2 /= ((f2 - 2.5) + (f2 -= 17.5));
```

Try to figure out on your own what the values of f1 and f2 will be.

Did you get f1=3.0 and f2=0.9? You are good! But let's explain it anyway, particularly why they did not have the same value. If we ignore the -= operator and use - instead, the two variable would have the same value because the order of the operand for the + operator does not matter. But the -= changes the value of the variable, and this is the reason for the difference.

Since the compound assignment operators look similar to the increment/decrement operators, they are also exposed to the same dangers. Notice the different value for j2 in the following example:

```
int j1 = 7, j2 = 7, j3 = 7;
j1 += ((j1 += 1) + j1);
j2 += ((j2++) + j2);
j3 += ((++j3) + j3);
```

The values of j1 and j3 will be 23, but j2 will be only 22 because the result of j2++ was not stored immediately in j2 so the evaluation of (j2++) + j2 uses the original value of j2 on the left-hand side rather than the incremented value. Try to do those calculations yourself, step by step, and make sure that you understand how the results are arrived at.

In general, it is a good practice *not* to use embedded assignments – the side-effects are too confusing and dangerous.

And Your Assignment Is...

The following program includes all the little example we saw in the previous sections:

```
01  // Example 13, file 'Assign.java'
02  // This program demonstrates the use of
03  // assignment operators
04
05  public class Assign
06  {
07      public static void main(String[] args)
08      {
09
10          ///////////////////////////////////////
11          // Assignment operators
12          ///////////////////////////////////////
13
14          System.out.println("\nAssignment operators\n");
15
16          // Compound assignments
17
18          int l = 3;
19          l += 5;
20          System.out.println("l=" + l);
21
22          // "embeded" assignments
23
24          int i = 0, j = 0;
```

```
25          i = 5 * (j = 8) + 11;
26          System.out.println("i=" + i + ", j=" + j);
27
28          // "embeded" compound assignments
29
30          int m = 3;
31          m *= (m = 5) * (m - 1);
32          System.out.println("m=" + m);
33
34          int j1 = 7, j2 = 7, j3 = 7;
35          j1 += ((j1 += 1) + j1);
36          j2 += ((j2++) + j2);
37          j3 += ((++j3) + j3);
38          System.out.println("j1=" + j1);
39          System.out.println("j2=" + j2);
40          System.out.println("j3=" + j3);
41
42          double f1 = 22.5, f2 = 22.5;
43          f1 /= ((f1 -= 17.5) + (f1 - 2.5));
44          f2 /= ((f2 - 2.5) + (f2 -= 17.5));
45          System.out.println("f1=" + f1);
46          System.out.println("f2=" + f2);
47      }
48 }
```

It's output would be:

```
Assignment operators

l=8
i=51, j=8
m=60
j1=23
j2=22
j3=23
f1=3.0
f2=0.9
```

Go over this program carefully, making sure you understand exactly how the compound, embedded and chained assignments work. Then remember this rule, which is true for everything you do but is particularly important in programming: *keep it simple!* If a statement is difficult to understand, break it into smaller statements; it is more important to write programs that you and others can understand than to squeeze as many expressions as possible into a single statement!

MIXED-TYPE EXPRESSIONS – PROMOTIONS, CONVERSIONS AND CASTS

Each of the expressions we used in previous examples involved only one data type; we never mixed data types in the same expression, and for a good reason: it's tricky and error-prone. But it's time now to overcome our fear of mixed-type expression, and show you why, how, and when to use them.

When you mix data types you have to understand how the program will transforms from one to the other in order to be able to perform the calculations. The way these transformations are done is by special code generated by the compiler; the compiler knows at compile time what needs to be done, based on the literals and variables involved in each operation.

Promotions and Conversions

There are two types of transformations: **promotions** and **conversions**. For all practical purposes, they are very similar. A conversion is the general term for any transformation among data types; a promotion is a specific case of *automatic* conversion of numeric values from a "lower" data type to a "higher" one, where the order (from low to high) is char, byte, short, int, long, float, double. In *"Casts"* below we will show you how to *force* promotions and conversions when they are not likely to be generated automatically.

The most common case of a promotion is when you use a type other than int when you really need an int, for example as the index of an array. When you write:

```
short s = 3;
double d[] = new double[5];
d[s] = 11;
```

The value of the variable s is promoted from short to int, because an index must be of type int. Types char and byte will also be promoted to int under similar circumstances, but this situation is not really meaningful since it hardly has any effect on the program's calculations. The dimension of an array, operands of a unary + or – operator, as well as those of the bitwise complement ~ and the shift operators >>, >>> and << are also promoted to type int. These promotions are called **unary promotions**, because they involve only one value.

A somewhat more interesting case of promotion is when we work with binary operators, and then we have – as you would expect – **binary promotions**. There is a rule that says that each binary operator must have both operands of the same type. So if we write:

```
float f = 1.234;
double d = 9.78654321;
double sum = d + f;
```

the value of f is promoted to a double so that the + will be happy with two doubles. We could have "demoted" d to a float rather than promote f to a double, but the compiler will never do it on its own: we are likely to lose information because the precision (the number of digits a number can have – remember *"Types and Values"* above?) of a float is smaller than that of a double. If the values we were using had a large number of digits, we would lose some digits on such demotions because they may not all fit in the smaller data type.

Another important rule is concerning integer operations: it states that all integer operations are performed with at least the type of int. For example:

```
byte b = 11;
short s =222;
int i = b * s;
```

Both b and s will be first promoted to int, before performing the multiplication. This is more demanding than the expected promotion of b to short and then the result to int.

It's easy when the promotion is between two member of the same "family," such as among integer numbers or floating-point numbers. More complex promotions are performed when the two types are from different families. Look at this example:

```
int i = 7;
double d = 11.95;
double x = d + i;
```

In order to add the 11.95 in d to the 7 in i, that int value has to be promoted to a double. No big deal – floating-point numbers can be much larger, and have much more precision, than integers; converting 11.95 is a no-brainer… The compiler easily produces the code to do it. If we used a literal value for the 7, instead of a variable, the compiler would just substitute 7.0 (in double) and won't have to bother with conversion code.

A trickier situation can come up when using the conditional operator:

```
double q = (n > 10 ? n : 100e30f);
```

If the value of n is larger than 10, its value has to be assigned to q – and that will require a promotion from int to double; if n is smaller or equal to 10, the floating-point literal value will be assigned – and this requires a promotion from float to double; because this is a literal, the compile will just substitute the value of the literal as a double, as if we wrote 100e30D; if we used a float variable, conversion code would have to be generated. You can count on the compile to generate the correct code for either situations of the conditional operator, knowing that at run-time only one of them will happen, depending on the value of n.

So far, it all makes sense but is still not terribly exciting… It gets a little more interesting when we realize that conversions occur *independently for each pair of operands*, not for the whole expression. Take this, for example:

```
int i = 4, j = 10;
double d = 15.0 - j / i;
```

If you thought d will be assigned the value 12.5, you were wrong. You might have expected this result assuming that if all operands are promoted to double, than j / i will be 2.5; but the promotion to double happens *after* j / i was calculated as an integer expression, and its value is only 2 (integer division, no remainder!) – and this is the value promoted to double. So d was assigned the value 13.

By the way, even if we wrote 15 instead of 15.0, the result would still be 13: the integer 2 coming out of the j / i will be subtracted from the integer 15, and then the resulting 13 will be promoted to double. This last promotion is called **assignment conversion**, which makes sure that whatever is assigned to a variable is of the correct type for it.

Some assignment conversions may cause the compiler to think twice, and complain. Here is one such case:

```
int m = 123L;
```

Seems innocent enough, doesn't it? But the compiler is going to complain about "possible loss of precision," because it realizes that it has to generate code to take a literal of type long and "stuff" it into a variable of type int, which may not be able to handle so many digits; it doesn't know that this particular number will fit – it only knows that because of the involved data types the value *may* not fit (apparently, sometimes the compiler is not that smart…). This is, in effect, a demotion of a long to an int; how embarrassing…

The most complex conversion we can talk about at this stage is from a numeric value to a String. When you write:

```
String message = "The value of pi is " + 3.1415;
```

The floating-point value 3.1415 is converted to type String so that it can be concatenated to the other string to create the full message. This is a rather complex conversion, but it's one that the compiler knows how to do for you.

There are other conversions, particularly between values of type reference to objects (which we only mentioned but haven't worked with, yet), but they are beyond the scope of this section.

Casts

Sometimes you must force a conversion from one data type to another. Suppose you want to divide one integer value by another, and you want the real result, not the integer division which gets rid of the fraction. You need to force a promotion of at least one of these integers to double, so that the division operator will be the floating-point operator rather than the integer operator. One way to do it is:

```
int i = 4, j = 10;
double d = 15.0 - j / (double)i;
```

Note that we are using the same example we used in the previous section, where we may have gotten an unexpected result. Now this will not happen. By using a **cast**, which is the (double) in front of i we tell the compiler we insist on promoting variable i to a double. So now the division operator has one int and one double as operands, and the compiler must promote the other int, variable j, to double as well. This division now yields 2.5, and the rest is history… You could have put the cast instead on j, or on both variables, but in this case it was enough to cast only one variable to force a promotion of the other one.

A cast takes the form of the name of the desired data type between parentheses, placed before the value you want to cast. That value does not have to be a variable; it can be a literal or even a whole expression (and then you will need to surround this expression in parentheses to let the compiler know what exactly is the cast applied to). Some examples may be helpful here:

```
int m = (int)123L;
```

This example just shows that you can tell the compiler to ignore its concern about loss of precision: here you tell it that you *do* want to take the `long` value 123L and stuff it into an `int` – this is why you cast it to `int`! But in most cases there is not much point in casting a literal – you might as well write the literal value in its correct type to begin with…

Let's look at another example: suppose you want to calculate the ratio of the numbers of boys to girls in your health, science and gym classes. After you gather the information, you can summarize it in the following table:

Class	Health	Science	Gym
Boys	9	10	12
Girls	7	13	8

Obviously, you need to divide the total number of boys by the total number of girls. This expression would be:

```
int boysHealth = 9, boysScience = 10, boysGym = 12;
int girlsHealth = 7, girlsScience= 13, girlsGym = 8;
double ratio = (boysHealth + boysScience + boysGym) /
   (girlsHealth + girlsScience + girlsGym);
```

Assuming that the variables with the counts are all of type `int`, we should remember the difficulty we had with integer division: we are likely to get an integer number as a result of this division even if the ratio is not a whole number! We need to cast to `double` at least one of the operand of the division operator:

```
double ratio = (boysHealth + boysScience + boysGym) /
   (double)(girlsHealth + girlsScience + girlsGym);
```

And that will force the other one to be promoted as well, and we will get the desired ratio as floating-point number. By the way, without the cast the ratio will come up as 1.0, indicating the same number of boys and girls; that's clearly wrong – there are more boys than girls in these classes!

Mixed Results…

Since most conversions, and promotions in particular, happen automatically, it is difficult to show examples of them when they work properly. So the program that follows is intended to show the situations where they do not work as expected or where casts are used to force them.

```
01 // Example 14, file 'Mixed.java'
02 // This program demonstrates the use of
03 // mixed-type expressions
04
05 public class Mixed
06 {
07    public static void main(String[] args)
08    {
09
10       /////////////////////////////////////////
11       // Mixed-type expressions
12       /////////////////////////////////////////
13
14       System.out.println("\nMixed-type expressions\n");
15
16       // cast to int to override long
17
18       int m = (int)123L;
19
20       // Use cast on a variable to force
21       // floating-point division
```

```
22
23          int i = 4, j = 10;
24          double d1 = 15.0 - j / i;
25          System.out.println("d1=" + d1);
26          double d2 = 15.0 - j / (double)i;
27          System.out.println("d2=" + d2);
28
29          // Use cast on an expression to force
30          // floating-point division
31
32          int boysHealth = 9, boysScience = 10, boysGym = 12;
33          int girlsHealth = 7, girlsScience= 13, girlsGym = 8;
34          double ratio1 = (boysHealth + boysScience + boysGym)
35            / (girlsHealth + girlsScience + girlsGym);
36          System.out.println("ratio1=" + ratio1);
37          double ratio2 = (boysHealth + boysScience + boysGym)
38            / (double)(girlsHealth + girlsScience + girlsGym);
39          System.out.println("ratio2=" + ratio2);
40      }
41 }
```

This program's output is as follows:

```
Mixed-type expressions

d1=13.0
d2=12.5
ratio1=1.0
ratio2=1.1071428571428572
```

The difference between the values of d1 and d2, as well as between ratio1 and ratio2, shows the difference between expression without a cast and those with it. You are welcome to try and change values in both groups to see how integer division behaves when you don't cast…

What you learned in this chapter:

⋏ Expressions *are like formulas, telling the computer to perform a calculation*

⋏ *Expressions are made of variables, literals, operators and parentheses*

⋏ Operators *define what calculations are to be performed between variables and literals*

⋏ *Expressions are* usually *evaluated* left-to-right

⋏ *Some operators have* precedence *over others, so they are performed first*

⋏ Parentheses *re-define the order of calculations if it needs to be different than order of precedence*

⋏ Assignment *operators are used to store results of calculations in variables*

⋏ Compound assignments *also perform a calculation with the variable before the assignment*

⋏ Chained assignments *are used to assign the same value to several variables*

⋏ Embedded assignments *are used to perform assignments during the calculation of a larger expression*

⋏ *Each binary operator requires that both its operands to be of the same data type*

⋏ Conversions *and* promotions *are used to transform between data types*

⋏ *The compiler usually generate automatically the required code for conversions and promotions*

⋏ Casts *are used to force a conversion of an expression, variable or literal to a desired data type*

Let's Put All This To Some Simple Uses

> *You now have enough knowledge to try your hand at some simple programs, and we will show you how to write them. These programs will perform some calculations and process some data, producing results that make sense.*
>
> *What you will learn in this chapter:*
> - ➤ *How to write programs that perform numerical calculations*
> - ➤ *How to write programs that manipulate texts*

VOLUME AND SURFACE AREA

Let's start with programs based on some math that you probably already know. Don't worry – this is not a math lesson; if you don't know the formulas we want to use, just take them as is – you'll probably learn them soon enough anyway.

Pyramid-in-a-Prism

The first program calculates the volume and surface of a prism and a pyramid enclosed in it. Its input are the dimension of the prism, namely its length (*l*), width (*w*) and height (*h*). The formulas we will use are below:

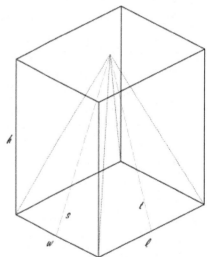

$$V_{Prism} = wlh$$

$$S_{Prism} = 2(hw + hl + lw)$$

$$V_{Pyramid} = \frac{1}{3}wlh$$

$$S_{Pyramid} = wl + ws + lt$$

$$s = \sqrt{h^2 + \left(\frac{l}{2}\right)^2}$$

$$t = \sqrt{h^2 + \left(\frac{w}{2}\right)^2}$$

V is the volume and *S* is the surface area; *s* and *t* are the slant heights of the sides of the pyramids, which are the heights of the triangles making up the sides. They are calculated using Pythagoras' formula from the length and width of the base of the pyramid and its height, which are the same as those of the prism.

The program asks the user to enter the three measurements (*l*, *w*, *h*) as inputs, and prints out the volumes and surface areas as outputs.

```
01  // Example 15, file 'Pyramid.java'
02  // This program calculates the volume
03  // and surface area of a prism and a
04  // pyramid
05
06  import java.io.*;
07  import java.lang.Math;
08
09  public class Pyramid
10  {
11     public static void main(String[] args)
12        throws IOException
13     {
14        BufferedReader inputReader = new BufferedReader(
15           new InputStreamReader(System.in));
16        String line;
17
18        /////////////////////////////////////
19        // Prism and Pyramid calculations
20        /////////////////////////////////////
21
22        System.out.println("\nPrism and Pyramid " +
23           "calculations\n");
24
25        System.out.print("Enter length (l): ");
26        line = inputReader.readLine();
27        double l = new Double(line).doubleValue();
28        System.out.print("Enter width  (w): ");
29        line = inputReader.readLine();
30        double w = new Double(line).doubleValue();
31        System.out.print("Enter height (h): ");
32        line = inputReader.readLine();
33        double h = new Double(line).doubleValue();
34
35        double s = Math.sqrt((h * h) + (l / 2) * ( l / 2));
36        double t = Math.sqrt((h * h) + (w / 2) * ( w / 2));
37        double vPrism = w * l * h;
38        double sPrism = 2 * (h * w + h * l + l * w);
39        double vPyramid = (w * l * h) / 3;
40        double sPyramid = w * l + w * s + l * t;
41        System.out.println("Prism volume is    " + vPrism);
42        System.out.println("Prism surface is   " + sPrism);
43        System.out.println("Pyramid volume is  " +
44           vPyramid);
45        System.out.println("Pyramid surface is " +
46           sPyramid);
47     }
48  }
```

Here are two possible "sessions" with this program:

```
Prism and Pyramid calculations

Enter length (l): 8
Enter width  (w): 6
Enter height (h): 3
Prism volume is    144.0
Prism surface is   180.0
Pyramid volume is  48.0
Pyramid surface is 111.94112549695427
```

```
Prism and Pyramid calculations

Enter length (l): 2.5
Enter width  (w): 1.2
Enter height (h): 2.75
Prism volume is    8.25
```

```
Prism surface is   26.35
Pyramid volume is  2.75
Pyramid surface is 13.661647764597157
```

The mysterious `Math.sqrt()` on lines 35 and 36 are calls to **functions**. We will discuss this programming element in depth later in *"It's How You Function – Using Functions or Methods;"* for now, let's just say that functions work like the buttons on a calculator: when you press the button, the calculator performs the calculation on the current number in the display; the function performs its calculation on whatever is between the parentheses; in this case, we use the equivalent of the √ button, to calculate a square root.

Like many programs, this one has three parts: *input*, where the program reads in the data with which it has to work; *processing* – where the program performs its calculations or any other activity; and *output* – where the program prints out the results.

Stuffed Cone

The second program in this series is similar – it calculates the volume and surface are of a prism and of a cone inside it. This time, the prism's base is a square, and we also need the value of π – whenever circles are involved, this guy pops up… The program's inputs are the prism width (w) and height (h). The formulas we use are:

$$V_{Prism} = w^2 h$$

$$S_{Prism} = 4hw + 2w^2$$

$$V_{Cone} = \frac{1}{3}\pi r^2 h$$

$$S_{Cone} = \pi rs + \pi r^2$$

$$r = \frac{1}{2}w$$

$$s = \sqrt{h^2 + r^2}$$

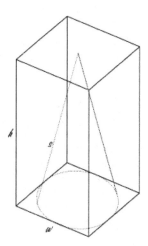

V is the volume and S is the surface area; s is the slant height of the side of the cone, and is calculated using Pythagoras' formula from the radius of the base of the cone, which is half the width of the prism, and the cone's height, which is the same as that of the prism.

Similar to the previous example, the program asks the user to enter the two measurements (w and h) as inputs, and prints out the volumes and surface areas as outputs.

```
01 // Example 16, file 'Cone.java'
02 // This program calculates the volume
03 // and surface area of a prism and a
04 // pyramid
05
06 import java.io.*;
07 import java.lang.Math;
08
09 public class Cone
10 {
11    public static void main(String[] args)
12       throws IOException
13    {
14       BufferedReader inputReader = new BufferedReader(
15          new InputStreamReader(System.in));
16       String line;
17
18       double pi = Math.PI;
```

```
19
20          /////////////////////////////////////
21          // Prism and Cone calculations
22          /////////////////////////////////////
23
24          System.out.println("\nPrism and Cone " +
25            "calculations\n");
26
27          System.out.print("Enter width  (w): ");
28          line = inputReader.readLine();
29          double w = new Double(line).doubleValue();
30          System.out.print("Enter height (h): ");
31          line = inputReader.readLine();
32          double h = new Double(line).doubleValue();
33
34          double w2 = w * w;
35          double r = w / 2;
36          double r2 = r * r;
37          double s = Math.sqrt(h * h + r2);
38          double vPrism = w2 * h;
39          double sPrism = 4 * h * w + 2 * w2;
40          double vCone = (pi * r2 * h) / 3;
41          double sCone = pi * (r * s + r2);;
42          System.out.println("Prism volume is  " + vPrism);
43          System.out.println("Prism surface is " + sPrism);
44          System.out.println("Cone volume is   " + vCone);
45          System.out.println("Cone surface is  " + sCone);
46      }
47  }
```

Here are a couple of outputs:

```
Prism and Cone calculations

Enter width  (w): 6
Enter height (h): 4
Prism volume is  144.0
Prism surface is 168.0
Cone volume is   37.69911184307752
Cone surface is  75.39822368615503
```

```
Prism and Cone calculations

Enter width  (w): 52.875
Enter height (h): 73.40625
Prism volume is  205226.67041015625
Prism surface is 21116.953125
Cone volume is   53728.21667343672
Cone surface is  8675.965960680629
```

In this program you can see an example of **optimization**: you optimize your program by avoiding repeated calculations. For that purpose, we calculated the radius r as half-the-width once, because we knew we need that value a few times and did not want to calculate every time; in the same spirit, we also calculated w^2 and r^2 – we also need those a few times. Some compilers are very talented on optimizing on their own, but you never know; it's better to at least do it when it is obvious to you; it also saves on coding, and thus on errors, because you use variables rather than expressions when the calculated values are needed.

Another interesting item you'll find in this program is Math.PI. This is a constant with the best possible value of π; this constant is part of the math library, the same one from where we pulled out the function Math.sqrt() to calculate square root.

As always, you are invited to play with this program, enter various values or experiment with the formulas. Can you add the calculations for the volume and surface of a cylinder bound by the same prism?

AGE VALIDATION

As you well know, the legal age for driving is different from one state to another. We are going to write a program that will read in the legal driving age for a particular state, and then the date of birth of a person, and determine if this person is allowed to drive in that state.

```java
01  // Example 17, file 'Age.java'
02  // This program verifies if a person
03  // is of legal driving age
04
05  import java.io.*;
06
07  public class Age
08  {
09      public static void main(String[] args)
10          throws IOException
11      {
12          BufferedReader inputReader = new BufferedReader(
13              new InputStreamReader(System.in));
14          String line;
15
16          /////////////////////////////////////////
17          // Legal driving age verification
18          /////////////////////////////////////////
19
20          System.out.println("\nLegal driving age " +
21              "verification\n");
22
23          System.out.print("Enter legal driving age: ");
24          line = inputReader.readLine();
25          int drivingAge = new Integer(line).intValue();
26
27          System.out.println("Enter verification date - ");
28          System.out.print("  Year:  ");
29          line = inputReader.readLine();
30          int yearCheck = new Integer(line).intValue();
31          System.out.print("  Month: ");
32          line = inputReader.readLine();
33          int monthCheck = new Integer(line).intValue();
34          System.out.print("  Day:   ");
35          line = inputReader.readLine();
36          int dayCheck = new Integer(line).intValue();
37          yearCheck = (yearCheck > 99 ? yearCheck :
38              yearCheck + 1900);
39
40          System.out.println("Enter birth date - ");
41          System.out.print("  Year:  ");
42          line = inputReader.readLine();
43          int yearBirth = new Integer(line).intValue();
44          System.out.print("  Month: ");
45          line = inputReader.readLine();
46          int monthBirth = new Integer(line).intValue();
47          System.out.print("  Day:   ");
48          line = inputReader.readLine();
49          int dayBirth = new Integer(line).intValue();
50          yearBirth = (yearBirth > 99 ? yearBirth :
51              yearBirth + 1900);
52
53          boolean legal =
54              yearBirth + drivingAge > yearCheck ? false :
55              yearBirth + drivingAge < yearCheck ? true :
56              monthBirth > monthCheck ? false :
57              monthBirth < monthCheck ? true :
58              dayBirth > dayCheck ? false :
59              dayBirth < dayCheck ? true :
60              true;
61
```

```
62          System.out.println("\nA person born on " +
63             monthBirth + "/" +
64             dayBirth + "/" +
65             yearBirth + " is " +
66             (!legal ? "NOT " : "") +
67             "\n allowed to drive on " +
68             monthCheck + "/" +
69             dayCheck + "/" +
70             yearCheck);
71      }
72  }
```

And some sample sessions:

```
Legal driving age verification

Enter legal driving age: 17
Enter verification date -
   Year:   2001
   Month:  11
   Day:    14
Enter birth date -
   Year:   84
   Month:  11
   Day:    15

A person born on 11/15/1984 is NOT
 allowed to drive on 11/14/2001
```

```
Legal driving age verification

Enter legal driving age: 18
Enter verification date -
   Year:   2002
   Month:  1
   Day:    10
Enter birth date -
   Year:   54
   Month:  9
   Day:    26

A person born on 9/26/1954 is
 allowed to drive on 1/10/2002
```

```
Legal driving age verification

Enter legal driving age: 16
Enter verification date -
   Year:   99
   Month:  6
   Day:    23
Enter birth date -
   Year:   83
   Month:  6
   Day:    23

A person born on 6/23/1983 is
 allowed to drive on 6/23/1999
```

The last session demonstrates that the program is smart enough to figure out the situation down to the day – in this session the question was asked on the person's 16th birthday. One important aspect of programming is to make sure that your programs cover all case, not only the easy one. This case is called an "edge condition," because the person's birth date is at the "edge" of the range for which the program is checking.

There isn't much to say about this program; it's relatively simply. The whole logic of the program is in the one expression on lines 53–60. This expression, using the conditional operator several times, is comparing the person's birth date with to the date of the verification. It is done by first finding out if the person's legal driving age falls exactly in the year in question; if not, it's easy to decide – it's illegal for the person to drive if the driving age's year is later, it's legal if it's earlier. If, however, the driving age year is the same as the verification year, the same logic is applied to the birth month compared to the verification month and then to the specific day. That's all it takes.

You may have noticed other uses of the conditional operator on lines 37–38 and 50–51. In these expression, we are trying to take care of people who are used to typing only the last two digits of a year – 98 for 1998, for example; if we get as input a number less than 99, we assume that the user meant a year prior to the 2000.

We employ another useful gimmick on line 66: we decide if the word NOT is required or not based on our decision regarding the person's legal driving status. If it is required, we use it; if it is not, we use an empty string, often called a "null" string. The printed output will have the word NOT only if the variable `legal` is `false` – that's way we use the complement operator `!` on the variable (a reminder from *"Logical Operators"* above: the value of `!legal` is `true` when the value of `legal` is `false`).

What you learned in this chapter:

⋏   *Most programs have three parts:* input, processing *and* output

⋏   *Mathematical formulas can be easily coded as numerical expressions*

⋏   *You can use the* math library *to perform special functions or get the values of special constants*

⋏   *Boolean variables are handy when you need to test conditions and make decisions*

It's a Matter of Control – Using Control Statements

> *Not every processing assignment can be expressed as a straightforward series of expressions. Most often, you need to describe more complex procedures, which perhaps repeat some sequences of computations, check for certain conditions and decide what to do based on these tests, etc. This is called the "logic" of a program, and we will learn how to use several different forms of control statements to describe this logic.*
>
> *What you will learn in this chapter:*
> - ➤ *How to tell the computer to make decisions*
> - ➤ *How to repeat a group of statements*

WHAT IF – CONDITIONAL EXECUTION

You make decisions every day; actually, even several times an hour. Some are trivial: What bubble gum should I buy? Do I want cereal or toast for breakfast? Some are more important: Should I pull my hair up or keep it loose? Do I need to clean up my room, so that my mom won't be mad at me? And some are really, really important: Should I try out for the basketball team or for track? Who should I ask to go with me on a date?

One thing is common to all these decisions: you ask yourself the question, make the decision, and then go on that path, most probably making other decisions on the way, decisions that may or may not be required based on previous ones. But once you made a decision *and act on it*, you cannot go back and undo it. You can make another decision to try and correct the results of the wrong one, but you cannot make it as if it did not happen – at least not in real life…

In programming, it is the same yet different… First, all decisions are equally important – there is no concept of less or more importance, because each decision makes the program go on a certain path, and that's that. Second, all decisions are "yes/no" decisions: you examine a situation by asking if a certain condition exists, and decide what to do if it does and if it doesn't; there is always a decisions for both the "yes" situation and the "no" situation – even if you decide to do nothing, it is still a decision! This type of a decision is called a **binary decision**, because it has two options. The Boolean values `true` and `false` represent the result of the test for the condition.

So how do we do it? How do we test a condition and make a decision? The statement that does that is called an **if statement**, and its structure is like this:

```
if (<Condition>)
   <what to do if the condition is true>
else
   <what to do if the condition is not true (is false)>
```

The key words are `if` and `else`, and the parentheses around the `condition`.

It would make sense once we apply it to a real problem, and we will start with a problem we already solved using the conditional operator: remember the calculation of the absolute value of a number in *"The Conditional Operator"* above? We wrote:

```
double x, absX;
absX = (x >= 0 ? x : -x);
```

Another way to do it would be:

```
double x, absX;
if (x >= 0)
  absX = x;
else
  absX = -x;
```

It may seem a little longer, but on the other hand it is easier to understand. You can actually read it out loud: "if x is greater than or equal to zero, its absolute value is itself; else it is its negative."

An if statement does not have to have an else part. For example, suppose a parent wants to add $1 to his child's $4 weekly allowance if the child was good that week:

```
int allowance = 4;
if (good)
  allowance += 1;
```

The if statement is more useful when the conditional operator *cannot* be used – when the whole expression, not just one operand, depends on the condition; based on the example in *"Pyramid-in-a-Prism"* above, here is a way to calculate *either* the volume *or* the surface area:

```
int type;
int typeV = 1, typeS = 2;
double result;
if (type == typeV)
  result = w * 1 * h;
if (type == typeS)
  result = 2 * (h * w + h * 1 + 1 * w);
```

There is no else here – so the value of result will be undefined if type was neither 1 nor 2 – generally not a good programming practice. Most likely, the compiler will notice this and tell you variable result might not have been initialized. To make sure that we always assign a value to result, we might change this program fragment to be:

```
int type;
int typeV = 1, typeS = 2;
double result;
if (type == typeV)
  result = w * 1 * h;
else
if (type == typeS)
  result = 2 * (h * w + h * 1 + 1 * w);
else
  result = -1;
```

This code now tests for both possible values of type, and if we don't find either we assign a negative value to result – that serves as an indication that we did not calculate any of the possible values (volume or area) because these values can *never* be negative! You might want to add another if statement to print out the result or an error message:

```
if (result < 0)    // wrong choice for calculation
  System.out.println("Error: you did not enter a valid choice!");
else
  System.out.println("Result is " + result);
```

But the if statement is not limited to having only one statement after the condition or after the else part; if you want to have more than one value, you can use a *block*. Then the code may look like this:

```
int typeV = 1, typeS = 2;
String what = "";
if (type == typeV)
{
  result = w * 1 * h;
  what = "Volume";
}
else
if (type == typeS)
{
```

```
      result = 2 * (h * w + h * l + l * w);
      what = "Surface area";
   }
   else
      result = -1;
   if (result < 0)    // wrong choice for calculation
      System.out.println("Error: you did not enter a valid choice!");
   else
      System.out.println(what + " is " + result);
```

Here we assign a string to the variable what, so that when we print the result we can say what it was that we calculated.

The { and } are bracketing the block. You will learn all about blocks later, in *"Playing with Blocks – grouping statements,"* but for now we will just say that a block can be used practically everywhere a single statement can be used, and that's what we did here: we needed to say more than what a single statement could say (we needed two statements), so we put it in a block. Inside a block we can put almost any statement, including additional if statements.

By the way, the reason we assigned the null string "" to what when we declared it is to make sure that it has a value even if type does not have a valid value, to avoid the compiler error we mentioned earlier regarding result.

if statements can come in handy when you have complex conditions to test. For example, remember the test for age in *"The Conditional Operator"* above? We used two conditional expressions. Here is code doing a similar thing with an if statement:

```
   int senior = 55, youth = 18;
   int age;
   String ageGroup;
   . . .
   if (age < youth)
      ageGroup = "Youth";
   else
   if (age < senior)
      ageGroup = "Adult";
   else
      ageGroup = "Senior";
```

If we wanted to only identify the "adult" age group, we could have used a more complex conditional expression:

```
   if (age >= youth  &&  age < senior)
      ageGroup = "Adult";
```

(It wasn't necessary to do it in the previous example because the first if statement already tested that, and by coming to the second if, after the else, we already know that age is not less than 18.)

Note the use of && instead of the & we learned about previously to perform the "and" operation. It behaves the same way regarding the Boolean value of the expression, but it has an additional feature, very useful in conditional expressions such as an if statement, which we will discuss later. Similarly, the "or" operation for conditional expressions is indicated by || rather than the |.

Let's look at even "heavier" conditions. Let's say that school policy is that C students cannot participate in sports without approval by their homeroom teacher or the guidance counselor; D students need also approval by the principal. How will we test if a particular student is allowed to participate in tomorrow's football game?

```
   char grade;
   boolean homeroomOK, guidanceOK, principalOK;
   boolean participate;
   . . .
   if (grade == 'A'  ||  grade == 'B')
      participate = true;
   else
   if (grade == 'C'  &&  (homeroomOK  ||  guidanceOK))
      participate = true;
```

```
else
if (grade == 'D' && (homeroomOK || guidanceOK) && principalOK)
  participate = true;
else
  participate = false;
```

We put the tests for approval by the homeroom teacher or the guidance counselor in parentheses, to override the normal left-to-right order for the **&&** and **||** operators, which would be incorrect here: it would be evaluated as (grade == 'C' && homeroomOK) || guidanceOK.

As you noticed, we put the two easy cases (A and B grades) in one condition. It is even possible to put everything together in a single condition. Watch:

```
if (grade == 'A' || grade == 'B' ||
  (grade == 'C' && (homeroomOK || guidanceOK)) ||
  (grade == 'D' && (homeroomOK || guidanceOK) && principalOK))
  participate = true;
else
  participate = false;
```

This condition has four parts; if *any* of them is **true**, the student can participate – that's why we use the **||** ("or") operator. The four parts are:

- ❑ The student's grade is A, or
- ❑ The student's grade is B, or
- ❑ The student's grade is C and approval by either the homeroom teacher or the guidance counselor is obtained, or
- ❑ The student's grade is D and approval by either the homeroom teacher or the guidance counselor, and the principal, is obtained.

Note that we put parentheses around each of the conditions testing the grades C and D requirements, to make sure that they are figured out correctly in relation to the others.

It's time to gather all the important examples in this section into one program. Watch out, this is a really long one, the longest so far!

```
01 // Example 18, file 'IfExample.java'
02 // This program demonstrates the use of
03 // the 'if' statement
04
05 import java.io.*;
06
07 public class IfExample
08 {
09   public static void main(String[] args)
10     throws IOException
11   {
12
13     BufferedReader inputReader = new BufferedReader(
14       new InputStreamReader(System.in));
15     String line;
16
17     ///////////////////////////////////////
18     // The 'if' statement
19     ///////////////////////////////////////
20
21     // Display list of examples and ask user
22     // to select which example to run
23
24     System.out.println("\nThe 'if' statement\n");
25
26     System.out.println("List of examples: ");
27     System.out.println("1. Absolute value");
28     System.out.println("2. Volume or surface area");
```

```
29          System.out.println("3. Grades and sports");
30          System.out.print("Enter example number: ");
31          line = inputReader.readLine();
32          int example = new Integer(line).intValue();
33
34          // Run the selected example
35
36          if (example == 1)   // Absolute value
37          {
38              double x, absX;
39
40              // Get number
41
42              System.out.print("Enter a number: ");
43              line = inputReader.readLine();
44              x = new Double(line).doubleValue();
45              if (x >= 0)
46                  absX = x;
47              else
48                  absX = -x;
49              System.out.println("|" + x + "|" + " = " + absX);
50          }
51          else
52          if (example == 2)   // Volume and surface area
53          {
54              double result;
55
56              // Get prism dimensions
57
58              System.out.print("Enter length (l): ");
59              line = inputReader.readLine();
60              double l = new Double(line).doubleValue();
61              System.out.print("Enter width  (w): ");
62              line = inputReader.readLine();
63              double w = new Double(line).doubleValue();
64              System.out.print("Enter height (h): ");
65              line = inputReader.readLine();
66              double h = new Double(line).doubleValue();
67
68              // Get choice of volume or surface area
69
70              int typeV = 1, typeS = 2;
71              String what = "";
72              System.out.print("Enter " + typeV +
73                  " for volume or " + typeS +
74                  " for surface area: ");
75              line = inputReader.readLine();
76              int type = new Integer(line).intValue();
77
78              // Perform calculation based on user's choice
79
80              if (type == typeV)
81              {
82                  result = w * l * h;
83                  what = "Volume";
84              }
85              else
86              if (type == typeS)
87              {
88                  result = 2 * (h * w + h * l + l * w);
89                  what = "Surface area";
90              }
91              else
92                  result = -1;
93
94              // Check if choice of calculation was valid
95
96              if (result < 0)     // Wrong choice
```

```
 97              System.out.println("Error: " + type +
 98                 " is not a valid choice!");
 99           else
100              System.out.println(what + " is " + result);
101        }
102     else
103     if (example == 3)  // Grades and sports
104     {
105        boolean homeroomOK, guidanceOK, principalOK;
106        boolean participate;
107        int response;
108        int gradeA = 1, gradeB = 2,
109           gradeC = 3, gradeD = 4,
110           gradeF = 5;
111        int yes = 1, no = 0;
112
113        // Get grade
114
115        System.out.print("Enter student's grade " +
116           "(A=1, B=2, C=3, D=4, F=5): ");
117        line = inputReader.readLine();
118        int grade = new Integer(line).intValue();
119
120        if (grade == gradeF)
121           // Failing students cannot participate!
122           participate = false;
123        else
124        if (grade == gradeA || grade == gradeB)
125           // Student with A or B grades
126           // do not need any extra approvals
127           participate = true;
128        else
129        { // Students with C or D grades need
130           // at least homeroom teacher's
131           // or guidance counselor's approval
132
133           // Ask about homeroom teacher's approval
134           System.out.print(
135              "Did homeroom teacher approve? " +
136              "(Yes=1, No=0) ");
137           line = inputReader.readLine();
138           response = new Integer(line).intValue();
139           if (response == no)
140              homeroomOK = false;
141           else
142           if (response == yes)
143              homeroomOK = true;
144           else
145           {
146              System.out.println(response +
147                 " is not valid, assuming No");
148              homeroomOK = false;
149           }
150
151           // Ask about guidance counselor's approval
152           System.out.print(
153              "Did guidance counselor approve? " +
154              "(Yes=1, No=0) ");
155           line = inputReader.readLine();
156           response = new Integer(line).intValue();
157           if (response == no)
158              guidanceOK = false;
159           else
160           if (response == yes)
161              guidanceOK = true;
162           else
163           {
164              System.out.println(response +
```

```
165                       " is not valid, assuming No");
166                   guidanceOK = false;
167               }
168
169               if (!(homeroomOK  ||  guidanceOK))
170                   // If there was no approval from either
171                   // homeroom teacher or guidance counselor,
172                   // grade does not matter...
173                   participate = false;
174               else
175               if (grade == gradeC)
176                   // There is approval, and this is enough
177                   // for C students
178                   participate = true;
179               else
180               {  // Student with D grade also needs
181                  // the principal's approval
182
183                  // Ask about principal's approval
184                  System.out.print(
185                      "Did principal approve? " +
186                      "(Yes=1, No=0) ");
187                  line = inputReader.readLine();
188                  response = new Integer(line).intValue();
189                  if (response == no)
190                      principalOK = false;
191                  else
192                  if (response == yes)
193                      principalOK = true;
194                  else
195                  {
196                      System.out.println(response +
197                          " is not valid, assuming No");
198                      principalOK = false;
199                  }
200
201                  if (principalOK)
202                      participate = true;
203                  else
204                      participate = false;
205               }
206           }
207
208           // Print out the result
209
210           System.out.println("The student may " +
211               (participate ? "" : "not ") +
212               "participate in sports");
213       }
214       else       // Wrong choice of example
215           System.out.println("Error: " + example +
216               " is not a valid example number!");
217   }
218 }
```

This program is quite complex, and therefore has many potential inputs and outputs. Below are a few, but it would be fun for you to try many more.

```
The 'if' statement

List of examples:
1. Absolute value
2. Volume or surface area
3. Grades and sports
Enter example number: 1
Enter a number: -89.456
|-89.456| = 89.456
```

```
The 'if' statement

List of examples:
1. Absolute value
2. Volume or surface area
3. Grades and sports
Enter example number: 2
Enter length (l): 8
Enter width  (w): 5
Enter height (h): 11
Enter 1 for volume or 2 for surface area: 2
Surface area is 366.0
```

```
The 'if' statement

List of examples:
1. Absolute value
2. Volume or surface area
3. Grades and sports
Enter example number: 3
Enter student's grade (A=1, B=2, C=3, D=4, F=5): 4
Did homeroom teacher approve? (Yes=1, No=0) 1
Did guidance counselor approve? (Yes=1, No=0) 0
Did principal approve? (Yes=1, No=0) 1
The student may participate in sports
```

As deserving such a large program, we have quite a few notes about it... We will start with some general comments about programming, and then become more specific.

Building a complex program is almost like building a castle with Lego© blocks, and it's always a good idea to plan ahead. The first step is to settle on the major parts of the program. You do that by deciding what are the major activities the program should have. In our example, there are three examples we want to have: "absolute value," "prism volume and surface area," and "grades and sports." You might want to draw this as three blocks (their size is only an estimate of how complex each one will be).

How are these blocks related? Only one of them will be used at run-time, by selecting the example the user wants to run. So we put the blocks in a larger block, more like a frame, to hold them together; we will also write down how a block is selected for running.

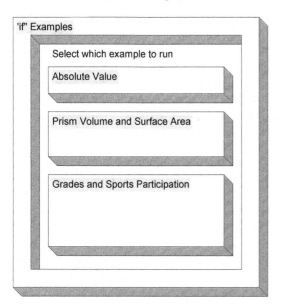

The next step is to look at each of the blocks, and decide what smaller blocks it should be built of. You can take that down to the level of the individual statements, but that is usually not necessary. We will stop at the next level, which is the top level of each of the major blocks (that's why we left the "..." in the lowest-level blocks).

This is how you build a complex program. The reverse is true when you study a complex program – you need to perform **reverse engineering** on the program to understand how it can be broken down. The author of the program – the person who engineered it – went through the process of putting it together much as we described before: building the program out of smaller blocks; now you have to do the reverse: take it apart to find out what these blocks are.

Let's look at our program and try to reverse-engineer it.

The first hint of which blocks make up the program is the if statement on line 36. It's obvious that there is a block following it, before the else part on line 51 – just look at the { and } around lines 38–49. Since there *is* an else part, followed by another if, that is a dead giveaway of another block, around lines 54–100. The same applies to the block around lines 105–212. You can use the same reasoning to identify the inside blocks. From this information, you could build the same diagram we built when we described how the program was designed.

A great help in identifying the blocks is the fact that we put matching { and } on separate lines and they have the same **indent** (the empty space at the beginning of the line), which puts them one below the other. You can even draw a vertical line from the { to the } and actually see the blocks! It is *extremely* important to indent properly – without it, it would be awfully hard to match the braces when you try to figure out where a block begins and where it ends.

Now, for a few more specific notes about the program itself.

On lines 72–74 we ask the user to select volume or surface area as the desired calculation. We build this question in a **dynamic** way, which means that the numbers we ask the user to type in are not coded as part of the question at compile-time, but are "pulled" into it from the variables typeV and typeS when it is constructed at run-time. Why the extra work on our part? Is it worth it? Definitely! It allows us to later change the specific numbers (now 1 and 2, later 3 and 6, or whatever…) without having to remember to change the text of the question as well. The advantage in building things dynamically in this case is that we can reduce the number of places where the program has to be modified when we change the way it talks with the user. The same idea can be applied in many programming situation; the rule is: *define everything that may change in only* one *place, and use those definition everywhere else*. The opposite of dynamic is **static**, which means that it's fixed as part of the program's code at compile-time and cannot be changed at run-time.

Another aspect of dynamic programming is on lines 83 and 89. There we *dynamically* assign a text to the variable what which names the calculation we just performed, so that this information can be *dynamically* inserted into the message we print on line 100. We could have used another if statement or a conditional expression to test the value of type again when we got to the printing point, and have two separate println() statements; but that would be extra work for the program, as well as yet *another* place where the test is made – which would be at risk of being forgotten if later we have to change that test (such as adding another type of calculation).

We probably should have done the same with lines 115–116 as well as on lines 135–136, 153–154 and 185–186. Try doing it yourself.

'if' Examples

Select which example to run:

Absolute Value
☐ Get input number
☐ Calculate absolute value
☐ Print result

Prism Volume and Surface Area
☐ Get prism's dimensions
☐ Select volume or surface area:
Volume
Calculate volume
Surface Area
Calculate surface area
Print out result

Grades and Sports Participation
☐ Get grade
☐ Check grade:
F
Forbid participation
A or B
Allow participation
C or D
Check approvals:
…
…
Print out result

Let's move on. The third example, "Grades and Sports," shows a common programming technique – grouping and elimination. The program has to deal with five different grades, with mostly different rules for each but some common rules too. This is handled by grouping together those that have common rules, and testing for them so that if they are not true they can be eliminated. So the program tests for F grade (line 120) to eliminate it first; then for A and B (line 124), which have the same simple rule. At this point, the program knows that the grade must be C or D (by the elimination of the other grades); these grades have one common rule – approval by either the homeroom teacher or the guidance counselor is required. If neither was given, the program can eliminate the student (line 169); if at least one approval was given, then the last rule, principal's approval, has to be applied – but only if the grade was *not* C (line 175). This process of elimination, or narrowing-down of the options, actually simplifies the program because once the program dealt with a specific case it does not have to consider it any more.

WHILE YOU CAN – REPETITIVE EXECUTION

Much of the work computers need to do is repetitive – doing the same thing over and over again. It's good they don't have any feelings, because they would be bored to tears… For example, a program may need to go over a mailing list and generate labels for the envelopes, or sort the names of all the football players in all the school participating in a championship tournament, or even calculate the grade averages for all the students in the school for the marking period report cards. None of these tasks is complex on its own, but the monotony of repeating it over and over again can discourage a normal human being; but computers don't mind – that's what they were born to do.

The only question we face now is: how do we tell the computer to repeat some activities? How do we write a program that performs a repetitive task?

One way to program repetition is the while statement, also called a **while loop**. It tells the computer to repeat, loop over, a block of statements as long as a certain condition is true. It looks like this:

```
while (<condition>)
    <what to do as long as the condition is true>
```

The key word is while, and the parentheses around condition are required. The condition part is a Boolean expression; the what can be a single statement or a block (bracketed by { and }).

The while statement works like this:

1. The condition is evaluated.

2. If it is false, the what part is skipped and the computer moves on to next statement.

3. If it is true, the what part is executed and the computer returns to evaluate the condition again in step 1. Each pass through the what part is called an iteration.

Let's work through an example. Suppose you have a list of grades, and you want to find what is the highest grade and which student received it. A common way to store the grades is in an array, where the index of each grade element is the student number. The last element of the array will have a grade of -1 to indicate the end of the list (you have to be really "out-of-it" to get such a grade…); this last element is called a **sentinel** because is "guards" the end of the array. So the code will be as follows:

```
int[] grade = {82, 67, 45, 89, 91, 96, 43, 78, 97, 81, -1};
int indexStudent = 0;      // running index
int indexHighest = -1;     // index of highest grade
int gradeHighest = -1;     // value of highest grade
while (grade[indexStudent] > 0)
{
  if (grade[indexStudent] > gradeHighest)
  {
    gradeHighest = grade[indexStudent];
    indexHighest = indexStudent;
  }
  indexStudent++;
}
```

Let's examine this program fragment carefully. First, our "inventory" of data: we have an array of 11 elements, indexed 0 to 10; the element at index 10 is the sentinel, so we only have 10 grades. We also have three int variables: w, which will run through all the index values for the array, indexHighest, where the program will store the index of the highest grade found so far, and gradeHighest, where the program will store the highest grade so far.

`indexStudent` starts at 0, so when the program first goes into the `while` statement and checks the condition it finds that `grade[0]` is greater then 0; the condition is `true` and it goes into the block following the `while`. Now it check if `grade[0]` is greater than the highest grade found have so far. Since `gradeHighest` was initialized to -1, the condition is `true` and so it takes `grade[0]` as the highest grade and stores both its value (82) and its index (0). It then increments the running index by 1, and goes to the beginning. `grade[1]` is also greater than 0, so the program again goes into the block. Now, however, the program finds that `grade[1]` (whose value is 67) is not larger than `gradeHighest` (whose value is 82), so the two statements in the `if` block are skipped. The index is incremented again, and the program goes once more to the beginning of the while. The if block will be executed again when the index is 3 and the grade at that index is 89 (larger than the 82 remembered so far), and so on: every time the program hits a higher grade, it remembers it. The `while` loop will terminate when the sentinel is hit – the element with index 10 has a value of -1, so the condition of the `while` will be `false` and the block after it will be skipped. By that time, `gradeHighest` and `indexHighest` will have the value (97) and the index (8) of the highest grade. It is rather boring, this "looping" over and over again, isn't it?

In a real program you are likely to read the grades, rather than have them "hard-coded" as part of the program. Putting the sentinel at the end of the array will be done by the input part of the program, when it knows that the last grade was read.

By the way, going over an array in the order of its elements is called sequential order, because the elements are accessed in sequence ("one after the other").

Here is a more complex example. Let's say we have a list of names, in an array of `Strings` called `name`, all belonging to the same family. The names do not tell us who is a descendent of whom, so we have another array, of type `int` and called `child`, to give us that information: each element of `child` corresponds to the element of `name` with the same index; it contains the index of the element of `name` who is the child of the person whose name is in the corresponding element of `name`. Confused? Perhaps a diagram will help:

Index	Name	Child
0	John	5
1	Jennifer	0
2	Thomas	3
3	Mark	-1
4	Sara	2
5	George	4

What does this diagram tell us? It shows the two arrays, `name` and `child`, side by side. It also shows how each element of `child` *points* to another element – this is called (surprise!) a pointer. The pointer points to the child of the person with the same index as the pointer. So we can see that John is Jennifer's child (Jennifer's index is 1, since her name is in `name[1]`; `child[1]` contains 5, which is John's index in `name`), Mark is Thomas' child, and Mark has no child (that's what the -1, an invalid index, must mean). In order to list the family members in order of parent-to-child, we only need to know where to begin; in this case, we know by looking at the table that it's Jennifer at index 0, because she is nobody's child) no one has a 1 as it's child). (We will later see how to write a program that will find that out on its own.) This is a very simple family, since each person has only one child – but it's good enough for our example.

The program fragment that lists the names in the correct order is as follows:

```
String[] name = {"John", "Jennifer", "Thomas",
  "Mark", "Sara", "George"};
int[] child = {5, 0, 3, -1, 2, 4};
int index = 1;      // Where to start
System.out.println("List of family members, " +
  "from parent to child");
while (child[index] != -1)
{
  System.out.println(name[index]);
  index = child[index];
}
System.out.println(name[index]);
```

Unlike the previous example of the while statement, this code does not go through the array in sequential order, but "bounces around" in the order of the pointers. The program sets up index to be the index of the first element (1). Then, as long as it does not hit the person with no child (marked by a -1 in its child element), it prints out the name and changes the index to go to the element pointed to by the current element (index = child[index]). When the loop ends, the last thing to do is to print the name of the last person, the one who has no child.

Let's put those two example together in one program, with all the trimmings...

```
01  // Example 19, file 'WhileExample.java'
02  // This program demonstrates the use of
03  // the 'while' statement
04
05  import java.io.*;
06
07  public class WhileExample
08  {
09    public static void main(String[] args)
10      throws IOException
11    {
12
13      BufferedReader inputReader = new BufferedReader(
14        new InputStreamReader(System.in));
15      String line;
16
17      /////////////////////////////////////////
18      // The 'while' statement
19      /////////////////////////////////////////
20
21      // Display list of examples and ask user
22      // to select which example to run
23
24      System.out.println("\nThe 'while' statement\n");
25
26      System.out.println("List of examples: ");
27      System.out.println("1. Highest grade");
28      System.out.println("2. Family list");
29      System.out.print("Enter example number: ");
30      line = inputReader.readLine();
31      int example = new Integer(line).intValue();
32
33      // Run the selected example
34
35      if (example == 1)  // Highest grade
36      {
37        int[] grade =
38          {82, 67, 45, 89, 91, 96, 43, 78, 97, 81, -1};
39        int indexStudent = 0; // running index
40        int indexHighest = -1;   // index of highest grade
41        int gradeHighest = -1;   // value of highest grade
42
43        while (grade[indexStudent] > 0)
44        {
45          if (grade[indexStudent] > gradeHighest)
46          {
```

```
47              gradeHighest = grade[indexStudent];
48              indexHighest = indexStudent;
49            }
50            indexStudent++;
51          }
52          System.out.println(
53            "Highest grade is " +
54            gradeHighest);
55          System.out.println(
56            "Student with highest grade is " +
57            indexHighest);
58        }
59      else
60      if (example == 2)  // Family list
61        {
62          String[] name = {"John", "Jennifer", "Thomas",
63            "Mark", "Sara", "George"};
64          int[] child = {5, 0, 3, -1, 2, 4};
65          int index = 1; // Where to start
66
67          while (child[index] != -1)
68            {
69              System.out.println(name[index]);
70              index = child[index];
71            }
72          System.out.println(name[index]);
73        }
74      else       // Wrong choice of example
75          System.out.println("Error: " + example +
76            " is not a valid example number!");
77    }
78 }
```

Because this program does very little, there are only two possible runs:

```
The 'while' statement

List of examples:
1. Highest grade
2. Family list
Enter example number: 1
Highest grade is 97
Student with highest grade is 8
```

```
The 'while' statement

List of examples:
1. Highest grade
2. Family list
Enter example number: 2
Jennifer
John
George
Sara
Thomas
Mark
```

Since we covered these examples already, there is nothing to add here. Just a couple of suggestions: first, try to change the grades for the first example, may be even add grades to the list; second, try to change the relationships in the second example, and perhaps even add more names.

FOR NOW AND AGAIN – LOOP CONTROL

For many repetitive tasks, you know how many times you want to do it. The programming "gizmo" that does that is called a **for loop**, because it loops around for as many times as you tell it to and is coded using a for statement. It looks like this:

```
for (<initialization>; <condition>; <update>)
  <what to do>
```

The key word is `for`, and the parentheses are required. Since this statement is more complex than the `while` statement, pay attention! `initialization` is a series of one or more expression statements separated by commas (,); `condition` is a Boolean expression; `update` is also a series of one or more expression statements separated by commas. Any one, or even all, of the ports can be left empty. In most cases, the `initialization` and `update` parts are only one statement. `what` can be a single statement or a block (bracketed by { and }).

The way it works is as follows:

1. The `initialization` part is evaluated (if not empty) by evaluating each expression statement from left to right.

2. The `condition` is evaluated (if not empty). If it is `true` (or if it *is* empty), the what part is execute; if it is `false`, the `for` statement ends and the next statement (after the what) is executed.

3. The `update` part is evaluated (if not empty) by evaluating each expression statement from left to right.

4. The computer goes back to step 2 to see if it has to go through the loop again.

How about an example? Here goes…

Let's calculate the sum of all the numbers from 1 to 10 (of course, there is a simple formula to do that, but we are going to do it the hard way…):

```
int sum, i;
for (sum = 0, i = 1; i <= 10; i++)
  sum += i;
```

For this code fragment, we use the variable `sum` to hold the sum of the numbers as we add them up and the variable `i` to hold the current number to add. The `initialization` part sets `sum` to 0 and `i` to 1 – at the beginning, the sum is 0 (we haven't added any numbers yet), and we intend to start with the number 1. The `condition` tests if the number we want to add is still less than or equal to the last number we plan to add (10 in this case). The `update` part moves up by 1 the number to add. The statement that makes up the actual loop just adds the current number (in `i`) to the accumulates sum (in `sum`).

Because the number of times the program goes through the loop (number of iterations) is controlled by `i`, this variable is sometimes called the **loop index**."

Need another example? Here it comes…

Suppose you need a table of powers of 2 for the numbers 1 through 100. Here's how you can calculate and print it out:

```
int power, i;
for (i = 1; i <= 100; i++)
{
  power = i * i;;
  System.out.println(
    i + " to the power of 2 is " + power);
}
```

Simple enough, isn't it? Besides the calculation itself, the only difference between this fragment and the previous one is that the *what* part is made up of two statements, and therefore is enclosed by curly braces. See if you can improve this program to also calculate powers of 3, etc.

One more example: let's take the example we used for the while loop, finding the highest grade, and re-write it using a for loop:

```
int[] grade = {82, 67, 45, 89, 91, 96, 43, 78, 97, 81};
int indexStudent = 0;   // running index
int indexHighest = -1;  // index of highest grade
int gradeHighest = -1;  // value of highest grade
int countStudents = grade.length;

for (indexStudent = 0;
  ndexStudent < countStudents;
  ndexStudent++)
{
  if (grade[indexStudent] > gradeHighest)
  {
    gradeHighest = grade[indexStudent];
    indexHighest = indexStudent;
  }
}
```

The difference between this approach and the `while` approach is that we do not need a sentinel (the -1) at the end of the array. Instead, we use an **attribute** of the array – its length – to know how many time to go through the loop; the attribute is used by putting a period (`.`) between its name (`length`) and the name of the array (`grade`): `grade.length`.

Many objects have attributes, just as people have them. For example, a person's height or weight are attributes, as can be education, mood, favorite color or practically anything that may help in describing that person. Arrays have other attributes as well, but we will not discuss them now. The `length` attribute is particularly important because it allows us to loop through an array without the need for any "gimmicks" to figure out its length.

`for` loops are very useful in dealing with arrays. Remember the class schedule in the program in *"Arraying It All For Review?"* The schedule for one day was printed by coding a `println()` statement for each line (AM and PM), specifically coding all array elements that were needed, and turned out to be quite long. Imagine if you had to print the schedule for the whole week, or if you had more than four classes to deal with! That's were "loops within loops" comes in handy. Here is the code:

```
final int AM = 0, PM = 1;
final int Monday = 0, Tuesday = 1, Wednesday = 2,
          Thursday = 3, Friday = 4;
int day, block, room;
for (day = Monday; day <= Friday; day++)
{
  for (block = AM; block <= PM; block++)
  {
    for (room = 0;
      room < weekSchedule[0][0].length;
      room++)
    {
      System.out.print(
        weekSchedule[day][block][room] + " ");
    }
    System.out.print("\n");
  }
}
```

This code fragment will print out the full weekly schedule (but not as nicely as the code in the full example below) in much fewer lines than if you coded printing each and every array element separately. One flaw of this code is that it relies on the day numbers to be in the proper order and on the values of AM and PM to be 0 and 1 exactly.

To put it all together, here is a program the includes all the examples:

```
01  // Example 20, file 'ForExample.java'
02  // This program demonstrates the use of
03  // the 'for' statement
04
05  import java.io.*;
06
07  public class ForExample
08  {
09     public static void main(String[] args)
10        throws IOException
11     {
12
13        BufferedReader inputReader = new BufferedReader(
14           new InputStreamReader(System.in));
15        String line;
16
17        /////////////////////////////////////
18        // The 'for' statement
19        /////////////////////////////////////
20
21        // Display list of examples and ask user
22        // to select which example to run
23
24        System.out.println("\nThe 'for' statement\n");
25
26        System.out.println("List of examples: ");
27        System.out.println("1. Sum of numbers from 1 to n");
28        System.out.println("2. Power of 2");
29        System.out.println("3. Highest grade");
30        System.out.println("4. Classroom schedules");
31        System.out.print("Enter example number: ");
32        line = inputReader.readLine();
33        int example = new Integer(line).intValue();
34
35        // Run the selected example
36
37        if (example == 1)  // Sum of numbers from 1 to n
38        {
39           int n;        // Highest number
40           int sum;      // Sum
41           int i;        // loop index
42
43           // Get value of n
44           System.out.print("Enter value of n: ");
45           line = inputReader.readLine();
46           n = new Integer(line).intValue();
47
48           // Calculate sum of numbers from 1 to n
49           for (sum = 0, i = 1; i <= n; i++)
50              sum += i;
51           System.out.println(
52              "Sum of numbers from 1 to " + n + " is " + sum);
53        }
54        else
55        if (example == 2)  // Powers of 2
56        {
57           int n;        // Highest number
58           int power;    // power of 2
59           int i;        // loop index
60
61           // Get value of n
62           System.out.print("Enter value of n: ");
63           line = inputReader.readLine();
64           n = new Integer(line).intValue();
65
66           // Calculate and print power of 2
```

```
67            // for numbers from 1 to n
68            for (i = 1; i <= n; i++)
69            {
70               power = i * i;;
71               System.out.println(
72                  i + " to the power of 2 is " + power);
73            }
74         }
75         else
76         if (example == 3)   // Highest grade
77         {
78            int[] grade =
79               {82, 67, 45, 89, 91, 96, 43, 78, 97, 81};
80            int indexStudent = 0; // running index
81            int indexHighest = -1;    // index of highest grade
82            int gradeHighest = -1;    // value of highest grade
83            int countStudents = grade.length;
84
85            // Find the highest grade and the
86            // student that got it
87            for (indexStudent = 0;
88               indexStudent < countStudents;
89               indexStudent++)
90            {
91               if (grade[indexStudent] > gradeHighest)
92               {
93                  gradeHighest = grade[indexStudent];
94                  indexHighest = indexStudent;
95               }
96            }
97            System.out.println(
98               "Highest grade is " +
99               gradeHighest);
100           System.out.println(
101              "Student with highest grade is " +
102              indexHighest);
103        }
104        else
105        if (example == 4)   // Classroom schedules
106        {
107           final int AM = 0, PM = 1;
108           final int Monday = 0, Tuesday = 1, Wednesday = 2,
109                  Thursday = 3, Friday = 4;
110           final String [] dayName =
111              {"Monday", "Tuesday", "Wednesday",
112              "Thursday", "Friday"};
113           int[][][] weekSchedule =
114           {
115              { // Monday
116                 {104, 106, 103, 205},   // AM block
117                 {104, 205, 105, 206}// PM block
118              },
119              { // Tuesday
120                 {206, 106, 103, 205},   // AM block
121                 {205, 104, 105, 103}// PM block
122              },
123              { // Wednesday
124                 {205, 206, 105, 104},   // AM block
125                 {104, 106, 103, 205}// PM block
126              },
127              { // Thursday
128                 {104, 106, 206, 205},   // AM block
129                 {105, 206, 103, 106}// PM block
130              },
131              { // Friday
132                 {206, 106, 103, 104},   // AM block
133                 {205, 104, 105, 103}// PM block
134              }
```

```
135            };
136
137            // Print out the classroom
138            // schedule for the whole week
139            System.out.println("Block   " +
140               "Class1  Class2  Class3  Class4");
141            int day, block, room;
142            for (day = Monday; day <= Friday; day++)
143            { // for each day
144               System.out.println(dayName[day] + ":");
145               for (block = AM; block <= PM; block++)
146               { // for each block
147                  System.out.print(
148                     (block == AM ? "AM" : "PM") +
149                     "       ");
150                  for (room = 0;
151                     room < weekSchedule[0][0].length;
152                     room++)
153                  { // for each class
154                     System.out.print(
155                        weekSchedule[day][block][room] + "       ");
156                  }
157                  System.out.print("\n");
158               }
159            }
160         }
161         else        // Wrong choice of example
162            System.out.println("Error: " + example +
163               " is not a valid example number!");
164      }
165 }
```

And here are the outputs from a few runs:

```
The 'for' statement

List of examples:
1. Sum of numbers from 1 to n
2. Power of 2
3. Highest grade
4. Classroom schedules
Enter example number: 1
Enter value of n: 20
Sum of numbers from 1 to 20 is 210
```

```
The 'for' statement

List of examples:
1. Sum of numbers from 1 to n
2. Power of 2
3. Highest grade
4. Classroom schedules
Enter example number: 2
Enter value of n: 5
1 to the power of 2 is 1
2 to the power of 2 is 4
3 to the power of 2 is 9
4 to the power of 2 is 16
5 to the power of 2 is 25
```

```
The 'for' statement

List of examples:
1. Sum of numbers from 1 to n
2. Power of 2
3. Highest grade
4. Classroom schedules
```

```
Enter example number: 3
Highest grade is 97
Student with highest grade is 8
```

```
The 'for' statement

List of examples:
1. Sum of numbers from 1 to n
2. Power of 2
3. Highest grade
4. Classroom schedules
Enter example number: 4
Block  Class1  Class2  Class3  Class4
Monday:
AM       104     106     103     205
PM       104     205     105     206
Tuesday:
AM       206     106     103     205
PM       205     104     105     103
Wednesday:
AM       205     206     105     104
PM       104     106     103     205
Thursday:
AM       104     106     206     205
PM       105     206     103     106
Friday:
AM       206     106     103     104
PM       205     104     105     103
```

Notice that the third run, finding the highest grade, is identical in results to the run using the `while` loop (in *"While You Can – Repetitive Execution"* above).

The fourth example, classroom schedule, produces a nice printout of the schedule. As in previous examples, we use an array for the names of the days (on line 144) and a conditional statement (on line 148) to choose between AM and PM.

TAKE A BREAK...

One problem loops have (both while and for) is that there seems to be no way to stop the loop until the condition is `false`. In most cases, you can "craft" the condition so that it will stop the loop when necessary, but you will run into a problem when it is in the *middle* of the what part that you have to make a decision if the loop should continue – this is called "breaking" the loop, and the statement that does it called, naturally enough, break.

Here's an example: let's find the prime numbers from 2 to 100. (Just a reminder: a prime number is a numbers that is divisible only by itself or by 1.) To do that, the program has to loop through all the numbers from 3 to 100 (we already know that 2 is a prime number), and for each one check if it is divided by any number from 2 to its square root. If it is divisible by another number – it's not a prime number and we stop checking; if it is not divisible by any number up to its square root – it is a prime number, so we print it and stop checking as well. The code to do it is as follows:

```
int i, j;
System.out.println(2);     // we know 2 is prime
for (i = 3; i <= n; i = i + 1)
{
  for (j = 2; j < i; j = j + 1)
  {
    if (i % j == 0)
      break;                // number is not prime
    if (j > Math.sqrt(i))
    {                       // number is prime
      System.out.println(i);
      break;
    }
  }
}
```

The variable i runs from 3 to 100 in the "outer" loop; the variable j runs from 2 to i in the "inner" loop. The test for divisibility is i % j == 0: if the remainder of the division is 0, the number is divisible – it is not a prime number – and we "break" the inner loop; that means we skip the rest of the what part, just as if the condition part turned out to be false – and this brings us to the next round of the outer loop, ready to test the next number. We also break the inner loop if we reach the square root of the tested number and it was still indivisible, but then we happily print it out because it *is* a prime number.

Note: the rules of "Structured Programming" (which we are not discussing in this book) prohibit the use of a break statement, so you would have to structure your program differently.

The complete program is below:

```
01 // Example 21, file 'Break.java'
02 // This program demonstrates the use of
03 // the 'break' statement
04
05 import java.io.*;
06 import java.lang.Math;
07
08 public class Break
09 {
10    public static void main(String[] args)
11       throws IOException
12    {
13
14       BufferedReader inputReader = new BufferedReader(
15          new InputStreamReader(System.in));
16       String line;
17
18       ////////////////////////////////////////
19       // The 'break' statement
20       ////////////////////////////////////////
21
22       System.out.println("\nThe 'break' statement\n");
23
24       // Get value of n
25       System.out.print("Enter value of n: ");
26       line = inputReader.readLine();
27       int n = new Integer(line).intValue();
28
29       int i, j;
30
31       System.out.println("List of prime numbers from 2 to " +
32          n + ":");
33       System.out.print(2);     // we know 2 is prime
34
35       for (i = 3; i <= n; i++)
36       {
37          for (j = 2; j < i; j++)
38          {
39             if (i % j == 0)     // number is not prime
40                break;
41             if (j > Math.sqrt(i)) // number is prime
42             {
43                System.out.print(", " + i);
44                break;
45             }
46          }
47       }
48    }
49 }
```

And the output would be:

```
The 'break' statement

Enter value of n: 30
List of prime numbers from 2 to 30:
2, 3, 5, 7, 11, 13, 17, 19, 23, 29
```

CONTINUE, PLEASE...

Similar to the break statement, there are situations when you need to make a decision to skip the rest of the what part of a loop; you don't want to break the loop, only to rush to the end to start another iteration. This is accomplished by the continue statement: it tells the program to go to back the beginning of the loop, to evaluate the condition for the next iteration.

Let's look at an example: here's a table of the results of the class' fund-raising for the school trip: it shows the number of items each student sold. Of course, all students get a "thank you," but those who sold 10 items or more are getting a certificate. Our task is to go through the list and print out the certificates.

Student Number	Items
0	6
1	4
2	1
3	19
...	
14	0
15	5

And here is the code to do it:

```
int[] item =
  {6, 4, 1, 19, 8, 21, 0, 9,
   8, 7, 10, 15, 3, 6, 0, 5};
int i;
for (i = 0; i < item.length; i++)
{
  if (item[i] < 10)
    continue;
  // This is where the code to print the
  // certificates will be placed. It could
  // be quite long and complicated.
}
```

The continue statement tells the program to go back to the beginning of the loop, to perform the update part (i++). We could have reversed the condition of the if statement to say item[i] >= 10 and put the certificate printing as the true part of the if, but the logic is cleaner if we say "let's skip and ignore those that do not get a certificate, and then concentrate on printing the certificates for those that deserve it."

Note: the rules of "Structured Programming" (which we are not discussing in this book) prohibit the use of a continue statement, so you would *have* to reverse the condition.

A complete program that prints out a more "respectable" certificate is right here:

```
01  // Example 22, file 'Continue.java'
02  // This program demonstrates the use of
03  // the 'continue' statement
04
05  import java.io.*;
06
07  public class Continue
08  {
09     public static void main(String[] args)
10        throws IOException
11     {
12
13        BufferedReader inputReader = new BufferedReader(
14           new InputStreamReader(System.in));
15        String line;
16
17        /////////////////////////////////////////
18        // The 'continue' statement
19        /////////////////////////////////////////
20
21        System.out.println("\nThe 'continue' statement\n");
22
23        while (true)
24        {
25           // Read in number of items sold
26           System.out.print("Enter number of items sold " +
27              "(-1 to end): ");
28           line = inputReader.readLine();
29           int num = new Integer(line).intValue();
30           if (num < 0)            // end of input
31              break;               // exit loop
32           if (num < 10)           // not enough sold
33           {
34              System.out.println("This student is not " +
35                 "entitled to a certificate.");
36              continue;       // continue with next student
37           }
38
39           // Read student's name for the certificate
40           System.out.print("Enter student's name: ");
41
42           // Print the certificate
43           line = inputReader.readLine();
44           System.out.println("+--------------------" +
45              "------------------------");
46           System.out.println("|     THIS IS TO CERTIFY THAT");
47           System.out.println("|        " + line);
48           System.out.println("|     Has sold " + num + " items in");
49           System.out.println("|     The School's Annual " +
50              "Fundraising Drive");
51           System.out.println("+--------------------" +
52              "------------------------");
53        }
54     }
55  }
```

And its output could be:

```
The 'continue' statement

Enter number of items sold (-1 to end): 8
This student is not entitled to a certificate.
Enter number of items sold (-1 to end): 35
Enter student's name: Jenny Hyper
+---------------------------------------------
|     THIS IS TO CERTIFY THAT
```

```
|          Jenny Hyper
|     Has sold 35 items in
|     The School's Annual Fundraising Drive
+---------------------------------------------
Enter number of items sold (-1 to end): 3
This student is not entitled to a certificate.
Enter number of items sold (-1 to end): 14
Enter student's name: Mark Salesman
+---------------------------------------------
|     THIS IS TO CERTIFY THAT
|        Mark Salesman
|     Has sold 14 items in
|     The School's Annual Fundraising Drive
+---------------------------------------------
Enter number of items sold (-1 to end): 9
This student is not entitled to a certificate.
Enter number of items sold (-1 to end): -1
```

Of course, in real life we would print the certificates on a printer with special certificate paper, and they would not be mixed with the input or the ineligibility notes.

Note the logic of the program: we first read the number of items sold; if it's less than the required minimum, we say so and continue with the next student – there is no point in reading the name of the student if we are not going to print a certificate!

MAKE THE SWITCH – SELECTIVE EXECUTION

Many programming tasks require testing for several conditions, with different action for each. Imagine writing a program that works as a calculator. It reads in two numbers and performs an arithmetic operation on them: addition, subtraction, multiplication, division, and perhaps others as well. After reading the two numbers, the program has to determine what operation was requested by testing the operator typed in. Here is a code fragment to do it:

```
char operator;      // the operator
int num1, num2;     // the two numbers
int result;         // the result
if (operator == '+')
  result = num1 + num2;
else
if (operator == '-')
  result = num1 - num2;
else
if (operator == '*')
  result = num1 * num2;
else
if (operator == '/')
  result = num1 / num2;
else
  // an unknown operator…
```

It's difficult enough to follow when we deal with only four options – imaging what it would look like if we had more: a very long sequence of if-then-else statements with no end in sight…

I am sure you are expecting us to come up with some magical solution to this problem… Well, here it is: the switch statement! With that statement, the same code fragment will look like this:

```
char operator;      // the operator
int num1, num2;     // the two numbers
int result;         // the result
switch (operator)
{
case '+':
  result = num1 + num2;
  break;
case '-':
  result = num1 - num2;
```

```
      break;
   case '*':
     result = num1 * num2;
     break;
   case '/':
     result = num1 / num2;
     break;
   default:
     result = 1 / 0;
   }
```

Let's explain: the switch statement tells the program to jump to the case whose value is equal to the value in the parentheses; for example, if the value of operator is the character *, than the program will go to the statement after the case '*': and continue processing from there. *It will not stop at the next* case, *but will "flow through" it* – this is why we need the break, to tell the program to get out of the switch.

The default part is where the program will go if there is no case matching the value in the parentheses of the switch; it is the "catcher" for all cases that were not specified, and it is always a good practice to have it, just in case… it helps in catching unexpected values in the switch, and avoids problems later; we coded a division by zero, which will cause the program to issue an error message and stop, rather than ignore the situation and end up with a result value that is not what we wanted.

The value between the parentheses of the switch can be any expression that can produce an int value. It can be as complex as you would want it to be.

Here is a complete program that pretends to be a calculator:

```
01 // Example 23, file 'Switch.java'
02 // This program demonstrates the use of
03 // the 'switch' statement
04
05 import java.io.*;
06 import java.lang.Math;
07
08 public class Switch
09 {
10    public static void main(String[] args)
11       throws IOException
12    {
13
14       BufferedReader inputReader = new BufferedReader(
15          new InputStreamReader(System.in));
16       String line;
17
18       //////////////////////////////////////////
19       // The 'switch' statement
20       //////////////////////////////////////////
21
22       System.out.println("\nThe 'switch' statement\n");
23
24       // Get first number
25       System.out.print("Enter first number: ");
26       line = inputReader.readLine();
27       int num1 = new Integer(line).intValue();
28       System.out.print("Enter operator (+ - * /): ");
29       // read operator (a single character)
30       char op = (char)inputReader.read();
31       // skip new line and carriage return ("Enter" key)
32       inputReader.read();
33       inputReader.read();
34       // Get second number
35       System.out.print("Enter second number: ");
36       line = inputReader.readLine();
37       int num2 = new Integer(line).intValue();
38
```

```
39         int result;
40
41         switch (op)
42         {
43         case '+':
44           result = num1 + num2;
45           break;
46         case '-':
47           result = num1 - num2;
48           break;
49         case '*':
50           result = num1 * num2;
51           break;
52         case '/':
53           result = num1 / num2;
54           break;
55         default:
56           result = 1 / 0;
57         }
58
59         System.out.println(num1 + " " + op + " " +
60           num2 + " = " + result);
61
62     }
63 }
```

And here is one possible output:

```
The 'switch' statement

Enter first number: 24
Enter operator (+ - * /): /
Enter second number: 8
24 / 8 = 3
```

As before, we will not discuss the "how and why" of the input; these will be explained later in *"Formatting Using Patterns."*

What you learned in this chapter:

⋏ Control statements *are used to describe decisions and repetition in the program*

⋏ *There are two types of control statement:* decisions *and* repetitions

⋏ *Decision statements describe different actions depending on different conditions*

⋏ *The most common decision statement is the* if *statement, which tests a condition and, depending on whether it is true or false, executes one group of statements or another*

⋏ *The* switch *statement tells the computer which group of statements to execute depending on the value of an expression*

⋏ *Repetition statement tell the program to repeat (loop) a group of statements; each time the group is executed is called an* iteration *of the loop*

⋏ *A* while *loop repeats a group of statements as long as a condition is true*

⋏ *A* for *loop also repeats a group of statements as long as a condition is true, but it also has an initialization part (before starting) and an update part (after each iteration)*

⋏ *The* break *statement stops a loop and takes the program out of it immediately*

⋏ *The* continue *statement stops the current iteration of a loop and goes back to the top of the loop (the condition or update part)*

Some More Serious Programs

> *Once more, it's time to see some more practical use for what you have learned so far.*
> *The examples in this chapter are more sophisticated, and the programs do a lot more*
> *than those we wrote before.*
>
> *What you will learn in this chapter:*
>
> ➤ *How to effectively use combinations of control statements*
> ➤ *What are algorithms*
> ➤ *What is pseudo-code*

SORT

One of the common procedures a program has to tackle is sorting. This is the process of taking a "pile" of information and putting it in a certain order. For example, arranging names in alphabetical order, putting people in date-of-birth order, listing town is order of population size, etc. The way to solve this is to apply a sort algorithm. An algorithm is a step-by-step procedure for solving a problem in a finite number of steps. The procedure can be used on any type of information, as long as the problem to be solved is the one for which the algorithm was designed. It is important that an algorithm has a finite number of steps, because we do not want to find ourselves in an *infinite* program, which would never end…

There are many sort algorithms, varying in complexity and efficiency (number of steps actually taken to sort the data) – usually the more complex algorithms are also more efficient, but more difficult to implement. For our program, we chose the simplest, and therefore least efficient, algorithm. It's advantage is that is a good example of an algorithm, and will show you how to build a program around an algorithm.

Before writing the program, it is a good practice to describe the algorithm in a form that is easier for non-programmer to understand but is close enough to a program; this is called pseudo code – "like code." So here is our sort algorithm in pseudo-code:

1. Start with the first element of the array.

2. Note that the current element is the minimum element so far.

3. Take the element following the current one as the next element to check.

4. If the next element to check is smaller than the minimum element, note that this is now the new minimum element.

5. Move to the element following the element we just checked, making it the next element to check; if you did not reach the end of the array yet, go to step 4.

6. Switch between the current element and the minimum element, which is the smallest one in the array.

7. Move to the element following the current element, making it the new current element; if you did not reach the end of the array yet, go to step 2.

8. The array is sorted!

How (and why) does it work? What we do is move the smaller elements to the beginning of the array one by one. First we move the smallest to the first position. Then we ignore it and look at the rest of the array, moving the smallest element there to the first position in the rest of the array, which is the second position in the array. Then we start with the third position and do the same, until we reach the end. This sorting algorithm is known as "Bubble Sort", because the smallest element rises to the to the first position just like bubbles in a liquid.

And here is the full program:

```
01  // Example 24, file 'Sort.java'
02  // This program sorts a list of positive numbers
03
04  import java.io.*;
05  import java.lang.Math;
06
07  public class Sort
08  {
09     public static void main(String[] args)
10        throws IOException
11     {
12
13        BufferedReader inputReader = new BufferedReader(
14          new InputStreamReader(System.in));
15
16        /////////////////////////////////////
17        // Sort numbers
18        /////////////////////////////////////
19
20        System.out.println("\nSorting numbers\n");
21
22        int[] number = new int[100];
23        int  cur,          // index of current item
24             min,          // index of minimum item
25             chk,          // index of item to check
26             cnt,          // count of items to sort
27             tmp;          // temporary item storage
28
29        // Read in the numbers
30        for (cur = 0; cur < number.length; cur++)
31        {
32           System.out.print("Enter a positive number " +
33              " (-1 if no more): ");
34           String line = inputReader.readLine();
35           number[cur] = new Integer(line).intValue();
36           if (number[cur] < 0)
37              break;
38        }
39        if (cur >= number.length)
40           System.out.println("No more numbers accepted, " +
41              number.length + " is the limit.");
42
43        cnt = cur;         // index of current item, which
44                           // is now just beyond last item,
45                           // is actually the count of items
46
47        // Print out unsorted numbers
48
49        System.out.println("Unsorted numbers:");
50        for (cur = 0; cur < cnt; cur++)
51           System.out.print(number[cur] + " ");
52        System.out.println("");
53
54        // Sort the numbers
55
56        for (cur = 0; cur < cnt; cur++)
57        {
58           min = cur;
59           for (chk = cur + 1; chk < cnt; chk++)
60           {
61                 if (number[chk] < number[min])
```

```
62                    min = chk;
63                }
64                // swap between current item and the
65                // one found to be the minimum
66                tmp = number[cur];
67                number[cur] = number[min];
68                number[min] = tmp;
69            }
70
71            // Print out sorted numbers
72
73            System.out.println("Sorted numbers:");
74            for (cur = 0; cur < cnt; cur++)
75                System.out.print(number[cur] + " ");
76            System.out.println("");
77        }
78 }
```

The algorithm itself is implemented in lines 56–69. Swapping the minimum element with the current is done in lines 66–68. You see how simple it really is!

On more note: line 39 is protecting us from an overflow of the array. We limit the array to a certain number of element, so we have to make sure that "we don't bite more than we can chew…" This is **defensive programming**.

We could have sorted arrays of any numbers, negative or even floating-point, but we would have had to figure out a way to indicate the end of the input step (right now any negative number marks the end). We could have sorted an array of texts, but for that we would need to know how to compare the *contents* of String elements – comparing the String elements themselves will just compare the references to them, which will never be equal!

Here is the output from one run of this program:

```
Sorting numbers

Enter a positive number (-1 if no more): 6
Enter a positive number (-1 if no more): 1
Enter a positive number (-1 if no more): 4
Enter a positive number (-1 if no more): 5
Enter a positive number (-1 if no more): 9
Enter a positive number (-1 if no more): 7
Enter a positive number (-1 if no more): 2
Enter a positive number (-1 if no more): 8
Enter a positive number (-1 if no more): 3
Enter a positive number (-1 if no more): -1
Unsorted numbers:
6 1 4 5 9 7 2 8 3
Sorted numbers:
1 2 3 4 5 6 7 8 9
```

MEDIAN AND AVERAGE VALUES

Let's move on to another example: we would like to help a teacher calculate the median and average of the grades given to the class in the last test. Calculating the average of a set of numbers is a "no brainer", but in order to figure out the median we have to first sort them and then find the middle number. One little difficulty, as you can see in the diagrams below, is the question of what to do if we have an even number of grades – there is no *single* middle number, but two; in that case we have to average their value, and the program takes care of that properly.

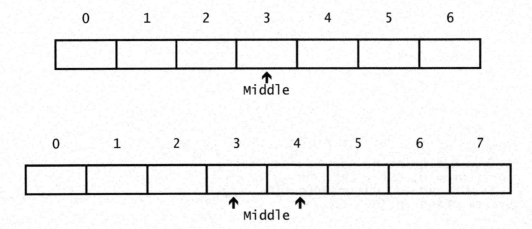

So here's the program:

```java
01  // Example 25, file 'Average.java'
02  // This program calculate average
03  // and median grades
04
05  import java.io.*;
06  import java.lang.Math;
07
08  public class Average
09  {
10    public static void main(String[] args)
11      throws IOException
12    {
13
14      BufferedReader inputReader = new BufferedReader(
15        new InputStreamReader(System.in));
16
17      ////////////////////////////////////////
18      // Calculate Average and Median Grades
19      ////////////////////////////////////////
20
21      System.out.println("\nCalculating Average and Median " +
22        "Grades\n");
23
24      int[] grade = new int[100];
25      int sum = 0;
26      int cur,            // index of current grade
27        min,            // index of minimum grade
28        chk,            // index of grade to check
29        cnt,            // count of grades to sort
30        tmp;            // temporary grade storage
31
32      // Read in the grades
33      for (cur = 0; cur < grade.length; cur++)
34      {
35        System.out.print("Enter a grade " +
36          "(-1 if no more): ");
37        String line = inputReader.readLine();
38        grade[cur] = new Integer(line).intValue();
39        if (grade[cur] < 0)
40          break;
41        sum += grade[cur]; // add them up, for later
42                          // calculation of average
43      }
44      if (cur >= grade.length)
45        System.out.println("No more grades accepted, " +
46          grade.length + " is the limit.");
47
48      cnt = cur;      // index of current grade, which
49                      // is now just beyond last grade,
```

```
50                            // is actually the count of grades
51
52         // Sort the grades
53
54         for (cur = 0; cur < cnt; cur++)
55         {
56            min = cur;
57            for (chk = cur + 1; chk < cnt; chk++)
58            {
59                  if (grade[chk] < grade[min])
60                min = chk;
61            }
62            // swap between current grade and the
63            // one found to be the minimum
64            tmp = grade[cur];
65            grade[cur] = grade[min];
66            grade[min] = tmp;
67         }
68
69         // Find median
70
71         double median;
72         if (cnt % 2 != 0)      // if we have an odd
73                                // number of grades,
74            {                   // we pick the one in the
75                                // middle of the array
76            median = grade[cnt / 2];
77            }
78         else                   // if we have an even
79            {                   // we average the two in
80                                // number of grades,
81                                // the middle of the array
82            median = (double)(grade[cnt / 2 - 1] +
83               grade[cnt / 2]) / 2.0;
84            }
85
86         double average = (double)sum / (double)cnt;
87
88         System.out.println("Read " + cnt + " grades");
89         System.out.println("Average is " + average);
90         System.out.println("Median is " + median);
91      }
92 }
```

And the results of one run:

```
Calculating Average and Median Grades

Enter a grade(-1 if no more): 69
Enter a grade(-1 if no more): 93
Enter a grade(-1 if no more): 45
Enter a grade(-1 if no more): 77
Enter a grade(-1 if no more): 98
Enter a grade(-1 if no more): 84
Enter a grade(-1 if no more): 72
Enter a grade(-1 if no more): 90
Enter a grade(-1 if no more): -1
Read 8 grades
Average is 78.5
Median is 80.5
```

A few comments (as if you didn't expect it…): notice the cast to double on lines 82 and 86? They are required to make sure that the calculations will be performed in floating-point rather than in integers; otherwise we would get rounded, instead of exact, results. Also, note the use of the remainder operator % on line 72; it is used to check if the number of grades is even or odd by dividing it by 2 and checking if there is a remainder (0 means even, 1 means odd). And lastly, note the use of cnt / 2 on lines 76 and 82–83; we know that the result is going to be truncated (rounded down) because of the integer division, and we use it to our advantage, knowing also that array indexes start from 0; try a few examples by hand and see how it works out.

MULTIPLICATION TABLE

The next problem we will solve is more about looks than substance... We want to print out a multiplication table, and the main challenge is getting the numbers aligned one under the other. The problem is that most numbers have more than one digit (what a great discovery...), and therefore we have to "pad" the smaller numbers with spaces to put them right above larger numbers, with more digits, in the same column. So most of this program is dealing with padding – we all know how to multiply anyway, don't we?

```
01  // Example 26, file 'Multiplication.java'
02  // This program prints out a multiplication table
03
04  import java.io.*;
05
06  public class Multiplication
07  {
08     public static void main(String[] args)
09        throws IOException
10     {
11
12        BufferedReader inputReader = new BufferedReader(
13           new InputStreamReader(System.in));
14
15        /////////////////////////////////////////
16        // Print out a multiplication table
17        /////////////////////////////////////////
18
19        System.out.println("\nPrinting a Multiplication Table\n");
20
21        final int min = 3, max = 30;
22        int num,           // number of rows and columns
23           col,            // column index
24           row;            // row index
25
26        // Read in table size
27
28        while (true)
29        {
30           System.out.print("Enter a number (between " +
31              min + " and " + max +
32              ")\n for multiplication table size: ");
33           String line = inputReader.readLine();
34           num = new Integer(line).intValue();
35           if (num > max)
36           {
37              System.out.println(num + " is too large");
38              continue;
39           }
40           else
41           if (num < min)
42           {
43              System.out.println(num + " is too small");
44              continue;
45           }
46           else
47              break;
48        }
49
50        System.out.println("\nMultiplication Table up to " +
51           num + " times " + num + "\n");
52
53        // Padding:
54        //    2 spaces for numbers between 1    and 9
55        //    1 space  for numbers between 10   and 99
```

```
56          //    0 space  for numbers between 100 and 999
57          String [] padding = {"   ", " ", ""};
58
59          // Print out the top line
60
61          System.out.print("   | ");
62          for (col = 1; col <= num; col++)
63          {
64              int pad = (col < 10 ? 0 : (col < 100 ? 1 : 2));
65              System.out.print(padding[pad] + col + " ");
66          }
67          System.out.println();    // a new line
68          System.out.print("---+");
69          for (col = 1; col <= num; col++)
70              System.out.print("----");
71          System.out.println();
72
73          // Print out the table
74
75          for (row = 1; row <= num; row++)
76          {
77              // Print number at begiining of row
78              int pad = (row < 10 ? 0 : (row < 100 ? 1 : 2));
79              System.out.print(padding[pad] + row + "| ");
80              // Calculate values and padding along row
81              for (col = 1; col <= num; col++)
82              {
83                  int val = row * col;
84                  pad = (val < 10 ? 0 : (val < 100 ? 1 : 2));
85                  System.out.print(padding[pad] + val + " ");
86              }
87              System.out.println();
88          }
89      }
90 }
```

Lines 28–48 read in the size of the table and make sure that the input is within the limits. Notice the use of the continue and break statements to control repetition of the input until the program gets a valid response.

Line 57 sets up the padding strings for the three expected sizes of numbers: 1, 2 or 3 digits. This is why we limit the size to 30 by 30 – to keep the maximum number to less than 999.

Lines 61–71 print out the top line of the table (the numbers across for the first multiplicand) and the separator line made up of dashes. On line 64 we calculate the index into the padding array based on the number we are about to print, and use this padding on line 65.

Lines 75–88 print out the table itself, starting with the second multiplicand at the beginning of each output line (lines 78–79) and then results of multiplying all the first multiplicands, column by column, by the second multiplicand for the current row (lines 81–86). We use the same technique as before to determine the necessary padding.

And the *beautiful* output of the program would be this:

```
Printing a Multiplication Table

Enter a number (between 3 and 30)
 for multiplication table size: 15

Multiplication Table up to 15 times 15

   |  1  2  3  4  5  6  7  8  9 10 11 12 13 14 15
---+--------------------------------------------------
  1|  1  2  3  4  5  6  7  8  9 10 11 12 13 14 15
  2|  2  4  6  8 10 12 14 16 18 20 22 24 26 28 30
  3|  3  6  9 12 15 18 21 24 27 30 33 36 39 42 45
  4|  4  8 12 16 20 24 28 32 36 40 44 48 52 56 60
```

5		5	10	15	20	25	30	35	40	45	50	55	60	65	70	75
6		6	12	18	24	30	36	42	48	54	60	66	72	78	84	90
7		7	14	21	28	35	42	49	56	63	70	77	84	91	98	105
8		8	16	24	32	40	48	56	64	72	80	88	96	104	112	120
9		9	18	27	36	45	54	63	72	81	90	99	108	117	126	135
10		10	20	30	40	50	60	70	80	90	100	110	120	130	140	150
11		11	22	33	44	55	66	77	88	99	110	121	132	143	154	165
12		12	24	36	48	60	72	84	96	108	120	132	144	156	168	180
13		13	26	39	52	65	78	91	104	117	130	143	156	169	182	195
14		14	28	42	56	70	84	98	112	126	140	154	168	182	196	210
15		15	30	45	60	75	90	105	120	135	150	165	180	195	210	225

A BETTER CALCULATOR

Remember the calculator we built when discussing the switch statement (in *"Make The Switch – Selective Execution"*)? It was somewhat primitive because we had to enter the two numbers and the operator separately – you had no way of reading in the complete expression and break it apart into the numbers and the operator. This is called **parsing** – to break something down into its components. Parsing requires the ability to deal with individual characters in a string, another challenge you have not mastered yet.

In this example we will show you a calculator that can read an input line containing an expression made up of two numbers and an operator and perform the required calculation. In order to do this we will parse the input text, isolate each number as a group of digits and figure out the value of that number. Once we have the two numbers, the rest is easy and you have seen it before...

```
01 // Example 27, file 'Calc.java'
02 // This program implements a simple calculator
03
04 import java.io.*;
05 import java.lang.Math;
06
07 public class Calc
08 {
09    public static void main(String[] args)
10       throws IOException
11    {
12
13      BufferedReader inputReader = new BufferedReader(
14        new InputStreamReader(System.in));
15
16      /////////////////////////////////////////
17      // A Simple Calculator
18      /////////////////////////////////////////
19
20      System.out.println("\nWelcome to The Simple Calculator!\n");
21
22      // Read in the complete expression
23      System.out.print("Enter expression: ");
24      String inputLine = inputReader.readLine();
25      char[] line = inputLine.toCharArray();
26
27      if (line.length == 0)
28      {
29        System.out.println("Empty expression");
30        return;
31      }
32
33      int epos,        // current position in expression
34          nstart,      // start of a number
35          nend,        // end of a number
36          digit,       // current digit
37          npos,        // position in number (going backwards)
38          num1,        // first number
39          num2,        // second number
```

```
40              p10,            // power of 10
41              result;         // result
42         char op;            // operator
43
44         // Find first number
45         for (epos = 0, nstart = 0, nend = -1;
46             epos < line.length;
47             epos++)
48         {
49             if (line[epos] >= '0'  &&  line[epos] <= '9')
50                 continue;       // a valid digit
51             nend = epos - 1;    // end of number
52             break;
53         }
54         if (epos == line.length)
55         { // 1st number is all we found
56             System.out.println("Invalid expression " +
57                 "(missing operator and 2nd number): '" +
58                 inputLine + "'");
59             return;
60         }
61         if (epos == nstart)
62         { // no number found
63             System.out.println("Invalid expression " +
64                 "(missing 1st number): '" +
65                 inputLine + "'");
66             return;
67         }
68
69         // Calculate value of first number
70         for (npos = nend, num1 = 0, p10 = 1;
71             npos >= nstart;
72             npos--)
73         {
74             // Calculate value of current digit
75             digit = line[npos] - '0';// current digit
76             // Add value of current digit,
77             // consideringits decimal place
78             num1 += digit * p10;
79             // Move to next power of 10 (decimal
80             // place) for next digit
81             p10 *= 10;
82         }
83
84         // Get operator
85         op = line[epos];
86
87         // Find second number
88         for (++epos, nstart = epos, nend = -1;
89             epos < line.length;
90             epos++)
91         {
92             if (line[epos] >= '0'  &&  line[epos] <= '9')
93                 continue;       // a valid digit
94             nend = epos - 1;    // end of number
95             break;
96         }
97         if (epos == nstart)
98         { // no number found
99             System.out.println("Invalid expression " +
100                "(no 2nd number): '" +
101                inputLine + "'");
102            return;
103        }
104        if (epos == line.length)    // 2nd number ended at
105            nend = epos - 1;    // end of expression
106
107        // Calculate value of second number
```

```
108        for (npos = nend, num2 = 0, p10 = 1;
109          npos >= nstart;
110          npos--)
111        {
112          // Calculate value of current digit
113          digit = line[npos] - '0';// current digit
114          // Add value of current digit,
115          // consideringits decimal place
116          num2 += digit * p10;
117          // Move to next power of 10 (decimal
118          // place) for next digit
119          p10 *= 10;
120        }
121
122        // Apply operator
123        switch (op)
124        {
125        case '+':
126          result = num1 + num2;
127          break;
128        case '-':
129          result = num1 - num2;
130          break;
131        case '*':
132          result = num1 * num2;
133          break;
134        case '/':
135          if (num2 == 0)
136          {
137            System.out.println("Cannot divide by 0");
138            return;
139          }
140          result = num1 / num2;
141          break;
142        default:
143          System.out.println("Invalid operator: '" + op + "'");
144          return;
145        }
146
147        System.out.println(num1 + " " + op + " " +
148          num2 + " = " + result);
149    }
150 }
```

The calculator assumes that its input is a number of at least one digit, followed by a single-character operator, followed by another number. Everything else will upset it and cause it to complain.

On lines 24–25 the program reads the expression and converts it into an array of chars so that it can work with each individual character. When parsing a string, you usually need pointers into various parts of the string so that you know where things begin and end; these pointers (indexes into the array), as well as some other variables the program needs, are defined on line 33–42.

Now we're off to capture the first number! This is done on lines 45–53: we start at the beginning of the string and check every character to see if it's a digit or not; we determine that by comparing the value of the characters to the digits 0 and 9, knowing that the values of all the digits are between those two (actually, these values are also in their proper sequence, a fact we will use later). By the way, notice the use of three initializer on line 45 – saving some extra lines. Before we continue processing the number, we check if the expression looks OK so far: on lines 54–67 we check if the number ended at the end of the input (meaning there was only that number, and the operator and the second number were missing), or if the input started with a non-digit (meaning there is not even a first number). Once we know the starting position of the number in the string and its ending position, we can go on to put it together. On lines 70–82, we go through the number back-to-front, from the units position to the 10's, 100's and so forth, multiplying each digit by the power of 10 corresponding to its position, and adding it all up. The way we figure out on line 75 the value of each digit is by subtracting the value of the digit 0 from each digit, knowing that the values of all the digits are **consecutive** (one after the other) beginning with the 0.

The rest is straightforward: we pick the operator on line 85; we get the second number on lines 88–120 using the same technique we used to get the first number; and then we perform the operator, using the switch statement (with a default, in case the operator is wrong – never leave anything to chance!), on lines 123–145.

The output of this program is simple:

```
Welcome to The Simple Calculator!

Enter expression: 1234*876
1234 * 876 = 1080984
```

What you learned in this chapter:

⋏   *An* algorithm *is a step-by-step procedure for solving a problem*

⋏   Pseudo-code *is a way to describe an algorithm without writing a program*

⋏   *How to combine control statements effectively*

Stay Organized – Using Statements and Blocks

> *Groups of statements and variables that are responsible for a specific task can be organized to be separate from other groups, so that each group is as independent as possible. In this chapter you will learn how to organize your program in such a way.*
>
> *What you will learn in this chapter:*
> ➤ *How to organize the statements in your program in blocks*
> ➤ *What are the rules for using variables among different blocks*

PLAYING WITH BLOCKS – GROUPING STATEMENTS

When you used a for statement, all the statements that were part of the loop had to be between braces ({ and }); statements before the opening brace or after the closing brace were not part of the loop. Such a group is called a **block**, and it has some special properties. The same rules apply to the group of statements following an if or an else, or the statements after the while. A block can be used anywhere a single statement can be – as you already saw, you can put either a single statement or a block of statements after an if.

The main use of the block construct is to tell the compiler that the group of statements are together in relation to other statements or groups, such as being the loop-controlled statements of a while loop: at the end of the block, the program will not continue – flow through – but will go back to the loop control part (between the parentheses after the keywords for or while) to decide if another iteration is necessary.

The break and continue statements also apply only to the block in which they appear. continue tells the program to skip the rest of the loop block and go immediately to the beginning of the loop for another possible iteration, and break tells it to go to the end of the loop or switch block and exit it. break can only be used in a loop, either for or while, or in a switch block; continue is only allowed in a loop.

ON THE SCOPE – VISIBILITY OF VARIABLES

But block have an even more important role – they allow you to control where and when variables are going to be recognized. Suppose you have tried to have these two statements in the same program (possibly by accident):

```
int value;
double value;
```

Even if they are not right next to each other, the compiler will come up with an error message like "value is already defined," pointing at the second definition of the variable. That's understandable: how can the compile know what you really want if you tell it that a variable is both an int and a double? But may be this is *exactly* what you want! What if in one part of the program you need an integer variable named value, and in another part you need a floating-point variable with the same name? Blocks to the rescue!

```
if (…)
{
  int value;
  // code using 'value' as an int
}
…
while (…)
{
  double value;
  // code using 'value' as a double
}
```

The blocks above could be those of an `if` statement (after the `if` or the `then`), loop blocks (after a `for` or a `while`), or just stand-alone blocks (which will be used rarely, usually only in order to take advantage of the new rules we are about to define).

The variable `value` appears in two different blocks having two different types. That's allowed, because the blocks limit the scope of the variable, namely the areas where it is recognized. The scope rule is for the compiler; it says that a variable's scope is limited to the block in which it is defined and any enclosed blocks (blocks within that block). What does it mean?

Let's look at the following code fragment:

```
{
  while (true)
  {
    int number = 7;
    System.out.println("number =" + number);
    break;
  }
  System.out.println("number =" + number);
}
```

The second `println` statement will not even pass compilation, *because there is no definition of the variable* number *outside the inner block* – it's like it never even existed! The moment the `while` block was closed, the compiler forgot all about the variables defined in it. Remember that it's the compiler who decides which variables to use, based on what it knows; if it doesn't remember a variable, it can't use it.

It is also important to remember that the initializers in a `for` statement are defined for the loop block only. For example:

```
for (int i = 0; i < 10; i++)
{
  if (i * i > 50)
    break;
}
System.out.println("i=" + i);
```

In case you wanted to find the first value of i whose power of 2 is greater than 50, this code wouldn't work… As a matter of fact, it wouldn't even pass compilation! The variable i is only known within the loop block, so the print statement will make the compiler unhappy – it wouldn't know what the i means.

What you learned in this chapter:

⅄ *Statements can be organized in* blocks *when they have to be grouped together*

⅄ *The group of statements belonging to a control statement (if, else, while, for) must be put in a block after the keyword and the control information in the parentheses which follow it*

⅄ *The continue and break statements apply to the block where they appear*

⅄ *Blocks also control the* scope *of a variable, which is the area where the variable is known*

⅄ *A variable's scope is the block within which it is defined and all enclosed blocks which do not re-define it*

⅄ *If the initializers in a for statements define new variables, their scope is only that loop's block*

It's How You Function – Using Functions or Methods

It's often the case that some logic you write is needed several times. Instead of repeatedly writing it every time you need it, someone has invented the idea of a function, or method to solve this problem. In this chapter we will study functions, why we need them and how best to use them.

What you will learn in this chapter:

> *What are functions and why you should use them*
> *How to define and write effective functions*

On a scientific calculator you have buttons to calculate absolute values, square roots, and many other special functions. How about getting something similar for programs? Isn't it quite annoying that you have to re-type the same code every time you want your program to calculate the absolute value of a number? To remind you, the code for one such calculation looks like this:

```
int absX = (x >= 0 ? x : -x);
```

And you would have to type the code between the parentheses, perhaps using different variable names, over and over again. But if you had a button with ABS on it, and you could just enter the value of x (or any other variable) and hit that button… Stop dreaming! Your wish has been granted. In programming, the concept of such a button is called a **function** or a **method**.

THE STRUCTURE OF A FUNCTION

The Simple Truth About Simple Functions

How does a calculator button work? You enter a value, press the button, and get the result. There is the input (the value you entered), the output (the value that comes back) and the calculation itself, which may be very complex.

A function is very similar in that it has these three parts. But it is smarter than a plain button because it can have more than one input value. The general format of a function definition is:

```
<type> <name>(<parameters>)
{
   <body>
}
```

If it seems a little complicated, don't worry. We'll explain everything.

First of all, every function must have a type, because it calculates a value and every value has a type. So the `type` part is just like the type of any regular variable.

Just like any variable, a function must have a name too, so that we can call it ("Hey, you!" wouldn't work…) The rules for the name of a function are the same as those for variables. That's what the `name` part is for.

The definitions for the types of values that the function takes as input are called **parameters**, and they make up the `parameters` part of the function's definition. Parameters are defined the same as you define variables, but are separated by commas instead of semi-colons.

Finally, the `body`. That's the code that performs the calculation. It is a group of statements in a block, following the same rules as any other block. It must have in it at least one return statement, which specifies the value to be returned.

It's time for an example. Let's define a function to compute the absolute value:

```
int abs(int v)
{
  return(v >= 0 ? v : -v);
}
```

Not that there is any advantage in it, but you could code this function differently:

```
int abs(int v)
{
  if (v >= 0)
    return(v);
  else
    return(-v);
}
```

This just shows you that you can use more than one return statement. You must remember, though, that when a return is executed the function terminates and returns the value computed – statements following the return will never be executed (and the compile will warn you about this). Also, a function *must* return a value, so all code paths must finish with a return statement.

So far, so good. But once you define a function, how do you use it? You **call** it (or **invoke** it). It's very simple – you write the name of the function, and follow it by its **arguments**, between parentheses and separated by commas. The arguments are the actual values for the function's parameters for this particular call (invocation), and must be specified in the same order as the parameters were defined and much them in their types. For example:

```
int twiceAbsX = abs(x) * 2;
```
or:

```
result = abs(top) / abs(bottom);
```

By the way, you can pass as argument a literal rather than a variable, such as abs(-7), but in this particular case it is silly because you know the result and can code it directly. But if we look at a function which calculates the square root of a number, it may make sense to code sqrt(3.1415926) if you don't know the square root of pi.

A function call can appear anywhere a simple variable is allowed to appear. It can even be an argument to another function. For example: sqrt(abs(x)).

Let's try a more sophisticated function: suppose we have an array of test grades, and we want to find the index of a specific grade. A function to do this is below:

```
int findGrade(int[] testGrades, int whichGrade)
{
  for (int i = 0; i < testGrades.length; i++)
    if (testGrades[i] == whichGrade)
      return(i);
  return(-1);
}
```

Note that we take advantage of the "finality" effect of the return statement: we know that if the loop completed, it means that the function didn't find the required grade – because if the function did find it the, the first return statement would have been executed and the loop terminated in the middle. We need the second return, though, because this function *must* return a value; we choose to return -1 because we know that this is an invalid index and thus will indicated failure to find the required grade.

Here's a code fragment that uses this function:

```
int[] grades = {88, 75, 44, 76, 69, 99};
int grade = findGrade(grades, 76);
```

This example will return the value 3; if we passed 77 as a second argument, we will get back a -1.

Throwing a Pass – Passing Arguments

Usually a function cannot change its arguments, but only access their values; so we say that the arguments are passed **by value**. In a case where the argument is a reference, such as a reference to an array, the argument is passed **by reference** and the function can not only access the value but can also change the contents of the array. In the following example, we have an array of temperatures in Fahrenheit; the function counts how many are below freezing, replaces each temperature with its Celsius equivalent and returns the count of sub-freezing temperatures:

```
int toCelsius(double[] temps)
{
  int count = 0;
  for (int i = 0; i < temps.length; i++)
  {
    if (temps[i] < 32.0)
      count++;
    temps[i] = (temps[i] - 32.0) * (5.0 / 9.0);
  }
  return(count);
}
```

Functions With No Value

There may be situations where a function is *not* expected to return a value, when the function's work does *not* produce a single calculated result to return – as may be the case with a function that only operates on an array but does not return any value. Such functions can be defined with the data type `void`, as in the following example:

```
void addInterest(double[] amounts, double interest)
{
  for (int i = 0; i < amounts.length; i++
    amounts [i] *= (1 + interest) + 100.0;
}
```

This functions goes over an array of amounts (such as in savings accounts) and adds to each account the interest that was earned. The array and the interest percentage are passed as arguments – the array by reference and the interest by value.

Even though we say that such functions have no value, it doesn't mean that they are useless…

WHERE FUNCTIONS CAN BE FOUND

One of the advantages of functions is called *encapsulation*. We will talk a lot more about this concept later (in Part Three) but another way to describe it is as "the black box effect:" A function can be viewed as a black box; you know *what* it does, but you don't have to know *how* it does it – just like a black box that you cannot see into. It's the same with your calculator: you know there is a button to calculate the square root of a number, and you don't care how it's done – obviously, you cannot look inside the calculator and figure it out. The benefit is that you can use a function anywhere you need its results, but you don't need to understand how it works or have to copy the same code and worry about the names of variables. One of the rules for writing functions is to keep them simple and have them do only one thing, so that there is no confusion regarding their "purpose in life."

It's time to tell you a secret: you have been using functions even without realizing it! Every time you used `System.out.println()` to print out something, you were calling a function; this function is provided with the run-time environment as part of a *library* (a concept we will discuss later); you have no clue how it works (very few people do…), but it's there for your use whenever you need it. When you needed to calculate a square root in previous examples (in *"Pyramid-in-a-Prism," "Stuffed Cone"* and *"Take a Break…"*) and coded `Math.sqrt(i)`, you were using a another function from the standard library.

It's also time to unravel another mystery encountered throughout all the examples: on the line saying

```
public static void main(String[] args)
```

you were defining a function called main, of type void (returning no value), with a single argument – an array of type String. This function is *required* in every program – it's the main function and where the program begins execution – it is called by the operating system when the program is run. (We will forget for the moment about the words public and static).

AN EXAMPLE FUNCTION (SORT OF...)

As a complete example of a truly useful function, let's take up sorting. We will "borrow" the sort algorithm from a previous example (in *"Sort"* above) and make it a function. Here goes:

```
01  // Example 28, file 'SortFunc.java'
02  // This program defines and uses a
03  // function to sort a list of positive numbers
04
05  import java.io.*;
06
07  public class SortFunc
08  {
09
10      // sort - a function to sort an array of numbers
11
12      static void sort(
13          double[] array,  // array of numbers to sort
14          int cnt)         // count of items to sort
15      {
16          int cur,          // index of current item
17            min,            // index of minimum item
18            chk;            // index of item to check
19          double tmp;       // temporary item storage
20
21          for (cur = 0; cur < cnt; cur++)
22          {
23              min = cur;
24              for (chk = cur + 1; chk < cnt; chk++)
25              {
26                      if (array[chk] < array[min])
27                      min = chk;
28              }
29              // swap between current item and the
30              // one found to be the minimum
31              tmp = array[cur];
32              array[cur] = array[min];
33              array[min] = tmp;
34          }
35      }
36
37      // main - the program's main function
38
39      public static void main(String[] args)
40          throws IOException
41      {
42
43          BufferedReader inputReader = new BufferedReader(
44              new InputStreamReader(System.in));
45
46          /////////////////////////////////////////
47          // Sort numbers using a function
48          /////////////////////////////////////////
49
50          System.out.println("\nSorting numbers\n");
51
52          double[] data = new double[100];
53          int count, item;
54
55          // Read in the numbers
56          for (item = 0; item < data.length; item++)
```

```
57      {
58         System.out.print("Enter a positive number " +
59            "(-1 if no more): ");
60         String line = inputReader.readLine();
61         data[item] = new Double(line).doubleValue();
62         if (data[item] < 0)
63            break;
64      }
65      if (item >= data.length)
66         System.out.println("No more numbers accepted, " +
67            data.length + " is the limit.");
68
69      count = item;  // index of current item, which
70                     // is now just beyond last item,
71                     // is actually the count of items
72
73      // Print out unsorted numbers
74
75      System.out.println("Unsorted numbers:");
76      for (item = 0; item < count; item++)
77         System.out.print(data[item] + " ");
78      System.out.println("");
79
80      // Sort the numbers
81
82      sort(data, count);
83
84      // Print out sorted numbers
85
86      System.out.println("Sorted numbers:");
87      for (item = 0; item < count; item++)
88         System.out.print(data[item] + " ");
89      System.out.println("");
90   }
91 }
```

This program is so similar to the one we borrowed from, that there is nothing to say about it. The only reason this program is better than the other is that it's easier to understand: the complex sort algorithm is encapsulated in the function, and when you read the main program you don't have to bother with it – you just know that it works. You could also use it multiple times if you need to sort several arrays without copying the same code over and over again.

This example demonstrates the two main reasons for writing a function: the first, which we have already discussed, is to avoid repetition – you take some code that is needed more than once and make it a function so that you don't have to copy it. The second reason for writing a function is clarity – by "packaging" a specific procedure into a function, it is easier to understand it apart from the rest of the program; even if you have code that is used only once, it may be wise to make it a function if it is complex enough, so that it will not "clutter" the program.

OVERLOADING A FUNCTION

You might recall that one of the rules for defining variables is that duplicates are not allowed (see *"On the Scope – visibility of Variables"* above) – you cannot use the same name for more than one variable (within the same scope). The rules for function names are slightly more forgiving, and it's called **overloading** of functions. This is needed to allow you to define functions with the same name but with *different number of parameters or the types of parameters*. And, might you ask, why is that useful?

A good example for functions with different number of parameters would be a sort function like the one we wrote before (in *"An Example Function (Sort Of...)"*). The definition we used was:

```
void sort(double[] array, int cnt)
```

But we could have defined another function using this definition:

```
void sort(double[] array)
```

and let the function find the length of the array to be sorted from its length attribute. The first function allows you to sort only part of the array, while the second function sorts the whole array. They are both named the same, and the compiler will pick the correct one based on the number of arguments when you call the function:

```
sort(ages);      // sort all ages in the array
sort(ages, 15);   // sort the first 15 ages
```

We could also define another pair of functions:

```
void sort(int[] array, int cnt)
void sort(int[] array)
```

To sort integer arrays, and again the compiler is smart enough to pick the correct function based on both the number *and* the types of the arguments.

One more thing worthy of note: even though we used the same names for the parameters (which is allowed because they are only known within the scope of the functions block), it is not required to do so. You could use different names for the same parameters in different definitions.

Another example of an overloaded function is the "substring" function. Let's define a function that takes a string as an argument and returns a portion of it, a sub-string, beginning at a requested position (beginning with 0) and with a requested length. The definition may look like this:

```
String subString(String input, int position, int length)
```

But what if we want to have a variation of this function that returns the "tail" of the string, that is the part from the requested position through the end of the string? We could define a function called `tail()`, but it makes more sense to define another `subString()` function which does not have a third parameter and thus assumes that the length is "to the end." This definition may look like this:

```
String subString(String input, int position)
```

Same name, different number of parameters. Logically, these two functions are the same – they return a substring. The only difference is how they know how far to go. These functions can be called in several ways:

```
String text = "Hello";
String ll = subString(text, 2, 2);   // returns "ll"
String llo = subString(text, 2); // returns "llo"
String middle = subString("This is a string", 5, 4); // returns "is a"
```

There is an actual substring function in the standard library, but it has different parameters, so don't get confused. This definition is just an example and we have not coded the actual function performing the task. We will show you the real one later (in Part Three).

What you learned in this chapter:

⋏ *A* function, *or a* method, *is a group of statements with a single, well defined purpose*

⋏ *Functions* encapsulate *procedures by hiding them from those who call the functions – the user of a function needs only to know its inputs and outputs, not how it works*

⋏ *A function is* called, *or* invoked, *when the program needs to execute the procedure which is the purpose of the function*

⋏ *When called, a function can accept* parameters, *which provide the function with the specific values to use in that particular invocation*

⋏ *Parameters are usually passed* by value, *which means that the function cannot change them*

⋏ *Sometimes a parameter is passed* by reference, *and then the function can change the original values that it refers to*

⋏ *It is allowed to* overload *function by defining more than one function with the same name, as long as the values retuned by these functions or their parameters are different*

⋏ *Functions can be grouped into* libraries *for everyone to use, and some useful functions are usually provided in* standard *libraries*

Can You Hear Me Now? – Input and Output

> *So now you know how to process data, calculate and compute. But what good is it if you cannot get the data into the program or the results to someone who can use them? That's the role of input and output. We will show you what are outside sources of data (inputs), what options you have for outside destinations for your results (outputs) and which functions you need to use in order to read from input sources and write to output destinations.*
>
> *What you will learn in this chapter:*
> - *What are inputs and outputs*
> - *How to use input functions*
> - *How to use output functions*

WHEN YOU HAVE SOMETHING TO SAY – OUTPUT

It is obvious why you need to know how to produce output from a program – what's the use of doing all the calculations and processing if no one can see them and use them?

There are two types of output we need to discuss. The first one is output for people to read, which is sometimes called **character output** because it is made up of the individual characters (letters, digits and symbols) that are exactly like those in a book; this type of output is directed at a computer screen or printer, where people can view it. The second type of output is for the computer itself – it is not meant for people to read, but for computers only, usually for other programs; it is frequently called **binary output** or **raw data** output, because it is usually in a form internal to the computer. Binary data is outside the scope of this book, so let us concentrate on character data.

We already know how to produce simple output, which we call **unformatted** because we have no real control over how it comes out. In some examples (such as in *"Multiplication Table"*) we used some tricks with "padding" to achieve an organized and neat printout of a table, but that was quite crude. It is true that most of today's programs do not produce printed reports, but instead use windows on the screen. But even if your program produces its output in a graphic window, you still have to control the appearance of each field. We are talking here about **formatted** output, called so because it uses a specific format, or structure, for each element.

Much of the output produced today by many programs is not directed at printers or at simple "character oriented" or "line oriented" devices like the DOS window in a Microsoft Windows environment. It mostly shows up as part of a graphic window, with plenty of buttons, input fields, selection boxes, and other controls. However, each element, whether it's a number or a text field, has to be formatted specifically to fit the area allocated to it on the window and to present its information correctly.

Formatting output is a relatively complex task, so we will focus only on some of the simpler ways to control how *numeric* output should look. We assume for the moment that text is not a big challenge to format, because all that is needed in most cases it only to put the text on the line, or the window, at the position where you want it to be. Date and time values are quite difficult, and we will not deal with them here either.

The challenge is telling the computer exactly how to print out numbers is in specifying the size of the area in which the number would be displayed, how many digits should appear before and after the decimal point, whether we want decimal or scientific notation, where we want to put a minus sign if the number is negative and if we want to have zeros or blanks filing up the area if there are not enough significant digits.

All these specifications are packaged into a **pattern**. This is a string which describes all the aspects mentioned above. That string is made up of special symbols, each representing a place for a digit or other information.

Decimal Notation

The symbol for a single digit is 0; a pattern for a three-digit number would be the string "000". It plainly says "at least three digits." So the number 123 will be displayed as 123, the number 1234 will show as 1234 (notice that it is more than 3 digits!), and 12 will be 012 (the 0 added to make sure that it's going to occupy three digits).

If you don't want **leading zeros** (those that come to the left of the first significant digit, not zeros that are part of the number), such as in the case of the 012 above, you can use the pattern symbol #, which will eliminate any leading zero. So if you use the pattern "##0", the number 987 will still produce 987, but 7 will produce just 7 (the three-zeros pattern would have produced 007). Using a pattern of "####" would cause a 0 to show up as a single 0, and this is because something must be displayed – you cannot ignore the last 0. Remember, however, that the # symbol only deals with leading zeros, so using the "#####" pattern, the number 1001 will show up as 1001.

Negative numbers are normally displayed with a minus sign to their left, just as you would expect: the pattern "0" will cause -4545 to be displayed as -4545.

And what about a decimal point? No problem! Just put it in the pattern where you want it to be. Take the number 135.246; use the pattern "0.000", and you will get the expected 135.246; use the pattern "0.0000", and you will get the 135.2460; but use the pattern "0.00", and you will get 135.25 – because you didn't leave enough room for the digits after the decimal point, the number was rounded for you. Using a # before the decimal point will avoid a 0 if the number is smaller than 1: printing 0.9753 using the pattern "#.0000" will produce .9753.

Let's take all the examples we used in this section and look at them together, with two separate views:

Pattern	Number	Result
000	123	123
	1234	1234
	12	012
	7	007
##0	987	987
	7	7
####	0	0
#####	1001	1001
0	-4545	-4545

Number	Pattern	Result
1234	0000	1234
	00000	01234
	000	1234
135.246	0.000	135.246
	0.00	135.25
0.9753	#.0000	.9753
	#.00000	.97530
	#.00	.98
	000.00	000.98

Scientific Notation

The major difference between decimal and scientific notation is that you specify the exponent (the "power of 10" value). If you remember, when you specified a literal value in a scientific notation (see *"Literals"*), you might have coded 2.9856E6 to indicate the number 2985600 or 7.23e-4 for 0.000723. Therefore, when you use a pattern to describe the format of a number in scientific notation, you have to say how to display the exponent. This is done by adding the letter E followed by a pattern for the exponent. For example, "0.0000E0" is a pattern for a number is scientific notation with one digit before the decimal points, four digits after and an exponent of one digit. The number

2468 will be printed as 2.4680E3. Using the pattern "0.0000E00" it will show as 2.4680E03. The pattern "00.0000E00" will cause the same number to print as 24.6800E02.

As you can see, the placement of the decimal point in the pattern forces the formatting to adjust the printed value of the exponent: when we specified one digit to the left of the decimal point, the exponent was 3; when we forced two digits, it was adjusted to be 2. This is one of the nice features of the scientific notation.

One more note: the pattern for the exponent must be made up of 0s only – no # allowed.

To summarize the scientific notation formatting, look at this table:

Number	Pattern	Result
2468	0.0000E0	2.4680E3
	0.0000E00	2.4680E03
	00.0000E00	24.6800E02

Formatting Using Patterns

There was one questions we left unanswered in the last two sections: how do we apply the pattern to a number to get it formatted? This section will provide the answer, but will still leave some mystery to it – mystery that will be unraveled later.

In order to format a number, you first have to create the pattern, and then use it on a number. The first step is done like this:

```
DecimalFormat numberFormat = new DecimalFormat("0.0000");
```

Then you apply it to a number like this:

```
System.out.println(numberFormat.format(2468));
```

The numberFormat variable is a reference that indirectly represents the pattern (as a matter of fact, it is a reference to an object of type DecimalFormat, but this is not the place to explain what it means). In order to apply the pattern, you invoke the method format() that somehow belongs to that pattern, and the result is a string with the formatted number; this string is then printed by the standard printing function println().

You can define as many patterns as you wish, but you can also use the same pattern to format several numbers. And you can specify a variable of any numeric type as the argument to the format() function.

Output to Files

It is possible that you may want to send the output of a program to a file (remember your visit to Computer Park in Part One?) rather than to the screen. This can be because you want to preserve this output, or send it to a few people, or even process it later by another program.

Coming to think of it, the screen is considered a file. We used the method call System.out.println() to send output to the screen, and System.out represented the system's standard output. So the only thing we have to learn is how to substitute another file for the screen, namely for System.out. We will replace it with a "creature" belonging to a family called *streams*. We will deal with this family later, in Part Three, but for now let's just settle for the fact that these guys are objects designed to take care of "streams" of characters, either input or output.

To use a stream, we first have to create it. Creating a stream for output to a file called OutputFile might look like this:

```
PrintStream output = new PrintStream(
  new FileOutputStream("OutputFile"));
```

Now you can use this stream the same way you used the standard output:

```
output.println("Hello!");
```

Instead of going to the screen, the output will go to a file named `OutputFile`. That's all there is to it. Of course, if you want to work with more than one file, you can have more than one stream.

LISTEN TO OTHERS – INPUT

As was the case with output, we are interested here in formatted input of numeric values, and not in raw input. You had some experience with formatted input in examples beginning in *"An Interactive Calculator."* If you'll go back there and take another look, you'll notice that we used a stream there to read a line from the standard input `System.in`. After we read in the line, we assumed that it contained one number and converted the contents of the line to a number of the type we expected. It became more interesting in *"A Better Calculator,"* where we expected more than a single number on the input line. In order to deal with this, we had to convert the line to an array of characters and then parse the line – analyze it character by character and "build" the numbers digit by digit. Perhaps it was a good exercise, but it was quite tedious. There were actually two challenges in doing it the hard way: first, finding the end of the number, so that we can look for the next element in the input following it (the operator, in the case of the calculator example), and assembling the number from its individual digits.

We solve this two problems by using the parsing function that belongs to an object of type `NumberFormat`. It is a relative of `DecimalFormat`, which we have met in *"Formatting Using Patterns."* The beauty of the parsing function is that it not only gets the number, it also tells us where it ends. Unfortunately, using all this power requires better understanding of objects, which you don't have yet. Therefore, consider all we have said in this section only an "appetizer," and you will find the "main course" later, in Part Three.

One more note regarding input: just as output was going to a stream, and there is a standard stream that goes to the screen, so is input coming from a stream and there is a standard stream that comes from the keyboard – `System.in`. Other input streams can come from files, and are defined similarly to output streams.

What you learned in this chapter:

⅄ Input *is the data the program needs to work with*

⅄ Output *is what a program produces to show the results of its work*

⅄ Character *input and output are readable by people*

⅄ Binary *or* raw *input and output are for other programs*

⅄ *Output is produced by using* output functions

⅄ *Numbers can be printed in decimal or scientific notation*

⅄ Patterns *are used to tell output functions how to format numbers*

⅄ Parsing *is used to extract numbers and other elements from input lines*

⅄ *The destination of output is a* stream

⅄ *There is a standard output stream which goes to the screen and a standard input stream that comes from the keyboard*

Finally, Real Programs

> *This is like a review for a final exam... We will write programs that uses almost everything you learned in this chapter – real programs that process data like any production program in real life.*
>
> *What you will learn in this chapter:*
> - *How to combine everything you learned so far to write real programs*

THE GRADES REPORT

This program is a simple data-processing program. It reads input, does some processing, and prints out a report.

The purpose of this program is to produce a report on students' grades. For each student, the program will report the student's name, average grade and grades in all the subjects the student took.

The input for this program is from files – there is too much data to ask the user to type it in every time the program needs to be run. By using files, the user can update the grades, as well as the participating students and the available subjects, whenever necessary without having to re-type everything. There are three files involved:

- ❏ Subjects file: for each subject, its id is listed together with its full name. Each line in this file has two fields: a subject id and a subject name (between quotes), separated by spaces or tabs. For example:
  10 "Algebra"
  This means that the subject "Algebra" has an id of 10.
  The first line of the file is different: it contains the number of subjects listed in the rest of the file.

- ❏ Students file: for each subject, the student's id is listed together with the student's full name. Each line in this file has two fields: a student id and a student name (between quotes), separated by spaces or tabs. For example:
  18791 "Einstein, Albert"
  This means the Albert Einstein has a student id of 18791.
  The first line of the file is different: it contains the number of students listed in the rest of the file.

- ❏ Grades file: each line in this file describes the grade information for one student in one subject. Each line contains three fields: a student id, a subject id, and a grade. For example:
  18791 10 63
  This means that Albert Einstein's grade in Algebra was 63. Well, even though he was a mathematical genius, his school work wasn't that great...
  Unlike the two other files, there is no first line with a count. The end of the list is indicated by a line with the single character '@'.

The beginning of the program, like most programs, is defining the variables that will by used throughout the program (constants and globals). Of particular interest are the arrays, which will hold the information we will read from the files. Some programs do their processing *while* reading their input, but we chose to first read all the data and then perform the calculations. Therefore, on lines 25–33 we have defined arrays to hold the names of the students and the subjects, and in parallel their ids. We also defined arrays for the grades and the averages. But notice one interesting facts: none of the arrays has been allocated, namely we did not reserve any space for the data, only defined the types of data we will need. There is a good reason for this – we wouldn't know how much data we will have until we read the first lines from the subjects and students files. These lines will tell us how many subjects and students we have, and from that we can calculate the maximum number of grades we will have (one grade for each subject for each student) and the number of averages (one average for each student).

The program itself can be divided into the following parts:

❑ Input master files – subjects and students (lines 45–103). This part reads the "subjects" and "students" files and saves their contents in the appropriate arrays. The file are processed in a similar way, in the following steps:

  ○ Read the first line, to know how many items (subjects or students) the file contains (lines 52–53, 82–83).

  ○ Allocate the arrays for the names and ids for as many items as there are (lines 64–65, 94–95).

  ○ Read the lines (records) from the files into the arrays. This requires parsing each line to extract the id and the name (lines 67–72, 97–102).

Notice that both files are processed using the same set of functions (methods); the file-specific information, such as the name of the file and the arrays to be used, is passed as arguments to those functions. This approach reduces the size of the program by re-using the same methods to deal with both files instead of coding almost identical code twice.

❑ Report the contents of the master files (lines 105–137). This section is executed only if there were no problems with reading the files. Otherwise, there is no point in continuing and the program terminates (line 136). Before printing, though, we sort the data (lines 111–114) so that it will be easier to work with it later.

❑ Read in the grades (lines 139–158). First, the "grades" array is allocated and initialized to invalid grades (lines 143–153). Then, the "grades" file is read in (line 158).

❑ Calculate the averages (lines 160–186). After all the preparations, we are finally ready for the program to perform its task. It turns out to be quite simple. First, an array for the averages is allocated (line 165), and then the averages are calculates by going through the grades array row by row – student by student – and calculating the average of the student's grades.

❑ Report the results (lines 188–218). Here we print a full, nicely formatted, report of the results.

As you can see, all this is in the main() function, which takes up only about two thirds of the program. The rest are functions that do small, well defined jobs. There are functions that perform parsing and conversions (lines 221–411), functions that read files (lines 413–571) and sorting (lines 573–639). We will not go into details regarding these functions – each is simple enough and you should be able to understand them on your own. If you have some difficulty understanding any function, you can copy it into another program and write some calls to it to experiment and see how it works.

```
92  //////////////////////////////////////////////////////////////////
01  // Example 29, file 'Grades.java'
02  // This program calculates grades
03  //////////////////////////////////////////////////////////////////
04
05  import java.io.*;
06
07  public class Grades
08  {
09
10      //////////////////////////////////////////////////////////////
11      // Constants
12      //////////////////////////////////////////////////////////////
13
14      final static int iStart = 0;
15      final static int iEnd = 1;
16      final static String subjectsFileName = "subjects.txt";
17      final static String studentsFileName = "students.txt";
18      final static String gradesFileName = "grades.txt";
19
20      //////////////////////////////////////////////////////////////
21      // Global variables
22      //////////////////////////////////////////////////////////////
23
24      static String[] subjectNames;
25      static String[] studentNames;
26      static int[] subjectIds;
27      static int[] studentIds;
28      static int subjectsCount;
29      static int studentsCount;
```

```
30
31   static int[][] grades;
32   static int[] averages;
33
34   ////////////////////////////////////////////////////////////
35   // main - the program's main function
36   ////////////////////////////////////////////////////////////
37
38   public static void main(String[] args)
39      throws IOException
40   {
41
42      boolean ReadOk = true;
43
44      ////////////////////////////////////////////////////////////
45      // Input subjects information
46      ////////////////////////////////////////////////////////////
47
48      // read record count for subjects file
49      BufferedReader subjectsIn =
50         new BufferedReader(new FileReader(subjectsFileName));
51      subjectsCount = readRecordCount(
52         subjectsFileName, subjectsIn);
53
54      // read subjects file
55      if (subjectsCount <= 0)
56      { // invalid count
57         System.out.println("Error: Invalid subjects file '"
58            + subjectsFileName + "'.");
59         ReadOk = false;
60      }
61      else
62      { // allocate arrays for subject records
63         subjectNames = new String[subjectsCount];
64         subjectIds = new int[subjectsCount];
65         // read subject records
66         readRecords(
67            subjectsFileName,
68            subjectsIn,
69            subjectsCount,
70            subjectNames,
71            subjectIds);
72      }
73
74      ////////////////////////////////////////////////////////////
75      // Input students information
76      ////////////////////////////////////////////////////////////
77
78      // read record count for students file
79      BufferedReader studentsIn =
80         new BufferedReader(new FileReader(studentsFileName));
81      studentsCount = readRecordCount(
82         studentsFileName, studentsIn);
83
84      // read studenst file
85      if (studentsCount <= 0)
86      { // invalid count
87         System.out.println("Error: Invalid students file '"
88            + studentsFileName + "'.");
89         ReadOk = false;
90      }
91      else
92      { // allocate arrays for student records
93         studentNames = new String[studentsCount];
94         studentIds = new int[studentsCount];
95         // read student records
96         readRecords(
97            studentsFileName,
```

```
 98              studentsIn,
 99              studentsCount,
100              studentNames,
101              studentIds);
102        }
103
104        ///////////////////////////////////////////////////////////
105        // Reprt results of reading subjects and students
106        ///////////////////////////////////////////////////////////
107
108        if (ReadOk)
109        {
110          // sort students by id
111          sortById(studentNames, studentIds, studentsCount);
112          // sort subjects by name
113          sortById(subjectNames, subjectIds, subjectsCount);
114          // report contents of files
115          System.out.print("\nMaster Files Contents");
116          System.out.print("\n=====================\n\n");
117          System.out.print("Number of subjects is "
118            + subjectsCount);
119          System.out.println(". Subjects are:");
120          for (int i = 0; i < subjectsCount; i++)
121            System.out.println(subjectIds[i] + "\t"
122              + subjectNames[i]);
123          System.out.println("");
124          System.out.print("Number of students is "
125            + studentsCount);
126          System.out.println(". Students are:");
127          for (int i = 0; i < studentsCount; i++)
128            System.out.println(studentIds[i] + "\t"
129              + studentNames[i]);
130          System.out.println("");
131        }
132        else
133        {
134          System.out.println("Error: Failed to read master files.");
135          return;
136        }
137
138        ///////////////////////////////////////////////////////////
139        // Input grades
140        ///////////////////////////////////////////////////////////
141
142        // allocate array for grades
143        grades = new int[studentsCount][subjectsCount];
144        int studentIndex, subjectIndex;
145        // initialize all grades to invalid value
146        for (studentIndex = 0;
147          studentIndex < studentsCount;
148          studentIndex++)
149          for (subjectIndex = 0;
150            subjectIndex < subjectsCount;
151            subjectIndex++)
152            grades[studentIndex][subjectIndex] = -1;
153
154        // read grades
155        BufferedReader gradesIn =
156          new BufferedReader(new FileReader(gradesFileName));
157        readGrades(gradesFileName, gradesIn, grades);
158
159        ///////////////////////////////////////////////////////////
160        // Calculate averages
161        ///////////////////////////////////////////////////////////
162
163        // allocate array for averages
164        averages = new int[studentsCount];
165        for (studentIndex = 0;
```

```
166            studentIndex < studentsCount;
167            studentIndex++)
168        {
169            int sum = 0;
170            int count = 0;
171            for (subjectIndex = 0;
172               subjectIndex < subjectsCount;
173               subjectIndex++)
174            {
175               if (grades[studentIndex][subjectIndex] >= 0)
176               {
177                  sum += grades[studentIndex][subjectIndex];
178                  count++;
179               }
180            }
181            if (count > 0)
182               averages[studentIndex] = sum / count;
183            else
184               averages[studentIndex] = -1;
185        }
186
187        ////////////////////////////////////////////////////////////
188        // Report grades
189        ////////////////////////////////////////////////////////////
190
191        System.out.print("Grades Report\n");
192        System.out.print("=============\n");
193
194        for (studentIndex = 0;
195            studentIndex < studentsCount;
196            studentIndex++)
197        {
198            System.out.println("\nName: " + studentNames[studentIndex]
199               + " (" + studentIds[studentIndex] + ")");
200            if (averages[studentIndex] < 0)
201               System.out.println("No grades available.");
202            else
203            {
204               System.out.println("Average: "
205                  + averages[studentIndex]);
206               for (subjectIndex = 0;
207                  subjectIndex < subjectsCount;
208                  subjectIndex++)
209               {
210                  if (grades[studentIndex][subjectIndex] >= 0)
211                     System.out.println(
212                        grades[studentIndex][subjectIndex]
213                        + "\tin " + subjectNames[subjectIndex]
214                        + " (" + subjectIds[subjectIndex] + ")");
215               }
216            }
217        }
218    } // main
219
220    ////////////////////////////////////////////////////////////
221    // findChar - find a character in a string
222    ////////////////////////////////////////////////////////////
223
224    static boolean findChar(    // returns: true if character found,
225                               //    false otherwise
226        char[] string,         // the string to search in
227        int[] pos,             // [0] (In): starting position
228                               //    for the search
229                               // [1] (Out): position where
230                               //    character was found
231        char what)             // character to search for
232    {
233        pos[iEnd] = pos[iStart];
```

```
234          while (pos[iEnd] < string.length
235             &&  string[pos[iEnd]] != what)
236             pos[iEnd]++;
237          return(pos[iEnd] < string.length);
238       } // findChar
239
240       ////////////////////////////////////////////////////////
241       // findNum - find a number in a string
242       ////////////////////////////////////////////////////////
243
244       static boolean findNum(       // returns: true if number found,
245                                     //    false otherwise
246          char[] string,             // the string to search in
247          int[] pos)                 // [0] (In): starting position
248                                     //   for the search
249                                     // [1] (Out): position where
250                                     //   character was found
251       {
252          pos[iEnd] = pos[iStart];
253          while (pos[iEnd] < string.length
254             &&  (string[pos[iEnd]] < '0'
255              || string[pos[iEnd]] > '9')
256             &&  string[pos[iEnd]] != '+'
257             &&  string[pos[iEnd]] != '-')
258             pos[iEnd]++;
259          return(pos[iEnd] < string.length);
260       } // findNum
261
262       ////////////////////////////////////////////////////////
263       // getNum - get a number from a string
264       ////////////////////////////////////////////////////////
265
266       static int getNum(            // returns: the number's value
267          char[] string,             // the string to search in
268          int[] pos)                 // [0] (In): starting position
269                                     //   for the search
270                                     // [1] (Out): position where
271                                     //   character was found
272       {
273          int num = 0;               // the number
274          int p10 = 1;               // powers of 10
275          int dpos;                  // digit's position
276          int spos = pos[iStart];    // number's starting position
277          int sign = 1;              // number's sign
278
279          // check if number has a sign
280          if (string[spos] == '+')
281          {
282             sign = 1;
283             spos++;
284          }
285          else
286          if (string[spos] == '-')
287          {
288             sign = -1;
289             spos++;
290          }
291          pos[iEnd] = spos;
292
293          // Find end of number
294          while (pos[iEnd] < string.length
295             &&  string[pos[iEnd]] >= '0'
296             &&  string[pos[iEnd]] <= '9')
297             pos[iEnd]++;
298          pos[iEnd]--;        // last digit of number
299
300          if (pos[iEnd] >= spos)
301          {
```

```
302              // Calculate value of first number
303              for (dpos = pos[iEnd];
304                dpos >= pos[iStart];
305                dpos--)
306              {
307                int digit;
308                // Calculate value of current digit
309                digit = string[dpos] - '0';   // current digit
310                // Add value of current digit,
311                // considering its decimal place
312                num += digit * p10;
313                // Move to next power of 10 (decimal
314                // place) for next digit
315                p10 *= 10;
316              }
317          }
318
319          return(num * sign);
320      } // getNum
321
322      //////////////////////////////////////////////////////////
323      // getId - get an id
324      //////////////////////////////////////////////////////////
325
326      static int getId(              // returns: index of id
327          String fileName,           // name of file being read
328          String targetName,         // name of target
329          int lineNum,               // line number
330          int[] ids,                 // array of ids
331          int count,                 // number of ids in array
332          char[] inputLine,          // the input line to search in
333          int[] pos)                 // 0 (In): number's starting position
334      {
335          int id;
336          int index = -1;
337          if (findNum(inputLine, pos))
338          { // get id
339            pos[iStart] = pos[iEnd];
340            id = getNum(inputLine, pos);
341            pos[iStart] = pos[iEnd] + 1;
342            index = findId(ids, count, id);
343            if (index < 0)
344              System.out.println("Error: File '"
345                + fileName + "', Line "
346                + (lineNum + 1)
347                + ": Invalid " + targetName + " id: " + id);
348          }
349          else
350            System.out.println("Error: File '"
351              + fileName + "', Line "
352              + (lineNum + 1)
353              + ": Missing " + targetName + " id.");
354          return(index);
355      } // getId
356
357      //////////////////////////////////////////////////////////
358      // findId - find an id in an array of ids
359      //////////////////////////////////////////////////////////
360
361      static int findId(             // returns: index of id
362          int[] ids,                 // array of ids
363          int count,                 // number of ids in the array
364          int id)                    // the id to look fo
365      {
366          int index = -1;
367          boolean found = false;
368
369          for (int i = 0; i < count  &&  !found; i++)
```

```
370        {
371           if (ids[i] == id)
372           {
373              index = i;
374              found = true;
375           }
376           else
377           if (ids[i] > id)
378              i = count;           // terminate loop
379        }
380
381        return(index);
382     } // findId
383
384     ///////////////////////////////////////////////////////////
385     // getGrade - get a grade
386     ///////////////////////////////////////////////////////////
387
388     static int getGrade(          // returns: grade
389        String fileName,           // name of file being read
390        String targetName,         // name of target
391        int lineNum,               // line number
392        char[] inputLine,          // the input line to search in
393        int[] pos)                 // 0 (In): number's starting position
394     {
395        int grade = -1;
396        if (findNum(inputLine, pos))
397        { // get grade
398           pos[iStart] = pos[iEnd];
399           grade = getNum(inputLine, pos);
400           pos[iStart] = pos[iEnd] + 1;
401           if (grade < 0  || grade > 100)
402              grade = -1;
403        }
404        else
405           System.out.println("Error: File '"
406              + fileName + "', Line "
407              + (lineNum + 1)
408              + ": Missing " + targetName + " id.");
409        return(grade);
410     } // getGrade
411
412     ///////////////////////////////////////////////////////////
413     // readRecordCount - read the number of records in the file
414     //
415     // The record count is a single number on the first line
416     // of the file.
417     ///////////////////////////////////////////////////////////
418
419     static int readRecordCount(    // returns: number of records
420        String fileName,            // name of file being read
421        BufferedReader reader)      // reader for that file
422        throws IOException
423     {
424        String inputString = reader.readLine();
425        char[] inputLine = inputString.toCharArray();
426        int[] pos = {0, -1};
427        int count = 0;
428
429        if (inputLine.length > 0)
430        { // line is not empty
431           if (findNum(inputLine, pos))
432              // get number of records
433              count = getNum(inputLine, pos);
434           else
435              System.out.println("Error: File '"
436                 + fileName + "': Invalid record count.");
437        }
```

```
438          else
439             System.out.println("Error: File '"
440                + fileName + "': Missing record count.");
441          return(count);
442       } // readRecordCount
443
444       ////////////////////////////////////////////////////////////
445       // readRecords - read records from master files
446       //
447       // Each record has the following format:
448       // * Id - an integer number
449       // * Name - text surrounded by quotes.
450       // Example:
451       // 20 "Language Arts"
452       ////////////////////////////////////////////////////////////
453
454       static void readRecords(
455          String fileName,         // name of file being read
456          BufferedReader reader,   // reader for that file
457          int count,               // count of records to be read
458          String[] names,          // array of names to be read
459          int[] ids)               // arrays of ids to be read
460          throws IOException
461       {
462          for (int lineNum = 0; lineNum < count; lineNum++)
463          {
464             // read in next line
465             String inputString = reader.readLine();
466             char[] inputLine = inputString.toCharArray();
467             int[] pos = {0, -1};
468             // look for id
469             if (findNum(inputLine, pos))
470             { // get id
471                pos[iStart] = pos[iEnd];
472                int id = getNum(inputLine, pos);
473                ids[lineNum] = id;
474                pos[iStart] = pos[iEnd] + 1;
475                // search for openning quote of text
476                if (findChar(inputLine, pos, '\"'))
477                {
478                   // position of first character of text
479                   pos[iStart] = pos[iEnd] + 1;
480                   // search for closing quote of text
481                   if (findChar(inputLine, pos, '\"'))
482                   {
483                      // length of text
484                      int len = pos[iEnd] - pos[iStart];
485                      names[lineNum] =
486                         new String(inputLine, pos[iStart], len);
487                   }
488                   else
489                      System.out.println("Error: File '"
490                         + fileName + "', Line "
491                         + (lineNum + 1)
492                         + ": Invalid text.");
493                }
494                else
495                   System.out.println("Error: File '"
496                      + fileName + "', Line "
497                      + (lineNum + 1)
498                      + ": Missing text.");
499             }
500             else
501                System.out.println("Error: File '"
502                   + fileName + "', Line "
503                   + (lineNum + 1)
504                   + ": Missing text.");
505          }
```

```
506     } // readRecords
507
508     /////////////////////////////////////////////////////////////
509     // readGrades - read grades
510     //
511     // Each record has the following format:
512     // * Student Id - an integer number
513     // * Subject Id - an integer number
514     // * Grade - an integer number between 0 and 100
515     // Last record should begin with the single character '@'
516     // to mark end-of-file
517     // Example:
518     // 19351 20 87
519     /////////////////////////////////////////////////////////////
520
521     static void readGrades(
522        String fileName,           // name of file being read
523        BufferedReader reader,     // reader for that file
524        int[][] grades)            // array of grades
525        throws IOException
526     {
527        int studentIndex, subjectIndex, grade;
528        boolean endOfFile = false;
529        int lineNum = 0;
530
531        while (!endOfFile)
532        {
533           int[] pos = {0, -1};
534           // read in next line
535           String inputString = reader.readLine();
536           char[] inputLine = inputString.toCharArray();
537           if (inputLine[0] != '@')
538           {
539              lineNum++;
540              // get student id
541              studentIndex = getId(gradesFileName, "student", lineNum,
542                 studentIds, studentsCount, inputLine, pos);
543              if (studentIndex >= 0)
544              { // get subject id
545                 subjectIndex = getId(
546                    gradesFileName, "subject", lineNum,
547                    subjectIds, subjectsCount, inputLine, pos);
548                 if (subjectIndex >= 0)
549                 { // get grade
550                    grade = getGrade(gradesFileName, "grade", lineNum,
551                       inputLine, pos);
552                    if (grade >= 0)
553                    {
554                       grades[studentIndex][subjectIndex] = grade;
555                       /*System.out.println(studentIds[studentIndex] + "/"
556                          + subjectIds[subjectIndex] + "/"
557                          + grade);*/
558                    }
559                    else
560                       System.out.println("Error: File '"
561                          + fileName + "', Line "
562                          + (lineNum + 1)
563                          + ": Missing or invalid grade.");
564                 }
565              }
566           }
567           else
568              endOfFile = true;
569        }
570     } // readGrades
571
572     /////////////////////////////////////////////////////////////
573     // sortById - sort records by id
```

```
574    ////////////////////////////////////////////////////////////
575
576    static void sortById(
577       String[] names,          // array of names to sort
578       int[] ids,               // array of ids
579       int cnt)                 // count of items to sort
580    {
581       int cur,                 // index of current item
582          min,                  // index of minimum item
583          chk;                  // index of item to check
584       String tmpName;          // temporary string item storage
585       int tmpId;               // temporary numeric item storage
586
587       for (cur = 0; cur < cnt; cur++)
588       {
589          min = cur;
590          for (chk = cur + 1; chk < cnt; chk++)
591          {
592             if (ids[chk] < ids[min])
593                min = chk;
594          }
595          // swap between current item and the
596          // one found to be the minimum
597          tmpName = names[cur];
598             names[cur] = names[min];
599             names[min] = tmpName;
600          tmpId = ids[cur];
601             ids[cur] = ids[min];
602             ids[min] = tmpId;
603       }
604    } // sortById
605
606    ////////////////////////////////////////////////////////////
607    // sortByName - sort records by name
608    ////////////////////////////////////////////////////////////
609
610    static void sortByName(
611       String[] names,          // array of names to sort
612       int[] ids,               // array of ids
613       int cnt)                 // count of items to sort
614    {
615       int cur,                 // index of current item
616          min,                  // index of minimum item
617          chk;                  // index of item to check
618       String tmpName;          // temporary string item storage
619       int tmpId;               // temporary numeric item storage
620
621       for (cur = 0; cur < cnt; cur++)
622       {
623          min = cur;
624          for (chk = cur + 1; chk < cnt; chk++)
625          {
626             if (names[chk].compareTo(names[min]) < 0)
627                min = chk;
628          }
629          // swap between current item and the
630          // one found to be the minimum
631          tmpName = names[cur];
632             names[cur] = names[min];
633             names[min] = tmpName;
634          tmpId = ids[cur];
635             ids[cur] = ids[min];
636             ids[min] = tmpId;
637       }
638    } // sortByName
639
640 } // Grades
```

Look at the three files supplied with the examples (subjects.txt, students.txt, grades.txt) and run the program to see its results. Then, you can improve the program by sorting the final report in a different way (by student name rather than id), or by changing the "students" and "subjects" files to have more or less or different students and subjects – just remember to change the "grades" file accordingly. By the way: can you figure out how the student ids were assigned?

Another interesting experiment would be to put in errors: bad counts for the "students" or "subjects" files, forget the @ at the end of the "grades" file, use a student or subject id that is not defined in the corresponding master file, badly formed input lines (no opening or closing quotes for a name, no space between id and name, etc.). As a matter of fact, this is the way you ought to test you program – not only with good, valid data, but also with bad input. This way you can ensure that the program will work "for better or worse…"

LET'S PLAY CHECKERS

The program in this example is a little bit more fun, although less typical of day-to-day programming. It is a program to play Checkers. Because it is intended only as an example, it is not really capable of playing on its own; it cannot think up a move or respond to an opponent's move. All it can do is performing moves that the user enters. The program validates that the move is legal, and moves the Checkers piece to its new place; it will also remove a piece that was skipped over. (Adding "intelligence" to this program is quite difficult, and requires a lot more knowledge of mathematics and games theory than you currently have. Despite that, once you understand how this program works, you will be able to find ways to improve it.)

Lines 14–32 show how the board is set up and how each square is referenced. On lines 70 and 71, we set up the board and draw it on the screen, respectively. Lines 73–95 are the body of the program, continuously reading a move (line 76) and parsing it (lines 82–86), then validating it while moving the piece (lines 87–88) and finally performing the special actions of removing a piece or crowning (lines 91 and 92, respectively). A valid move causes the board to be re-drawn (line 93).

The rest of this relatively long program is the functions that actually do all the work (it's sort of funny: the first few lines take all the glory, but the real work is done by the slave function…). Many of these functions are very short, perhaps only one statement, but they allow us to isolate an action or a test of a condition so that when used, it is much more readable (for example, the function l2i on lines 232–237, which converts the letter of the row A–H into an index 0–7). This technique, although appearing to need more coding, actually saves a lot of aggravation later – when something is *not* working right, which *does* happen more often than programmers like to admit, it is easy to identify where it is happening – there is only one place where that action occurs; and when a change is needed to fix the problem, it can be made in only one place, instead of having to locate all the places in the program where the action was coded.

We will not analyze this program in details here. The best way for you to study it and understand how it works is to follow the chain of function calls: every time you encounter a call to a function you have not seen before, go study that function and then go back to where it was called and continue your journey from there – in a sense, you'll be following the same path the computer would be following when executing the program.

```
01 ///////////////////////////////////////////////////////////////////
01 // Example 30, file 'Checkers.java'
02 // This program plays checkers
03 ///////////////////////////////////////////////////////////////////
04
05 import java.io.*;
06
07 public class Checkers
08 {
09
10     /* This is how the Checkers board will
11        look at the start of a new game:
12
13        A   B   C   D   E   F   G   H
14      +---+---+---+---+---+---+---+---+
15   8 |   |:b:|   |:b:|   |:b:|   |:b:| 8
16      +---+---+---+---+---+---+---+---+
```

```
17   7 |:b:|    |:b:|    |:b:|    |:b:|    |  7
18     +---+---+---+---+---+---+---+---+
19   6 |   |:b:|   |:b:|   |:b:|   |:b:| 6
20     +---+---+---+---+---+---+---+---+
21   5 |:::|    |:::|    |:::|    |:::|    | 5
22     +---+---+---+---+---+---+---+---+
23   4 |   |:::|   |:::|   |:::|   |:::| 4
24     +---+---+---+---+---+---+---+---+
25   3 |:w:|    |:w:|    |:w:|    |:w:|    | 3
26     +---+---+---+---+---+---+---+---+
27   2 |   |:w:|   |:w:|   |:w:|   |:w:| 2
28     +---+---+---+---+---+---+---+---+
29   1 |:w:|    |:w:|    |:w:|    |:w:|    | 1
30     +---+---+---+---+---+---+---+---+
31       A   B   C   D   E   F   G   H
32
33   */
34
35   ///////////////////////////////////////////////////////////
36   // Constants
37   ///////////////////////////////////////////////////////////
38
39   final static char blackSquare = ':';
40   final static char whiteSquare = ' ';
41   final static char emptySquare = ' ';
42   final static char blackPiece = 'b';
43   final static char whitePiece = 'w';
44   final static char blackKing = 'B';
45   final static char whiteKing = 'W';
46   final static char bar = '|';
47   final static String sepLine =
48      "+---+---+---+---+---+---+---+---+";
49
50   ///////////////////////////////////////////////////////////
51   // Global variables
52   ///////////////////////////////////////////////////////////
53
54   static char[][] board = new char[8][8];
55   static char topColor = blackPiece;
56
57   ///////////////////////////////////////////////////////////
58   // main - the program's main function
59   ///////////////////////////////////////////////////////////
60
61   public static void main(String[] args)
62      throws IOException
63   {
64      BufferedReader inputReader = new BufferedReader(
65         new InputStreamReader(System.in));
66      String inputLine = ".";
67      char[] line;
68
69      boardSet();
70      boardDraw();
71
72      while (true)
73      {
74         System.out.print("\nEnter move: ");
75         inputLine = inputReader.readLine();
76         if (inputLine == null || inputLine.equals(""))
77            break;
78         line = inputLine.toCharArray();
79         if (line[0] == '/' && line[1] == '/')
80            continue;
81         char color = line[0];
82         int colFrom = l2i(line[1]);
83         int rowFrom = n2i(line[2]);
84         int colTo = l2i(line[3]);
```

```
 85            int rowTo = n2i(line[4]);
 86            boolean valid = movePiece(
 87              color, rowFrom, colFrom, rowTo, colTo);
 88            if (valid)
 89            {
 90              takePiece(rowFrom, colFrom, rowTo, colTo);
 91              crownPiece(rowTo, colTo);
 92              boardDraw();
 93            }
 94         }
 95      } // main
 96
 97      ///////////////////////////////////////////////////////////
 98      // boardSet - set the board
 99      ///////////////////////////////////////////////////////////
100
101      static void boardSet()
102      {
103         int row, col;
104         int firstSquare;        // first square to be filled on row
105         int nextSquare;
106
107         // set up an empty board
108         for (row = 7; row >= 0; row--)
109         {
110            for (col = 0; col < 8; col++)
111            {
112               board[row][col] = emptySquare;
113            }
114         }
115
116         // put the black pieces on the board
117         firstSquare = 1;
118         for (row = 7; row >= 5; row--)
119         {
120            for (col = firstSquare; col < 8; col+=2)
121            {
122               board[row][col] = blackPiece;
123            }
124            // change first square for next row
125            firstSquare = 1 - firstSquare;
126         }
127
128         // put the white pieces on the board
129         firstSquare = 0;
130         for (row = 2; row >= 0; row--)
131         {
132            for (col = firstSquare; col < 8; col+=2)
133            {
134               board[row][col] = whitePiece;
135            }
136            // change first square for next row
137            firstSquare = 1 - firstSquare;
138         }
139      } // boardSet
140
141      ///////////////////////////////////////////////////////////
142      // boardDraw - draw the board
143      ///////////////////////////////////////////////////////////
144
145      static void boardDraw()
146      {
147         int row, col;
148         boolean firstSquareWhite = true;   // top left square is white
149         boolean nextSquareWhite;
150         char square;
151
152         // print top column letters
```

```
153        System.out.println();
154        boardLetters();
155
156        // print top line
157        System.out.println("   " + sepLine);
158
159        // print squares
160        for (row = 7; row >= 0; row--)
161        {
162           // print row number at left and bar
163           System.out.print((row + 1) + " " + bar);
164
165           // print squares
166
167           // at the beginning, next square
168           // is the first square on line
169           nextSquareWhite = firstSquareWhite;
170           for (col = 0; col < 8; col++)
171           {
172              if (nextSquareWhite)
173                 square = whiteSquare;
174              else
175                 square = blackSquare;
176              System.out.print("" + square +
177                 (board[row][col] == ' ' ? square : board[row][col]) +
178                 square + bar);
179              // switch color for next square
180              nextSquareWhite = !nextSquareWhite;
181           }
182           // print row number on right
183           System.out.println(" " + (row + 1));
184           // print row's bottom line
185           System.out.println("   " + sepLine);
186           // switch color for first square of next line
187           firstSquareWhite = !firstSquareWhite;
188        }
189
190        // print bottom column letters
191        boardLetters();
192     } // boardDraw
193
194     //////////////////////////////////////////////////////////////////
195     // boardLetters - draw column letters
196     //////////////////////////////////////////////////////////////////
197
198     static void boardLetters()
199     {
200        System.out.print("     ");
201        for (int col = 0; col < 8; col++)
202           System.out.print((char)(col + 'A') + "   ");
203        System.out.println();
204     } // boardLetters
205
206     //////////////////////////////////////////////////////////////////
207     // isValCol - validate a column letter
208     //////////////////////////////////////////////////////////////////
209
210     static boolean isValCol(   // returns: true if valid column letter
211        char letter)            // column letter to be validated
212     {
213        return((letter >= 'a'  &&  letter <= 'h')
214           || (letter >= 'A'  &&  letter <= 'H'));
215     } // isValCol
216
217     //////////////////////////////////////////////////////////////////
218     // isValRow - validate a row number
219     //////////////////////////////////////////////////////////////////
220
```

```
221    static boolean isValRow(   // returns: true if valid row number
222      char number)             // row number to be validated
223    {
224      return((number >= '1'  &&  number <= '8'));
225    } // isValRow
226
227    //////////////////////////////////////////////////////////////
228    // l2i - convert a column letter into an index
229    //////////////////////////////////////////////////////////////
230
231    static int l2i(             // returns: index of column
232      char letter)             // letter - assumed to be valid
233                               // (a-h or A-H)
234    {
235      return(((byte)letter & 0x1F) - 1);
236    } // l2i
237
238    //////////////////////////////////////////////////////////////
239    // n2i - convert a row number into an index
240    //////////////////////////////////////////////////////////////
241
242    static int n2i(             // returns: index of row
243      char number)             // number - assumed to be valid
244                               // (1-8)
245    {
246      return(((byte)number & 0xF) - 1);
247    } // n2i
248
249    //////////////////////////////////////////////////////////////
250    // isPresent - validate presence of a piece at a square
251    //////////////////////////////////////////////////////////////
252
253    static boolean isPresent( // returns: true if piece
254                              // of specified color and type
255                              // is at specified square
256      int row,
257      int col,
258      char piece)             // piece's color
259    {
260      return(board[row][col] == piece);
261    } // isPresent
262
263    //////////////////////////////////////////////////////////////
264    // isSameColor - compare colors of two piece
265    //////////////////////////////////////////////////////////////
266
267    static boolean isSameColor(   // returns: true if piece
268                                  // of specified color
269                                  // is at specified square
270      int row,
271      int col,
272      char piece)             // piece's color
273    {
274      boolean result;
275      if (piece == whitePiece  ||  piece == whiteKing)
276        result = (board[row][col] == whitePiece
277          || board[row][col] == whiteKing);
278      else
279      if (piece == blackPiece  ||  piece == blackKing)
280        result = (board[row][col] == blackPiece
281          || board[row][col] == blackKing);
282      else
283        result = false;
284      return(result);
285    } // isSameColor
286
287    //////////////////////////////////////////////////////////////
288
```

```
289      static boolean isSameColor(   // returns: true if both
290                                    // pieces are of the same
291                                    // color
292         char piece1,
293         char piece2)
294      {
295         boolean result;
296         if (piece1 == whitePiece
297            || piece1 == whiteKing)
298            result = (piece2 == whitePiece
299               || piece2 == whiteKing);
300         else
301         if (piece1 == blackPiece
302            || piece1 == blackKing)
303            result = (piece2 == blackPiece
304               || piece2 == blackKing);
305         else
306            result = false;
307         return(result);
308      } // isSameColor
309
310      ///////////////////////////////////////////////////////////
311      // isEmpty - validate that a square is empty
312      ///////////////////////////////////////////////////////////
313
314      static boolean isEmpty(    // returns: true if square empty
315         int row,
316         int col)
317      {
318         return(board[row][col] == emptySquare);
319      } // isEmpty
320
321      ///////////////////////////////////////////////////////////
322      // isKing - check if a piece is a king
323      ///////////////////////////////////////////////////////////
324
325      static boolean isKing(     // returns: true if piece is a king
326         char piece)
327      {
328         return(piece == whiteKing || piece == blackKing);
329      } // isKing
330
331      ///////////////////////////////////////////////////////////
332      // isWhite - check if a piece is white
333      ///////////////////////////////////////////////////////////
334
335      static boolean isWhite(    // returns: true if piece is white
336         char piece)
337      {
338         return(piece == whiteKing || piece == whitePiece);
339      } // isWhite
340
341      ///////////////////////////////////////////////////////////
342      // isBlack - check if a piece is black
343      ///////////////////////////////////////////////////////////
344
345      static boolean isBlack(    // returns: true if piece is black
346         char piece)
347      {
348         return(piece == blackKing || piece == blackPiece);
349      } // isBlack
350
351      ///////////////////////////////////////////////////////////
352      // opposite - get color opposite to a piece's color
353      ///////////////////////////////////////////////////////////
354
355      static char opposite(          // returns: color opposite
356                                     // to color of piece
```

```
357        char piece)
358    {
359        return(isWhite(piece) ? blackPiece : whitePiece);
360    } // opposite
361
362    ////////////////////////////////////////////////////////////
363    // movePiece - validate a move and make it
364    ////////////////////////////////////////////////////////////
365
366    static boolean movePiece( // returns: true if move valid
367        char color,
368        int rowFrom,
369        int colFrom,
370        int rowTo,
371        int colTo)
372    {
373        boolean valid = false;  // expect the worst...
374
375        while (true)
376        {
377            char piece = board[rowFrom][colFrom];
378            // is there ia a piece (any piece) in that square?
379            if (isEmpty(rowFrom, colFrom))
380            {
381                System.out.println(
382                    "There is no piece there.");
383                break;
384            }
385            // is there is a piece of the correct
386            // color at the 'from' square?
387            if (!isSameColor(board[rowFrom][colFrom], color))
388            {
389                System.out.println(
390                    "This is not your piece.");
391                break;
392            }
393            // is the 'to' square empty?
394            if (!isEmpty(rowTo, colTo))
395            {
396                System.out.println(
397                    "This square is already occupied.");
398                break;
399            }
400            // is movement diagonally - both row and
401            // column are changing by the same amount?
402            int rowChange = rowFrom - rowTo;
403            int colChange = colFrom - colTo;
404            int rowChangeAbs = Math.abs(rowChange);
405            int colChangeAbs = Math.abs(colChange);
406            if (rowChange == 0 || colChange == 0
407                || rowChangeAbs != colChangeAbs)
408            {
409                System.out.println(
410                    "You must move diagonally.");
411                break;
412            }
413            // is piece not a king - can move only forward?
414            if (!isKing(piece))
415            {
416                // is piece moving in the right direction?
417                // (black pieces move 'downward',
418                // white pieces move 'upward')
419                if ((isBlack(piece) && rowChange < 0)
420                    || (isWhite(piece) && rowChange > 0))
421                {
422                    System.out.println(
423                        "You cannot move in that direction.");
424                    break;
```

```
425                    }
426               }
427               // is move too far (more than to adjacent
428               // square or a skip?
429               if (rowChangeAbs > 2  &&  colChangeAbs > 2)
430               {
431                  System.out.println(
432                     "You cannot move that far.");
433                  break;
434               }
435               // is move a valid skip?
436               if (rowChangeAbs == 2  &&  colChangeAbs == 2)
437               {
438                  // row of skipped square
439                  int rowSkip = rowFrom - rowChange / 2;
440                  // column of skipped square
441                  int colSkip = colFrom - colChange / 2;
442                  // does skipped square contain a piece?
443                  if (isEmpty(rowSkip, colSkip))
444                  {
445                     System.out.println(
446                        "You cannot skip an empty square.");
447                     break;
448                  }
449                  // is skipped piece of a different color?
450                  if (isSameColor(board[rowSkip][colSkip], color))
451                  {
452                     System.out.println(
453                        "You cannot skip over your own piece.");
454                     break;
455                  }
456               }
457               board[rowTo][colTo] = board[rowFrom][colFrom];
458               board[rowFrom][colFrom] = emptySquare;
459               valid = true;
460               break;
461            }

463         return(valid);
464      } // movePiece

466      /////////////////////////////////////////////////////////////
467      // takePiece - take a piece that was skipped over
468      // (assumes a valid move!)
469      /////////////////////////////////////////////////////////////

471      static boolean takePiece( // returns: true if piece taken
472         int rowFrom,
473         int colFrom,
474         int rowTo,
475         int colTo)
476      {
477         boolean skipped = false;
478         char piece = board[rowFrom][colFrom];
479         int rowChange = rowFrom - rowTo;
480         int colChange = colFrom - colTo;
481         int rowChangeAbs = Math.abs(rowChange);
482         int colChangeAbs = Math.abs(colChange);
483         // is move a skip?
484         if (rowChangeAbs == 2  &&  colChangeAbs == 2)
485         {
486            // row of skipped square
487            int rowSkip = rowFrom - rowChange / 2;
488            // column of skipped square
489            int colSkip = colFrom - colChange / 2;
490            // remove the skipped piece
491            board[rowSkip][colSkip] = emptySquare;
492            skipped = true;
```

```
493        }
494     return(skipped);
495   } // takePiece
496
497   ////////////////////////////////////////////////////////////
498   // crownPiece - crown a piece if it arrives at
499   // the opposite edge row (assumes a valid move!)
500   ////////////////////////////////////////////////////////////
501
502   static boolean crownPiece(// returns: true if piece crowned
503      int rowTo,
504      int colTo)
505   {
506      boolean crowned = false;
507      char piece = board[rowTo][colTo];
508      // is piece at the opposite edge row?
509      if ((isBlack(piece)  &&  rowTo == 0)
510        || (isWhite(piece)  &&  rowTo == 7))
511      {
512         board[rowTo][colTo] =
513            (isBlack(piece) ? blackKing : whiteKing);
514         crowned = true;
515      }
516      return(crowned);
517   } // takePiece
518
519 } // Checkers
```

PART TWO REVIEW:

⅄ *Programs use* Declarations *to define the tools and parts that the program needs, and* Statements *to tell the computer what to do with them in order to produce result*

⅄ Expressions *are used to describe calculations*

⅄ *Programs work with different* data types

⅄ *Specific values in a program are expressed as* literals, *while changing values are stored in named* variables

⅄ *Repeating data is stored in* arrays; *each element of an array can be accessed directly using its* index

⅄ *Arrays have one or more* dimensions

⅄ *Text data is stored in* strings

⅄ Reference variables *point to other variables or literals*

⅄ Operators *are used to describe calculations and other data manipulations*

⅄ *Operators operate on* operands

⅄ *Expressions are like formulas, telling the computer to perform a calculation*

⅄ *Expressions are made of variables, literals, operators and parentheses*

⅄ *Some operators have* precedence *over others, so they are performed first;* parentheses *re-define the order of calculations if it needs to be different than order of precedence*

⅄ Assignment *operators are used to store results of calculations in variables*

⅄ Conversions *and* promotions *are used to transform between data types*

⅄ *The compiler usually generate automatically the required code for conversions and promotions;* casts *are used to force a conversion*

⅄ Control statements *are used to describe decisions and repetition in the program*

⅄ *There are two types of control statement:* decisions *and* repetitions

⅄ Decision *statements describe different actions depending on different conditions*

⅄ Repetition *statement tell the program to repeat (loop over) a group of statements; each time the group is executed is called an iteration of the loop*

⅄ *An* algorithm *is a step-by-step procedure for solving a problem*

⅄ Pseudo-code *is a way to describe an algorithm without writing a program*

⅄ *Statements can be organized in* blocks *when they have to be grouped together*

⅄ *A variable's* scope *is the block within which it is defined and all enclosed blocks which do not re-define it*

⋏ *A* function, *or a* method, *is a group of statements with a single, well defined purpose*

⋏ *A function is* called, *or* invoked, *when the program needs to execute the procedure which is the purpose of the function*

⋏ *When called, a function can accept* parameters, *which provide the function with the specific values to use in that particular invocation*

⋏ Input *is the data the program needs to work with*

⋏ Output *is what a program produces to show the results of its work*

⋏ *Input can come from the keyboard or from a file*

⋏ *Output can go to the screen or to a file*

⋏ *In order to interpret input, it usually have to be* parsed

⋏ *In order to produce readable output, it has to be* formatted

PART THREE – OBJECT-ORIENTED PROGRAMMING

> *Object-oriented programming allows you to write programs that can be more easily understood, maintained and reused. We will explain what are the concepts of object-oriented programming and what are the advantages, and show you how to write programs using these techniques. What you learned in the previous chapter will fit right in – only packaged in a different way.*
>
> *What you will learn in this section:*
>
> ➢ *What is object-oriented programming (OOP)*
> ➢ *What are the advantages of OOP*
> ➢ *How to write object-oriented programs*

Every Object Is, Well, an Object...

> *You might guess that "object-oriented" means dealing with objects. But what is the meaning of an object in programming? This chapter will define the term and describe the concepts, highlighting the special things objects can do for your program.*
>
> *What you will learn in this chapter:*
>
> ➢ *What are objects*
> ➢ *What are they capable of doing for you*

WHAT'S IN AN OBJECT

We deal with objects every day. The world around us is full of object. If you want to be precise, the dictionary defines an object as "anything that is visible or tangible and is relatively stable in form." Nice, but what does it have to do with programming? Bear with me…

Let's take an everyday object as an example. How about your iPod? It's an object, for sure; a solid piece of electronics. And if we look at it closely we can see that it has certain attributes and behaviors, some of which we can influence from the outside. For example, we can decide what songs to download; we can choose which ones to play; or we can select the volume level; or we can do even more complex things, such as adjusting the equalizer.

In the next section, you'll see how this applies to programming.

SOME BIG WORDS – ENCAPSULATION, INHERITANCE, POLYMORPHISM

The first thing we noticed is that the iPod has properties and behaviors. Let's examine each separately.

A **property** (also called an **attribute**) is some characteristic of the object. Some of the attribute of an iPod would be its memory size (4GB, 160GB), the size of its screen (2", 2.5"), its thickness (0.41", 0.53"), etc. These attributes are **constant**, namely we cannot change them. But it may also have other attributes, which change as we use the iPod: the current volume level, the name of the current song, the total number of songs and videos on the device, is it showing video now or only playing audio, etc. Unless you are into electronics or are a hacker, you don't think about how these attributes are stored in the iPod. All you care is that you know what they are, and that you can change those that are not constant. This is what is known as **encapsulation** – we say that the iPod encapsulates the attributes: their meaning is known, but the internals of their storage is not (and is not of our concern either!).

But encapsulation has more to it than hiding the details of the attributes. It also relieves us of the concern for the **behavior**. You know that when you move your finger in a certain way over the click wheel, the iPod will move to the next song; move your finger a different way, and the menu pops up; move it yet again, and the volume changes. As a regular iPod user, you are not too curious how this is done; it's enough to know that it is. The iPod object encapsulates the behavior: you know how to get your iPod to do what you want it to do, without bothering with the hardware and software "hows." In object-oriented programming, behavior is described by **methods** or "**functions**".

Another aspect of objects (in programming) is called **inheritance**. We all know the old cliché "like father, like son." Most of us suffered an old aunt exclaiming "you look so much like your mother (or father)," or worse yet, adding, "but she (he) was prettier (better looking) than you when she (he) was younger…" In the real world, living things inherit some of their characteristics from their parents – it's called genetics. In the inanimate world, we can see similar family relationships. Let's go back to the iPod. It's a member of a family of "Portable Music Players." They all share many similarities, the most obvious is the ability to play music (those that are any good, that is…). Other characteristics are the ability to download music to them, to control volume, etc. But they may also have differences, such as the ability to play iTune files or MP3s, or whether they have a click wheel or buttons for control. In object-oriented language, we say the Portable Music Player is a parent, and the iPod is a child; there could be other children, such as the Zune or the SanDisk. But the family tree does not end here: the iPod itself can be considered a parent when you realize that the Nano, the Shuffle and the Classic are children of the iPod family (which is a child of the Portable Music Players family). A partial diagram of the family (like a "family tree") would look like the one on the next page.

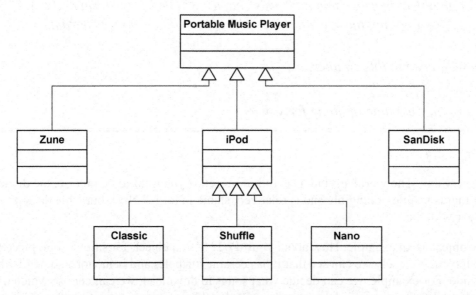

By using inheritance, you can focus on the common attributes and behaviors at the higher levels in the family tree, and only deal with the variations as you go "down" the tree. For example, understanding the concept of downloading a song is the same regardless of the type of player, although the process may be different for each player; most likely, the procedure for connecting the player to your computer is roughly the same as well. Furthermore, many players can be used with the same software on the PC or Mac (iTunes and Windows Media Player, for example, can work with iPods as well as with many other players). So the top level, the Portable Music Player object, is good enough. But when you come to more specific attributes (such as specific supported file formats), you have to deal with them at a lower level.

And this brings us to the last concept on our list. Wikipedia defines **polymorphism** as the ability of objects belonging to different types to respond to method calls of the same name, each one according to an appropriate type-specific behavior. So when you "change volume" on a Potable Music Player, the action has a single name regardless of the specific type or model, but the implementation is different – use the click wheel, click on a button – depending on the specific player's type and model. Similarly, "downloading" is the name of a method which is performed in different ways, and may be using different software, depending on the player.

Now that we have the concepts, let's see how we can apply them in programming. In doing so, we are going to take a "leap of faith" between physical actions on a real object, and programming actions on a software object. For example, when we talk about changing the volume on a physical "Portable Music Player," we mean clicking on buttons or sliding fingers on touch-sensitive pads; but when we discuss doing the same thing to a software "Portable Music Player," we may mean changing the numeric value that indicates the volume level. Let's try not to confuse the two – the physical object is just a "modcl" or a "blueprint" of the software one.

What you learned in this chapter:

ᴧ   *Objects in programming are used to represent object in real life*

ᴧ   *An object* encapsulates *attributes and behaviors via its properties and methods*

ᴧ   *An object can* inherit *attributes and behaviors from another object*

ᴧ   *Objects of different types can be* polymorphic, *each responding in its own way to the same set of requests*

In a Class of Its Own – The Making of an Object Class

> *The subject of this chapter is how to define objects. You will learn about the two types of members a class may have, and how to create objects of that class.*
>
> *What you will learn in this chapter:*
> ➢ *What is a class*
> ➢ *How to define classes*
> ➢ *What is the relationship between a class and an object*
> ➢ *How to create objects*

KNOW YOUR CLASS

Based on the previous section, we see that we can organize objects based on their class. That means that my iPod and yours both belong to the "iPod" class, while your friend's Zune belongs to the "Zune" class. If I have a Nano and you have a Classic, then mine belongs to the "Nano" class, which is a child of the "iPod" class, and yours belongs to the "Classic" class, which is also a child of the "iPod" class. And so on, and so forth… A **class** is the definition of the attributes and behaviors (methods) of a group of objects. All actual objects that share *each and every one* of those attributes and methods belong to that class.

Note that if an object does not share *all* attributes, it cannot belong to the class; it can, however, belong to a child class (also known as inherited class, **subclass** or a **derived class**) which has other attributes *in addition* to all the attributes of the parent class (also known as **superclass** or **base class**). For example, we may define the class "Portable Music Player" as not having the ability to play videos, but the sub-class "iPod" does have this attribute, in addition to the expected attribute of playing audio.

Let's leave music playing and go back to programming. Below is our first example from part 2:

```
01 // Example 1, file 'Wassup.java'
02 // This program displays 'Wassup?'
03 public class Wassup
04 {
05    public static void main(String[] args)
06    {
07       // Declare a string
08       String textWassup;
09       // Store the text in the string
10       textWassup = "Wassup?";
11       // Display "Wassup?"
12       System.out.println(textWassup);
13    }
14 }
```

Now some parts we did not want to talk about should make a little bit more sense… On line 3, we define a class called Wassup. This class has one member: a method called main, defined on line 5. (For now, let's ignore the public and static keywords.) It is a requirement of the Java language that each source file contains a class with the same name as the file. If this is the file with the code that you want executed first when you run your program (also known as the main class), that class must have a method named main, so that the Java Runtime Environment (JRE) knows where to start.

TAKING ATTENDANCE – CLASS MEMBERS

When we previously discussed objects and classes, we said that each object has attributes and methods. Since each object belongs to a class, these are really the class' attributes and methods. They are called class **members**. Each class has a collection of member attributes and member methods, which together define the class properties and behaviors. The specific values of attributes can vary from one object to another, but the methods are common to all objects. Since most methods manipulate attributes, the behavior of each specific object may depend on its specific properties.

Each class has its own members. When a derived class is defined, it has all of the base class' members, plus all those that are unique to it. But that's not all – it can also **override** methods in the base class! That means that a certain behavior that is defined in the base class is to be performed differently by the derived class. For example, if the base class "Portable Music Player" has a method "connect to PC" which is implemented by connecting a USB cable, the derived class "Zune" can override this method with one that connects via a wireless network.

Members are accessed using the **dot notation**. In order to access the member `objMem` of an object which is referenced by the variable `objRef`, you would write `objRef.objMem`. If the member is a method, it will be `objRef.objMem()`.

LIKE FATHER LIKE SON – INHERITANCE

In order to give examples of a class definition and inheritance, let's abandon our iPods (only figuratively speaking...) and take a look at our cell phones. They all belong to the class "Cell Phone". Derived classes can provide more specific properties and behaviors: for example, we can have a child class for each manufacturer ("LG", "Samsung", "Nokia", etc.) and each of those can have children classes based on specific models.

Here is a class diagram of a small part of the world of cell phones:

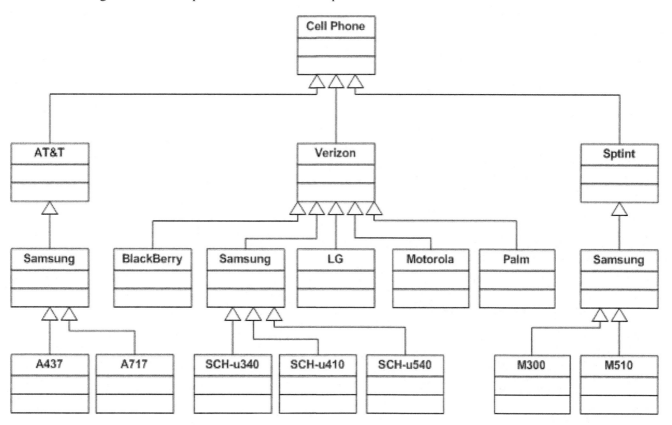

For illustration purposes, we went to the lowest level on the "Samsung" branches. This is to show that several classes for the same manufacturer can be defined as children, but they are distinct because they have different parents – just like not all kids named "Joe" are the same…

Now let's look at the definition of the parent class, `Cell Phone`:

```
01  // Example 31, file 'CellPhone.java'
02  // This file defines the class 'CellPhone'
03
04  import java.util.Date;
05
06  public class CellPhone
07  {
08      // attributes
09
10      private String carrier;
11      private String manufacturer;
12      private String model;
13      private int screenHeight;
14      private int screenWidth;
15      private int memorySize;
16      private int volume;
17      private Date now;
18
19      // methods
20
21      // constructors
22      CellPhone (
23        String carrierArg,
24        String manufacturerArg,
25        String modelArg,
26        int screenHeightArg,
27        int screenWidthArg,
28        int memorySizeArg )
29      {
30        carrier = carrierArg;
31        manufacturer = manufacturerArg;
32        model = modelArg;
33        screenHeight = screenWidthArg;
34        screenWidth = memorySizeArg;
35      }
36      // ...
37
38      // getters
39      public String getModel ()
40      {
41          return ( model );
42      }
43      public int getVolume ()
44      {
45          return ( volume );
46      }
47      public Date getNow ()
48      {
49          return ( now );
50      }
51      // ...
52
53      // setters
54      public void setVolume ( int volumeArg )
55      {
56          volume = volumeArg;
57      }
58      public void setDate ( Date nowArg )
59      {
60          now = nowArg;
61      }
```

```
62     // ...
63
64     // actions
65     public void volumeChange ( int changeArg )
66     {
67         volume += changeArg;
68     }
69 }
```

Mind you, this is not even the complete definition of the class. Everywhere you see // ..., it means there should me more lines there. These lines will be added later on, when you'll have a better understanding of what they mean. Let's analyze the part of the definition we have here. (Let's ignore the public and private keywords for now. They will be explained shortly.)

Lines 10-17 declare some of the member attributes of a cell phone. Lines 19-68 define member methods. This is all we need to know at this point. The real meaning of these definitions will be examined in the following sections.

The define the class Samsung, which is derived from CellPhone, you have to use the following definition:

```
public class Samsung extends CellPhone
{
 // ...
}
```

And the SCH-u410 class which will be defined like this:

```
public class SCH_u410 extends Samsung
{
 // ...
}
```

We left the "meat" of the definitions out for now. We will fill in the missing details shortly.

FOR INSTANCE... – CLASS INSTANTIATION

You might view a class definition as the plan for a class, very much like a "mold" out of which many objects can be made. A class has no substance – it's only an "idea" of what each object of this class would look like. You cannot use the electronic diagrams of an iPod to listen to music – Apple has to manufacture a real iPod for you to use. The terminology we use for "manufacturing" in object-oriented programming is instantiation. To instantiate an object of a certain class is to create a real (programming-wise) instance of the class, to build a real object based on the class definition. Once you instantiate an object, you have an actual "something" to work with. That object has specific values to its attributes (which may be different among different objects of the same class). For example, after instantiating two iPod objects, they can have different songs downloaded to them or have their volume set to different levels.

If you instantiate an object of a parent class, it may be "incomplete." For example, if a method is declared to change the volume in the "Cell Phone" class but is not defined (because we only know that we need it, but we don't know how it will be done on different models), you will not be able to tell the phone to raise the volume; you will only be able to do this if a method is defined, which in this case may be in the child "Treo" or "Samsung." If all Samsung phones change volume the same way, than we could have the method defined in the "Samsung" classes rather than in the model-specific children, and then we would not need to define it in the children.

The way to instantiate an object is to use the operator new. This operator returns a reference to the newly created object. Let's look at a simple class which describes a text message.

```
01 // Example 32, file 'TxtMsg.java'
02 // This file defines and instantiates the class 'TxtMsg'
03
04 import java.util.Date;
05
06 public class TxtMsg
```

```
07 {
08     // attributes
09
10     private int from;
11     private int to;
12     private String text;
13     private Date when;
14
15     // methods
16
17     // constructors
18     TxtMsg (
19        int fromArg,
20        int toArg,
21        String textArg,
22        Date whenArg )
23     {
24        from = fromArg;
25        to = toArg;
26        text = textArg;
27        when = whenArg;
28     }
29     // ...
30
31     public static void main ( String[] args )
32     {
33        // Declare a reference to TxtMsg and instantiate it
34        TxtMsg txtMsg = new TxtMsg (
35           2019871234, 2122349876, "Wassup?", new Date () );
36     }
37 }
```

Lines 10-11 declare the attributes of the text message. Lines 18-28 define the constructor for this class, which is a method that (you guessed it!) constructs an instance of the object. We will discuss constructors in much more details later, but I'm sure you get the idea of how it works by just looking at the code…

The crux of this example is lines 34-35. In these lines, an instance of TxtMsg is constructed and assigned the reference variable txtMsg. Note also that an instance of the Date class is also constructed (and will represent the date at which is was constructed).

(Please note that the main method would not usually be defined in a regular class unless this is the main class for an application. It is defined in this example only for demonstration purposes.)

> *What you learned in this chapter:*
>
> ⋏ *A* class *is a template for an object, defining its attributes and behaviors*
>
> ⋏ *Classes can be organized in a hierarchy, where* child *classes inherit (are* derived) *from* parent *classes*
>
> ⋏ *Individual objects are* instantiated *based on their class definition*

The Right to Privacy – Public and Private Members

> *Just like a class of students, the members of an object class may have different personalities. Some are shy and private, others like the public light. We will see what this means to the members themselves and to the relationships among classes.*
>
> *What you will learn in this chapter:*
> ➤ *What are the access attributes of class members*
> ➤ *How to use access attributes*
> ➤ *How to access private members*

THE PUBLIC VS. PRIVATE QUESTION

In example 31 above we have used the keywords `private` and `public`, and promised you that we'll explain them shortly. Now that "shortly" has arrived… The member attributes of the class were all declared as **private**. This means that no one outside the class can access them (neither look at them nor change them). This is part of the idea of encapsulation we discussed earlier – the class encapsulates the attributes, and has full control over them; no one else can access them directly. Obviously, when a member is declared as **public** it would mean that it *is* accessible from the outside. The member methods in the example are so declared, because it makes sense that if you want to get something done with the class you need access to its methods, which represent the actions and behaviors.

It is not required that attributes be `private` and methods `public`. It is a *very* good practice to have all attributes private, to maintain complete encapsulations, and you should be hard-pressed to justify a public attribute. Methods, on the other hand, can be of either type. Public methods are those that are accessible from the outside, and private ones are only accessible from other methods that belong to the class.

There is one more type of "privacy" – **protected**. It is somewhere between private and public, but its rules are complicated and somewhat confusing. For our purposes, suffice it to say that a protected member can be used by methods in the class that defines it and in its derived classes, but not by anybody else. We will demonstrate this in the next example.

ACCESS TO PRIVATE MATTERS

If all attributes are better kept private, how can we access them if we want to find their values or change them? Easy – with **getter** and **setter** methods. Their use is quite obvious: you use the getters (lines 38-52) to obtain the current values of the associated attributes, and the setters (lines 53-61) to set the values. This way, there are methods to do what we need, and we do not have to access the attributes directly. This is important, because if for some reason the implementation of a setter needs to be more complicated (like involving some calculations before storing the value), the user of the setter does not have to know about it. By the same token, if some calculations are needed to get the value of an attribute in a way that the caller expects (perhaps conversion of temperatures between Celsius and Fahrenheit), the caller of the getter method does not have to be aware of those calculations and they can be changes without affecting the callers.

Note that by the nature of the `CellPhone` class in the example, some attributes are not changeable (like the manufacturer or screen size), and some may be changeable (the volume level, and perhaps the carrier if you are not stuck with one of those phones which can only work on a single network). These differences manifest themselves in the member methods. Although we did not define *all* the getters and setters for this class, *some* omissions are intentional: there are no setters for attributes that cannot be changed; once the object exists (you have the cell phone in your hand), they cannot be changed (you cannot change the manufacturer, for example).

> *What you learned in this chapter:*
>
> ⋏   *An object's attributes can have different levels of access permissions,* public, protected *or* private
>
> ⋏   *The best way to access attributes is via* getter *and* setter *methods*

There Must Be a Method to This Madness – Class Methods

> *A method is another term for a function, but in the context of object-oriented programming methods may have some special duties. You will see the different types of methods that a class may have, and examine their special behavior.*
>
> *What you will learn in this chapter:*
>
> ➢   *The role of methods in a class*
> ➢   *Special methods that you must or may have in each class*
> ➢   *Common conventions for methods*

The class member methods can be classified in various ways. The following sections describe the different categories. The example below illustrates many of the ideas.

```
01  // Example 33, file 'TxtMsg.java'
02  // This file defines the class 'TxtMsg'
03
04  import java.util.Calendar;
05
06  public class TxtMsg
07  {
08      // attributes
09
10      private long from;
11      private long to;
12      private String text;
13      private Calendar when;
14      private boolean sent;
15      private boolean delivered;
16      private boolean replied;
17
18      // methods
19
20      // constructors
21      TxtMsg (
22          long fromArg,
23          long toArg,
24          String textArg,
25          Calendar whenArg )
26      {
27          from = fromArg;
28          to = toArg;
29          text = textArg;
30          when = whenArg;
31      }
32      TxtMsg (
33          long fromArg,
34          long toArg,
35          String textArg )
36      {
```

```
37          from = fromArg;
38          to = toArg;
39          text = textArg;
40          when = Calendar.getInstance();
41       }
42       TxtMsg (
43          TxtMsg txtMsg )
44       {
45          from = txtMsg.from;
46          to = txtMsg.to;
47          text = txtMsg.text;
48          when = txtMsg.when;
49       }
50
51       // getters
52       long getFrom ()
53       {
54          return ( from );
55       }
56       long getTo ()
57       {
58          return ( to );
59       }
60       String getText ()
61       {
62          return ( text );
63       }
64       Calendar getWhen ()
65       {
66          return ( when );
67       }
68       boolean getSent()
69       {
70          return ( sent );
71       }
72       boolean getDelivered()
73       {
74          return ( delivered );
75       }
76       boolean getReplied()
77       {
78          return ( replied );
79       }
80
81       // setters
82       void setText ( String textArg )
83       {
84          if ( !sent )
85             text = textArg;
86       }
87       void setFrom ( long fromArg )
88       {
89          if ( !sent )
90             from = fromArg;
91       }
92       void setTo ( long toArg )
93       {
94          if ( !sent )
95             to = toArg;
96       }
97       void setWhen ( Calendar whenArg )
98       {
99          when = whenArg;
100      }
101
102      // methods
103      void send ()
104      {
```

```
105        sent = true;
106        when = Calendar.getInstance();
107    }
108
109    void display()
110    {
111        System.out.println ( "Message '" + text +
112           "'\n from " + from + " to " + to );
113        String status;
114        if ( sent )
115           status = "sent";
116        else if ( delivered )
117           status = "delivered";
118        else if ( replied )
119           status = "replied to";
120        else
121           status = "created";
122        System.out.println ( " " + status +
123           " on " + when.getTime() );
124    }
125
126    public static void main ( String[] args )
127    {
128        TxtMsg txtMsg1 =
129           new TxtMsg ( 2019871234, 2122349876, "Wassup?" );
130        txtMsg1.display();
131        TxtMsg txtMsg2 = new TxtMsg ( txtMsg1 );
132        txtMsg2.setText ( "r u ready 4 my party?" );
133        txtMsg2.display();
134        txtMsg1.send();
135        txtMsg1.display();
136        Calendar whenever = Calendar.getInstance();
137        whenever.set( 2008, Calendar.APRIL, 01, 11, 11, 11 );
138        TxtMsg txtMsg3 =
139           new TxtMsg ( 4083456789L, 4159641357L, "Hi!",
140              whenever );
141        txtMsg3.display();
142    }
143 }
```

When you run this program, this is what you should get (with different dates, of course):

```
Message 'Wassup?'
 from 2019871234 to 2122349876
 created on Sun Apr 06 16:01:04 EDT 2008
Message 'r u ready 4 my party?'
 from 2019871234 to 2122349876
 created on Sun Apr 06 16:01:04 EDT 2008
Message 'Wassup?'
 from 2019871234 to 2122349876
 sent on Sun Apr 06 16:01:04 EDT 2008
Message 'Hi!'
 from 4083456789 to 4159641357
 created on Tue Apr 01 11:11:11 EDT 2008
```

If you are worried about the Calendar class, don't be. It should be quite obvious to figure out what it does, and the details do not matter at this point.

CONSTRUCTORS

In lines 18-28 of example 32, we saw a type of method called **constructor**. This particular type of method is distinguished by the fact that *it does not have a data type* (not even void) and that its name is the same as the class name. It is called when the program uses the new operator on the class, as in lines 34-35. Among other things, the new operator calls the constructor for the class to "initialize" the class. In most cases, it is used to assign initial or default values to some attributes. In many cases the values are obtained from the constructor's arguments, but they can also be determined internally. For example, we might have changed the constructor's argument list and dropped the last one (`Date`). Then we could change line 27 to:

```
When = new Date();
```

This would always set the date attribute to the construction date, without the need to pass a new `Date` object as a parameter. Of course, in that case it would not be possible to instantiate an object of class `TxtMsg` with any other date *but* the construction date. We will see later how we can get around this problem too.

This brings out the question: can we have both options? Namely, can we have one constructor that takes a date as an argument, and one that sets it to the current date? And the answer is… Yes! We can have more than one constructor. In example 33 below we have those two constructors. And more than that – we have three, the last of which is called a copy constructor, because it copies the attributes of another instance when it initializes its own. These constructors are on lines 20-49 of example 33.

If no constructor is defined for a class, a default parameter-less constructor is automatically created by the compiler. The default constructor calls the default parent constructor (`super()`) and initializes all instance variables to default value (zero for numeric types, null for object references, and false for Boolean). It does not do anything else; it's just there as a "placeholder". If you want it to do something, you must define it yourself as a constructor with no arguments, and then have it do whatever you need it to do.

One thing to remember is that the constructor is invoked after the object is created and memory for all attributes has been allocated. You can count on all the attributes to be there, but with undefined values.

There is an interesting aspect of constructors when it comes to derived classes. When the `new` operator is applied to a derived class, the *default* constructor of the base class is executed first, and then that of the derived class. If you want any other constructor to be called, you must call it explicitly in the constructor of the derived class. This can be done by calling the method `super()`, passing any arguments that will match one of the base class' constructors. The call to `super()` must be the first statement in the derived class' constructor.

Here is an example:

```
class Base
{
  int value;
  public Base()
  {
    value = 0;
  }
  public Base( int valueArg )
  {
    value = valueArg;
  }
  public String toString()
  {
    return ( value + "" );
  }
}

class Derived extends Base
{
  int num;
  public Derived()
  {
    num = 11;
  }
  public Derived( int numArg )
  {
    super( numArg );
    num = numArg;
  }
  public String toString()
```

```
    {
        return ( value + ":" + num );
    }
}
```

The two statement:

```
System.out.println( new Derived() );
System.out.println( new Derived( 123 ) );
```

Will produce the following two lines:

```
0:11
123:123
```

The reason is that the first constriction of `Derived` (with no arguments) calls, by default, the default constructor of `Base`, which assigns 0 to `value` and then `Derived`'s constructor assigns 11 to `num`. The second construction (with the argument 123) calls explicitly the second constructor of `Base`, which takes an argument and uses it to set `value`, in this case to 123; `Derived`'s constructor then uses the same value to set `num`. Without the call to `super(numArg)`, the default constructor of `Base` will be called here too, setting value to 0, and the output would have been 0:123.

ATTRIBUTES ACCESS – GETTERS AND SETTERS

We already discussed getters and setters when we talked about privacy, but there is a little bit more to say about them. First, their names: unlike the constructors, whose names *must* follow the rule described above, the naming of the getters and setters is only a convention. The name of a getter is made up of the word `get` in lower case, followed by the name of the attribute with the first letter capitalized (note that also by convention names of attributes start with a lower-case letter). So the getter for the attribute `memorySize` from example 31 is `getMemorySize`. Setters are named the same way, using the word `set` at the beginning.

Another rule regarding the getters and setters is their **signature** – the combination of return value, name and parameters that uniquely identify a method or a function. A getter must have *no arguments* (we are not passing any information to the method) and its return data type *must* be identical to that of the attribute (this is the type of the value we expect to get back). A setter *must not* have a return value (we do not expect anything back from the method), and the one and only argument *must* have the data type of the attribute (this is the value to which we want to set the attribute). We can define a setter that takes other types of arguments (more than one, or with a different data type) and set the attribute based on those values, but strictly speaking this is not a "basic" setter but a regular action method (although we may look at it as a setter from the privacy and encapsulation perspective). The same applies to getters: those that do more than just delivery of the values are not "basic" getters, but nevertheless can be accepted as getters because they support the privacy and encapsulation of the attributes. The getters for the `TxtMsg` class are on lines 52-79 and the setters are on lines 82-100. The getters are simple, but the setters go a little bit beyond "basic": we do not allow setting some attributes if the message has already been sent – you can not "unsay" what you already said!

One last rule: do not provide a setter for an attribute you do not want outsiders to change, or a getter for an attribute outsiders should not see. This is the whole idea of encapsulation and privacy – if there is no method to do it, it cannot be done! This is why we do not have setters for the `sent`, `delivered` and `replied` attributes – it is not reasonable to set them without another related action, such as actually sending a message (which is what the `send()` method on lines 103-107 is doing).

If you look now at how we use the `Calendar` object, you will see that we call a special getter called `getInstance()` to get a new calendar object (it has a hidden constructor in it), and a setter called `set()` to set the date in the calendar object. These do not follow the conventions, but there must be a perfectly valid explanation for it (I haven't found it yet though…) It serves to illustrate that these are only conventions; if you want be unconventional, no one (and in particular the Java environment) is going to stand in your way (except that many programmers will be puzzled or upset…)

OTHER METHODS

There is not much we can say about other methods. They are just supposed to do what they are supposed to do. The send() and display() methods in the example are just like that. Of course, some methods can be very complex, but their nature is still the same: performs some actions and calculations that affect the attributes of the object or other objects.

You can imagine that the send() method has a lot more to it than just setting the flag and the time, but since we are not covering "Cellular Network Communications" in this book, let's ignore this part of the method and leave it to the experts.

We could add another method the TxtMsg class: reply(). It may look like that:

```
TxtMsg reply ( String replyTxt )
{
  TxtMsg replyMsg =
    new TxtMsg ( to, from, replyTxt );
  return ( replyMsg );
}
```

Notice that we switched the to and the from – a reply is going in the opposite direction. Then you might add the following lines to the end of main():

```
TxtMsg txtMsg4 = txtMsg2.reply ( "sure!" );
TxtMsg4.send();
txtMsg4.display();
```

And the extra output will be:

```
Message 'sure!'
 from 2122349876 to 2019871234
 sent on Sun Apr 06 16:23:24 EDT 2008
```

By the way, the full example in the examples directory already includes these changes to the class.

What you learned in this chapter:

⋏ *Methods that are used when an object is created are called* constructors

⋏ *The constructor of the base class is called before the constructor of its derived class*

⋏ *Methods used to access attributes are called* getters *and* setters

---

Overloading is Good

> *Sometimes a method has to have different sets of arguments, but is still expected to perform the same actions. The method definition can be then overloaded.*
>
> *What you will learn in this chapter:*
> - ➤ *Why overloading is needed*
> - ➤ *How is overloading accomplished*
> - ➤ *The rules for proper overloading*

Two of the common functions in programming are functions to find the minimum or maximum among a set of values. They are commonly called, not surprisingly, `min()` and `max()`. But the values may be of different types: I may want to find the minimum of two integers, or doubles, or even strings (comparing lexicographically). Since the data type of a function's arguments are an integral part of its signature, it's impossible to have one function that will take any type of argument without losing something in the conversion process. (for example, if we only write a function to compare strings, how will we handle numbers?). One crude solution is to write several functions, such as:

```
int min_int(int num1, int num2);
double min_double(double num1, double num2);
String min_string(String str1, String Str2);
```

But this requires the user of your functions to know what your naming conventions are and remember all the names. It also adds more names to the general "clutter" of names in your program. All this points to the idea that we should be able to have only one name, but many different functions accepting different argument types, as in:

```
int min(int num1, int num2);
double min(double num1, double num2);
String min(String str1, String Str2);
```

Now it seems we are violating the rule that names in the same scope must be unique (look back at "On the Scope – Visibility of Variables" in part 2). But that's fine: we have special permission for this, thanks to a feature called **overloading**, and it is one way of providing the polymorphism we discussed earlier. What we are doing is overloading the single name of the function with multiple meanings. The rule is simple: you can use the same name to define multiple functions as long as the *arguments* are different. That means the number and/or the types of the arguments must be different. So,

```
int min(int num1, int num2);
int min(int num1, int num2, int num3);
int min(short num1, short num2);
int min(int num1, short num2);
int min(short num1, int num2);
```

are all good. However,

```
int min(short num1, short num2);
short min(short num1, short num2);
```

are *not* acceptable, because the only difference between the two functions is in the return type, and that is not a factor in telling apart the overloaded functions.

Here is an example of a class that uses overloading:

```
01  // Example 34, file 'MinMax.java'
02  // This file defines the class 'MinMax'
03
04  public class MinMax
05  {
06    // methods
07    int min(int num1, int num2)
08    {
09     System.out.println("int");
10      if ( num1 < num2 )
11        return ( num1 );
12      else
13        return ( num2 );
14    }
15    long min(long num1, long num2)
16    {
17     System.out.println("long");
18      if ( num1 < num2 )
19        return ( num1 );
20      else
21        return ( num2 );
22    }
23    double min(double num1, double num2)
24    {
25     System.out.println("double");
26      if ( num1 < num2 )
27        return ( num1 );
28      else
29        return ( num2 );
30    }
31    String min(String str1, String str2)
32    {
33     System.out.println("String");
34     int compare = str1.compareTo( str2 );
35      if ( compare < 0 )
36        return ( str1 );
37      else
38        return ( str2 );
39    }
40    int max(int num1, int num2)
41    {
42     System.out.println("int");
43      if ( num1 > num2 )
44        return ( num1 );
45      else
46        return ( num2 );
47    }
48    long max(long num1, long num2)
49    {
50     System.out.println("long");
51      if ( num1 > num2 )
52        return ( num1 );
53      else
54        return ( num2 );
55    }
56    double max(double num1, double num2)
57    {
58     System.out.println("double");
59      if ( num1 > num2 )
60        return ( num1 );
61      else
62        return ( num2 );
63    }
64    String max(String str1, String str2)
65    {
66     System.out.println("String");
```

```
67       int compare = str1.compareTo( str2 );
68         if ( compare > 0 )
69           return ( str1 );
70         else
71           return ( str2 );
72       }
73
74       public static void main ( String[] args )
75       {
76         MinMax minMax = new MinMax();
77         System.out.println( minMax.min ( 1, 11 ) );
78         System.out.println(
79           minMax.min ( 9876543212345L, 1234567898765L ) );
80         System.out.println( minMax.min ( 111.111, 1.1 ) );
81         System.out.println( minMax.min ( "xyz", "abc" ) );
82         System.out.println( minMax.max ( "xyz", "abc" ) );
83       }
84 }
```

When running this program, these are the results:

```
int
1
long
1234567898765
double
1.1
String
abc
String
xyz
```

We added the `System.out.println()` calls in the `min()` and `max()` methods only to show which one was called; of course, a real class will not have these calls. Also, as in previous examples, the `main()` function is only included in order to be able to demonstrate the use the class and should not be considered a part of the class definition.

One thing to notice is that the `String` versions of `min()` and `max()` are different than the numerical versions; it has to use a different comparison mechanism than the numerical < and > operators. This demonstrates the power of the overloading: all the `min()` methods perform the same logical function, but the ways they accomplish their tasks are based on their arguments.

> *What you learned in this chapter:*
>
> ⋏ Overloading *lets us define multiple methods with the same name but with different parameters in the same class*
>
> ⋏ *Overloading allows us to implement polymorphism*
>
> ⋏ *Each overloaded method can handle its parameters in the most appropriate way for their types*

The Overriding Directive

> *When a derived class needs to re-define a method that is defined in its base class, it can override that definition with a new one.*
>
> *What you will learn in this chapter:*
>
> ➢ *Why overriding is needed*
> ➢ *How is overriding accomplished*
> ➢ *The rules for effective overriding*

Suppose you volunteered to write a program to control the teleprompter in your school's auditorium. It's a simple gizmo: you give it text, and it displays it in a certain size and scrolls it at a certain speed. So you write a simple class, aptly named `Teleprompt`, which has one main method: `show()`. This method takes one argument, the text to be displayed, and sends the text out to the device in **XML** (Extensible Markup Language) format. (Since we are not learning XML here, you'll have to take my word on what is proper XML. Since I invented this teleprompter, you'll also have to trust me when I define what is the format of the XML document that it expects... But don't you worry; we will use *very* simple XML here. A good place to start learning more about XML is http://en.wikipedia.org/wiki/XML and the many links available there). The main thing the method does, then, is create the correct XML for our gizmo. Since we don't really have a teleprompter (sorry to disappoint you...), we will just print out what would otherwise be sent to the device. So the class may look something like that:

```
public class Teleprompt
{
  void showText ( String text )
  {
    String outText = "<Text>" + text + "</Text>";
    System.out.println ( outText );
  }
}
```

All the `showText()` method does is add the XML tags around the text. But things are never that simple, are they? The teleprompter has a limit on the size of the text it can accept each time (10 characters), and you must wait some time (1/2 a second) before you send each "chunk". So now the class gets a little more complicated:

```
01 // Example 35, file 'Teleprompter.java'
02 // This file defines the class 'Teleprompt'
03
04 import java.lang.Math;
05 import java.lang.Thread;
06
07 public class Teleprompter
08 {
09    int maxSize = 10;  // in characters
10    int waitTime = 500; // in miliseconds
11
12    public void showText ( String text )
13      throws InterruptedException
14    {
15      String outText = "<Text>" + text + "</Text>";
16      sendText ( outText );
17    }
18    protected void sendText ( String text )
19      throws InterruptedException
20    {
21      for ( int pos = 0; pos < text.length(); pos += maxSize )
22      {
23        int chunkSize = Math.min(
24          maxSize, text.length() - pos );
```

```
25        String chunk = text.substring (
26          pos, pos + chunkSize );
27        System.out.println ( chunk );
28        Thread.sleep ( waitTime );
29      }
30    }
31
32    public static void main ( String[] args )
33      throws InterruptedException
34    {
35      Teleprompter tele = new Teleprompter();
36      tele.showText (
37        "Good evening, ladies and gentlemen." );
38    }
39 }
```

The main logic is in the sendText() method in lines 18-30, with the heart of it in lines 23-26. the loop goes over the re-formatted string in increments of maxSize, and cuts the text into chunks before sending them out. Lines 21-22 are necessary to ensure that when we reach the last chunk we have its correct size, or else the substring method will be upset – you cannot specify an ending position (the pos + chunkSize) which is beyond the end of the string. The throws InterruptedException is there because the Thread.sleep() method needs it; we will cover exceptions at a later time. We use the keyword protected for sendText() in anticipation of some good news you'll receive shortly (hey, we can do this; we write the script here…).

Running this program, you should expect to see the following:

```
<Text>Good
 evening,
ladies and
 gentlemen
.</Text>
```

The complete XML document can be found in the file Text.xml in the examples. Notice that as you increase the value of waitTime, you will see the output lines showing up at a slower pace, which is exactly the desired effect.

After you completed this assignment, you were given the good news that the school just got another teleprompter, a more sophisticated one. The new one has the extra feature of displaying the text in various sizes and colors, and its maximum chunk size is bigger – 12 characters. So now you have to implement a new class to deal with the new teleprompter. But you really don't want to implement all the "complex" logic of sendText() again, so the best solution is to define the new class as derived from the old one. The XML for the new device is slightly more complex too, so the new class has to take care of it as well.

We will call the new class SmartTeleprompter, and will override both the class constructor and the showText() method of the base Teleprompter class. (You may think that the base Teleprompter class did not have a constructor; after all, we didn't write one! But you'd be wrong: because we did not write it, it was given to us automatically; it is called the **default constructor**.) So after all is said and done (or coded and tested), this is what we should have:

```
01 // Example 35, file 'SmartTeleprompter.java'
02 // This file defines the class 'SmartTeleprompter'
03
04 import java.lang.Math;
05 import java.lang.Thread;
06
07 public class SmartTeleprompter extends Teleprompter
08 {
09    public SmartTeleprompter ()
10    {
11      maxSize = 12;
12    }
13    public void showText ( String text, String Color, int size )
14      throws InterruptedException
15    {
```

```
16      String outText = "<Text color=\"" + Color +
17        "\" size=\"" + size + "\">" + text + "</Text>";
18      sendText ( outText );
19    }
20
21    public static void main ( String[] args )
22      throws InterruptedException
23    {
24      SmartTeleprompter tele = new SmartTeleprompter();
25      tele.showText (
26        "Good evening, ladies and gentlemen.", "Bright Red", 20 );
27    }
28 }
```

It is very important to remember that SmartTeleprompter cannot live on its own – it *must* have Teleprompter to rely on. That's why it is shorter – part of its intelligence is in its base class, so the "chunking" logic did not have to be rewritten. But obviously, some work had to be done… So this is what we did: first, we created a new constructor, which sets the maxSize attribute to a different value than the original. (We could have been a lot smarter, anticipating yet a more sophisticated generation of teleprompters, and passed the value as an argument to the constructor.) Secondly, we created a new version of showText(), which builds the necessary XML for the new gadget. In XML lingo, the change involved adding the color and size attributes to the Text tag.

Oh, and we didn't forget our promise to explain the **protected** keyword in front of sendText() in Teleprompter – this is so that its child SmartTeleprompter can use the method; if we left it private, it would not be accessible and the compiler would let you know; if we made it public, anyone would be able to use it and perhaps send badly-formatted XML to the device, which may cause it to choke.

So this is what the results should be:

```
<Text color=
"Bright Red"
 size="20">G
ood evening,
 ladies and
gentlemen.</
Text>
```

The complete XML document can be found in the file SmartText.xml in the examples. We certainly hope that the new teleprompter, once installed in the auditorium, displays the text in bright red and in letters of size 20, or you'll hear from the vice-principal…

What you learned in this chapter:

⋏ *Overriding is the replacement of a method in a superclass by a method in a subclass with the same signature*

⋏ *Overriding allows us to replace the logic of a method in a base class with one that is appropriate for the derived class*

Levels of Abstraction

> *When a base class does not define a method, but wants to ensure that its derived classes do define it, it makes the method an abstract method, and thus becomes abstract itself.*
>
> *What you will learn in this chapter:*
> ➢ *When abstract methods and classes are needed*
> ➢ *How to define and use them*

Imagine a class that encapsulates the behavior of an airplane. Let call the base class `Airplane`, and define derived classes of `Jet` and `Prop`. All airplanes have engines, but the process of starting them up would be different depending on the type of engine. If we name the starting procedure `startYourEngines()`, we will implement a different one for each of the derived classes. The code might look like this (please note that this example is incomplete and is not expected to compile and run!):

```
class Airplane
{
  String id;

  public Airplane( String idArg )
  {
    System.out.println( "Constructing airplane " +
      idArg + "." );
    id = idArg;
  }
  public String getId()
  {
    return ( id );
  }
}

class Jet extends Airplane
{
  public Jet( String idArg )
  {
    super( idArg );
    System.out.println( "It is a jet airplane." );
  }
  public void startYourEngines()
  {
    System.out.println( "Starting jet engines." );
  }
}

class Prop extends Airplane
{
  public Prop( String idArg )
  {
    super( idArg );
    System.out.println( "It is a propeller airplane." );
  }
  public void startYourEngines()
  {
    System.out.println( "Starting propeller engines." );
  }
}
```

Let's now put all the airplanes in the terminal. We will define `Terminal` class, which will have an array of gates (it's a small airport, so we have only 10 gates). Each airplane will be parked at a gate.

```
public Terminal ( int numGatesArg )
{
   System.out.println( "Constructing a terminal with "
      + numGatesArg + " gates." );
   gates = new Airplane[ numGatesArg ];
   numGates = numGatesArg;
}

public void park( Airplane airplane, int gateNum )
{
   System.out.println( "Parking " + airplane.getId() +
      " at gate " + gateNum + "." );
   gates[ gateNum ] = airplane;
}

public void startEngines()
{
   int gateNum;
   for ( gateNum = 0; gateNum < numGates; gateNum++ )
   {
      if ( gates[ gateNum ] != null )
         gates[ gateNum ].startYourEngines();
   }
}
}
```

To tie it all together, here is the main program:

```
public class Aviation
{
   public static void main( String[] args )
      throws IOException
   {
      Terminal terminal = new Terminal( 10 );

      Jet j1 = new Jet( "J1" );
      Jet j2 = new Jet( "J2" );
      Prop p1 = new Prop( "P1" );

      terminal.park( j1, 0 );
      terminal.park( j2, 1 );
      terminal.park( p1, 2 );

      terminal.startEngines();
   }
} // Aviation
```

When we run this program, we will get the following output:

```
Constructing a terminal with 10 gates.
Constructing airplane J1.
It is a jet airplane.
Constructing airplane J2.
It is a jet airplane.
Constructing airplane P1.
It is a propeller airplane.
Parking J1 at gate 0.
Parking J2 at gate 1.
Parking P1 at gate 2.
Starting jet engines.
Starting jet engines.
Starting propeller engines.
```

If we now define a new airplane type, let's say `TurbProp`, and we are not careful, we might forget to define a startYourEngines() method.

```
class TurboProp extends Airplane
{
  public TurboProp( String idArg )
  {
    super( idArg );
    System.out.println( "It is a turbo-prop airplane." );
  }
}
```

We now add the line:

```
    terminal.park( t1, 3 );
```

After the other calls to `park()`, and this is the output:

```
Constructing a terminal with 10 gates.
Constructing airplane J1.
It is a jet airplane.
Constructing airplane J2.
It is a jet airplane.
Constructing airplane P1.
It is a propeller airplane.
Constructing airplane T1.
It is a turbo-prop airplane.
Parking J1 at gate 0.
Parking J2 at gate 1.
Parking P1 at gate 2.
Parking T1 at gate 3.
Starting jet engines.
Starting jet engines.
Starting propeller engines.
Starting unknown engines.
```

What happened? Why do we have "unknown" engines? This is because we had a startrYourEngines() method in the `Airplane` class, even though this class is not expected to ne instantiated on its own. If we hadn't defined this method, we would not have been able to code gates[gateNum].startYourEngines(); because the method would have been defined only in derived classes, and this statement tries to invoke it from the base class.

Remember polymorphism? We saw how it applies to individual methods. Here we have an example how it applies to objects. The `gates` array takes in any object of the base class or its derived classes, allowing us to invoke a certain behavior (startYourEngines()) without knowing how it is implemented. Unfortunately, it seems to force us to define an unnecessary method.

This is where abstract classes and methods come into play. The example below shows how we can make sure that we do not have a case of "unknown" by forcing the derived class to define the necessary method.

```
01 // Example 43, file 'Aviation.java'
02 // This file defines the class 'Aviation'
03
04 import java.io.*;
05
06 abstract class Airplane
07 {
08    String id;
09
10    public Airplane( String idArg )
11    {
12      System.out.println( "Constructing airplane " +
13        idArg + "." );
14      id = idArg;
15    }
16
```

```
17     public String getId()
18     {
19        return ( id );
20     }
21
22     public abstract void startYourEngines();
23  }
24
25  class Jet extends Airplane
26  {
27     public Jet( String idArg )
28     {
29        super( idArg );
30        System.out.println( "It is a jet airplane." );
31     }
32
33     public void startYourEngines()
34     {
35        System.out.println( "Starting jet engines." );
36     }
37  }
38
39  class Prop extends Airplane
40  {
41     public Prop( String idArg )
42     {
43        super( idArg );
44        System.out.println( "It is a propeller airplane." );
45     }
46
47     public void startYourEngines()
48     {
49        System.out.println( "Starting propeller engines." );
50     }
51  }
52
53  class TurboProp extends Airplane
54  {
55     public TurboProp( String idArg )
56     {
57        super( idArg );
58        System.out.println( "It is a turbo-prop airplane." );
59     }
60
61     public void startYourEngines()
62     {
63        System.out.println( "Starting turbo-prop engines." );
64     }
65  }
66
67  class Terminal
68  {
69     Airplane gates[];
70     int numGates;
71
72     public Terminal ( int numGatesArg )
73     {
74        System.out.println( "Constructing a terminal with "
75           + numGatesArg + " gates." );
76        gates = new Airplane[ numGatesArg ];
77        numGates = numGatesArg;
78     }
79
80     public void park( Airplane airplane, int gateNum )
81     {
82        System.out.println( "Parking " + airplane.getId() +
83           " at gate " + gateNum + "." );
84        gates[ gateNum ] = airplane;
```

```
85      }
86
87      public void startEngines()
88      {
89         int gateNum;
90         for ( gateNum = 0; gateNum < numGates; gateNum++ )
91         {
92            if ( gates[ gateNum ] != null )
93               gates[ gateNum ].startYourEngines();
94         }
95      }
96 }
97
98 public class Aviation
99 {
100    public static void main( String[] args )
101    throws IOException
102    {
103       Terminal terminal = new Terminal( 10 );
104
105       Jet j1 = new Jet( "J1" );
106       Jet j2 = new Jet( "J2" );
107       Prop p1 = new Prop( "P1" );
108       TurboProp t1 = new TurboProp( "T1" );
109
110       terminal.park( j1, 0 );
111       terminal.park( j2, 1 );
112       terminal.park( p1, 2 );
113       terminal.park( t1, 3 );
114
115       terminal.startEngines();
116    }
117 } // Aviation
```

The important lines here are line 6 and line 22. Thank to them, we must define the startYourEngines() method for the TurboProp class. Line 6 makes the Airplane class an abstract class, thus ensuring that it can never be instantiated on its own. Line 22 defines the startYourEngines() method as abstract, forcing each derived class to define it (or the compiler will issue an error); this definition has no statements to execute, relieving us of the need to write code that should never be used anyway.

The output from this program is exactly what we would expect:

```
Constructing a terminal with 10 gates.
Constructing airplane J1.
It is a jet airplane.
Constructing airplane J2.
It is a jet airplane.
Constructing airplane P1.
It is a propeller airplane.
Constructing airplane T1.
It is a turbo-prop airplane.
Parking J1 at gate 0.
Parking J2 at gate 1.
Parking P1 at gate 2.
Parking T1 at gate 3.
Starting jet engines.
Starting jet engines.
Starting propeller engines.
Starting turbo-prop engines.
```

What you learned in this chapter:

⋏   *An* abstract *method is a method that has no implementation*

⋏   *A class that has abstract methods becomes an abstract class*

⋏   *An abstract class cannot be instantiated*

⋏   *An abstract class lets us define required methods for its derived classes without implementing any of them*

There May Be Some Exceptions

There are occasions when a program encounters a problem and must stop what it is doing. It is important to make sure that these exceptions are handled properly and not cause other failures or crashes.

What you will learn in this chapter:

➢ *How to define an exception handler*
➢ *What can, and should, an exception handlers do*
➢ *Some of the standard exceptions*

Imagine you write a program that performs some division of two values. What would happen if the denominator is zero? The most common result is (…drum roll…) – a crash! The term for this event is that an exception has been **thrown**. The program will suffer what is also known as "abnormal termination", usually with some nasty message that will have not much additional useful information. For example, if you have the following code in your program:

```
int numerator = 11;
int denominator = 0;
int result = numerator / denominator;
System.out.println( "Result = " + result );
```

The `println()` will never be executed. What you will get is a message similar to this one:

```
Exception in thread "main" java.lang.ArithmeticException: / by zero
```

Followed by the line number at which the "accident" occurred. But what if you want to have some more information, such as the value of the nominator? The answer is known as the **try-catch block**. It may look like this:

```
int result = 0;
int numerator = 11;
int denominator = 0;
boolean succeeded = true;
try
{
  result = numerator / denominator;
}
catch ( ArithmeticException exArith )
{
  System.err.println( "ArithmeticException: "
    + exArith.getMessage()
    + " (Numerator = " + numerator + ")." );
  succeeded = false;
}

if ( succeeded )
  System.out.println( "Result = " + result );
else
  System.out.println( "Division failed." );
```

And the result may look like this:

```
ArithmeticException: / by zero (Numerator = 11).
Division failed.
```

This is a little more useful, since we know what the numerator was. If you add a call to `exArith.printStackTrace()` in the `catch` block, a complete stack trace will be printed, which will show you exactly at what line the error occurred and all the methods called in order to get into that trouble spot.

Another useful exception to catch is `ArrayIndexOutOfBoundsException`. If you refer to an array element that is outside the definition of the array, you will get an exception. This code:

```
int List[] = { 0, 1, 2, 3 };
List[ 11 ] = 11;
```

Will cause the following exception:

```
Exception in thread "main" java.lang.ArrayIndexOutOfBoundsException: 11
```

One missing piece of information, useful for identifying the cause of the problem, may be how may elements are in the array. If we change the code to look like this:

```
int intList[] = { 0, 1, 2, 3 };
try
{
    intList[ 11 ] = 11;
}
catch ( ArrayIndexOutOfBoundsException exOutOfBound )
{
  System.err.println( "ArrayIndexOutOfBoundsException: "
    + exOutOfBound.getMessage()
    + " (Number of elements = " + intList.length + ")."
}
```

We will improve the error reporting to look like this:

```
ArrayIndexOutOfBoundsException: 11 (Number of elements = 4).
```

It is allowed to have multiple `catch` blocks, trapping different exceptions. When an exception occurs, the exception handler looks thought all the `catch` blocks to find one that bets matches the exception that just happened. For example, the following code is perfectly valid (although it does not make much sense…):

```
int intList[] = { 0, 1, 2, 3 };
try
{
  for ( int i = 0; i < intList.length; i++ )
    intList[ i ] = intList[ i - 1 ] / intList[ i ];
}
catch ( ArrayIndexOutOfBoundsException ex )
{
  System.err.println( "ArrayIndexOutOfBoundsException: "
    + ex.getMessage()
    + " (Number of elements = " + intList.length + ")." );
}
catch ( ArithmeticException ex )
{
  System.err.println( "ArithmeticException: "
    + ex.getMessage() );
}
```

The two `catch` blocks attempt to trap two possible exceptions: a potential divide by zero, which may happen when i is 0 and then the value of `intList[i]` is 0, and a possible array bounds issue when i-1 is less than 0, referring to an array element that does not exist. (This code snippet may be a good example of defensive programming, but a bad example of programming in general… A better approach is to validate the values before using them, and not "throw it up in the air" and expect that the exception handler will catch it. Exception management should be used only in cases where either there is no way to ensure that an operation can succeed, or there is no other way to notify the user that an error has occurred.).

By the way, in the above example, the exception that will be thrown (and caught) is the `ArrayIndexOutOfBoundsException`, because the reference to `intList[i-1]` occurs before the division by `intList[i]`.

The Java language defines a large number of exceptions, arranged in a hierarchy. We will not review that subject here, and will only note that the rules are relatively simple and it is worth while to learn them.

Example 36 contains the code fragments above, so we will not replicate it here. In order to demonstrate a realistic example, let's look at example 37. In this example, we are implementing a class representing fractions. In case you forgot, a fraction is composed of a numerator and a denominator: in ¾, 3 is the numerator and 4 is the denominator. So our class will have two integer members, not surprisingly named `numerator` and `denominator` (lines 14 and 15). The operation we would like to perform on fractions are the four basic arithmetic operations, so we define four methods: `add()`, `sub()`, `mul()` and `div()` (lines 26-66). Two other functions are `lcd()` (lines 68-81), which calculate the lowest common denominator of two number, and the function `adjustLcd()` (lines 83-88), which uses `lcd()` to reduce a fraction after a calculation to the smallest possible numerator and denominator. In order to be able to easily print out a fraction, we implanted the method `toString()` (lines 90-93), which is invoked every time the class appears in an expression with a `String` object (every primitive data type has such a method). The `toDouble()` method (lines 95-100) is used to convert a `Fraction` object to a `double`.

But to be perfectly honest, all this is just a setup… The interesting code is in the `main()` function, and the important class is `InvalidFractionException` (lines 4-10), which defines an exception for our very special application. We will throw this exception when we encounter "unbearable situations".

The first try-catch block (lines 108-131) is very peaceful, and no exception is thrown. It gets exciting in the next block (lines 133-147): the attempt to create a fraction with a denominator of zero is an "unbearable situation", and the `InvalidFractionException` exception is thrown. The third block throws an `ArithmeticException` because of the expression `2 / 0`, which is evaluated before the constructor of the Fraction is called (and thus the `InvalidFractionException` is never thrown), despite the fact that the denominator would have been zero if the numerator didn't cause an exception first.

The complete program is presented below.

```
01 // Example 37, file 'FracMath.java'
02 // This file defines the classes 'FracMath' and 'Fraction'
03
04 class InvalidFractionException extends Exception
05 {
06   public InvalidFractionException( String message )
07   {
08     super( message );
09   }
10 }
11
12 class Fraction
13 {
14   int numerator;
15   int denominator;
16
17   public Fraction( int numeratorArg, int denominatorArg )
18     throws InvalidFractionException
19   {
20     if ( denominatorArg == 0 )
21       throw new InvalidFractionException( "zero denominator" );
22     numerator = numeratorArg;
23     denominator = denominatorArg;
24   }
25
26   public Fraction add( Fraction right )
27     throws InvalidFractionException
28   {
29     Fraction result = new Fraction(
30         numerator * right.denominator
31         + right.numerator * denominator,
32         denominator * right.denominator );
33     adjustLcd( result );
34     return ( result );
```

```
35      }
36
37      public Fraction sub( Fraction right )
38         throws InvalidFractionException
39      {
40         Fraction result = new Fraction(
41             numerator * right.denominator
42             - right.numerator * denominator,
43             denominator * right.denominator );
44         adjustLcd( result );
45         return ( result );
46      }
47
48      public Fraction mul( Fraction right )
49         throws InvalidFractionException
50      {
51         Fraction result = new Fraction(
52             numerator * right.numerator,
53             denominator * right.denominator );
54         adjustLcd( result );
55         return ( result );
56      }
57
58      public Fraction div( Fraction right )
59         throws InvalidFractionException
60      {
61         Fraction result = new Fraction(
62             numerator * right.denominator,
63             denominator * right.numerator );
64         adjustLcd( result );
65         return ( result );
66      }
67
68      public static int lcd( int n1, int n2 )
69      { // lowest common denominato
70         while ( n1 > 0 )
71         {
72            if ( n1 < n2 )
73            {
74               int tmp = n1;
75               n1 = n2;
76               n2 = tmp;
77            }
78            n1 = n1 % n2;
79         }
80         return ( n2 );
81      }
82
83      private void adjustLcd( Fraction frac )
84      {
85         int fracLcd = lcd( frac.numerator, frac.denominator );
86         frac.numerator /= fracLcd;
87         frac.denominator /= fracLcd;
88      }
89
90      public String toString()
91      {
92         return ( numerator + "/" + denominator );
93      }
94
95      public double toDouble()
96      {
97         if ( denominator == 0 )
98            throw new ArithmeticException( "/ by zero" );
99         return ( (double)numerator / (double)denominator );
100     }
101 }
102
```

```
103  public class FracMath
104  {
105    public static void main ( String[] args )
106      throws Exception
107    {
108      try
109      {
110        Fraction f01 = new Fraction( 7, 9 );
111        Fraction f02 = new Fraction( 5, 18 );
112        Fraction f03 = f01.add( f02 );
113        Fraction f04 = f01.sub( f02 );
114        Fraction f05 = f01.mul( f02 );
115        Fraction f06 = f01.div( f02 );
116        System.out.println( "f03=" + f03 );
117        System.out.println( "f04=" + f04 );
118        System.out.println( "f03=" + f03.toDouble() );
119        System.out.println( "f05=" + f05 );
120        System.out.println( "f06=" + f06 );
121      }
122      catch ( ArithmeticException ex )
123      {
124        System.out.println( "ArithmeticException: " +
125          ex.getMessage() );
126      }
127      catch ( InvalidFractionException ex )
128      {
129        System.out.println( "InvalidFractionException: " +
130          ex.getMessage() );
131      }
132
133      try
134      {
135        Fraction f11 = new Fraction( 1, 0 );
136        System.out.println( "f11" + f11.toDouble() );
137      }
138      catch ( ArithmeticException ex )
139      {
140        System.out.println( "ArithmeticException: " +
141          ex.getMessage() );
142      }
143      catch ( InvalidFractionException ex )
144      {
145        System.out.println( "InvalidFractionException: " +
146          ex.getMessage() );
147      }
148
149      try
150      {
151        Fraction f21 = new Fraction( 2 / 0, 0 );
152        Fraction f22 = f21.sub( f21 );
153        System.out.println( "f22=" + f22 );
154      }
155      catch ( ArithmeticException ex )
156      {
157        System.out.println( "ArithmeticException: " +
158          ex.getMessage() );
159      }
160      catch ( InvalidFractionException ex )
161      {
162        System.out.println( "InvalidFractionException: " +
163          ex.getMessage() );
164      }
165    }
166  }
```

The output of this program is:

```
f03=19/18
```

```
f04=1/2
f03=1.0555555555555556
f05=35/162
f06=14/5
InvalidFractionException: zero denominator
ArithmeticException: / by zero
```

There is a special type of catch block called `finally`. This block is executed after the try block is completed, regardless if there was an exception (which caused one of the catch blocks to be executed) or not. It is used for unconditional cleanup after the try block, and is a very useful invention. You will see in later examples how this "gizmo" works.

What you learned in this chapter:

➤ *An* exception *is* thrown *when the program encounters an unexpected situation*

➤ *An exception handler can be defined to properly handle exceptions*

➤ *A* try-catch *block is used to define exception handlers*

➤ *There are standards Java exceptions, but you can define your own as well*

Classic Classes – Some Built-In Classes

> *The basic language ruled allow you to do only basic things. The Java language includes a very large library of classes that do much more, and saves the programmers lots of time. This section will expose some of those classes.*
>
> *What you will learn in this chapter:*
> - *How to add external classes to a program*
> - *What are some of the standard Java classes*
> - *How to use some of those classes*

The Java language is an extensible language by design. Instead of defining in the language all that a programmer will ever need (a somewhat impossible undertaking!), the language was designed to be easily extended by anybody who has something useful to contribute. This is done by allowing anyone to import classes developed by someone else. Here the principles of encapsulation, inheritance and polymorphism show their strength – you don't have to know how someone you don't even know implemented some capability. All you need to know is the **interface** to the class you want to use. The interface definition will tell you what methods are available (declared `public`), what are their signatures and what are their expected results. In some cases, a few attributes are also declared `public`, and the interface will describe those as well.

But your good fortunes do not end with that. A large number of good people have spent a lot of time developing very useful classes, and many of those are included as part of the Java environment. They are "part of the language" not in having special syntax, but in just being there, wherever Java is running.

In the following sections we will take a closer look at some of those classes. We chose those that we think are the most important to the beginning programmer, and we do not even cover all the capabilities of the classes we chose to review. If you want to get more information, go to http://java.sun.com/javase/6/docs/api. We chose classes from the java.lang, java.util and java.io packages, but there are many more packages. (The subject of packaging is beyond the scope of this book, so just take it as a way to organize classes.)

THE IMPORT BUSINESS

In order to include other people's classes in you program, you **import** them. The statement is quite simple:

```
import <classname>;
```

Where `<classname>` is the name of the class you want to include in your program. For example:

```
import SomeClass;
```

Very often the name of the class is prefixed by the name of the package to which it belongs:

```
import <packagename>.<classname>;
```

Where `<packagename>` is the name of the package. This name may actually be composed of several names separated by periods if there is a hierarchy of packages (as happens in most cases). For example:

```
import java.io.File;
```

If you want to import all the classes within a package, you can use the "wildcard" indicator *:

```
import java.io.*;
```

Most of the standard classes included in the Java environment have to be imported into your program. An exception is the package `java.lang`: classes in this package are imported automatically, so you do not have to use the `import` statement.

STRINGS

Strings are probably the most heavily used standard class. You need them any time you want to manipulate text, which is quite often. We already used some of their capabilities in many of our previous examples, and we asked you to take it on faith that we are not feeding you nonsense… Now is the time to go a little deeper into this class, so that we can turn faith into facts.

The `String` class is defined in the package `java.lang`. It represents character strings. All string literals in Java programs, such as `"abc"`, are implemented as instances of this class. An important fact to remember about Strings is that they are constants; their values *cannot* be changed after they are created; operations that appear to modify a string actually create a new string with the modified value.

Construction

There are many things we can do with strings, but the first thing we have to learn is how to create them. And it's very easy. The lines below will create two string with the value "Little Mary had a lamb":

```
String littleMary1 = "Little Mary had a lamb";
String littleMary2 = new String( "Little Mary had a lamb" );
```

Another way is to use a character array. The lines below will create a string with the value "lamb" from the character array:

```
char[] lambChar = { 'l', 'a', 'm', 'b' };
String lambStr1 = new String( lambChar );
```

A string can also be created from another string:

```
String lambStr2 = new String( lambStr1 );
```

The first form is the most popular one. The others are useful under different circumstances, particularly when using existing strings or character arrays (rather than literal values) to construct another one.

Length

Probably the most important attribute of a string is its length, which is the number of characters it contains. In order to find out this number, we use the `length()` method:

```
int littleMaryLen1 = littleMary1.length();
```

The value of `littleMaryLen` would be 22. If you use this method on a literal, you will get the literal's length:

```
int littleMaryLen2 = "Little Mary had a lamb".length();
```

Although it seems like this is just laziness – couldn't we just count the number of characters ourselves? – it is a good practice: if we count the characters and then use the number as a literal (22 in this example), and later change the string (by adding a period at the end, for example), we may be using the wrong number! The rule is: *never* use a literal if it can be obtained programmatically!

Comparison

A very important feature is the ability to compare two strings. The primary method for this is `compareTo()`. It returns an integer whose value reflects the lexicographic relationship between the two strings; the string on which we invoke the method is called "the object" and the one we pass as parameter to the method is called "the argument".

(Lexicographic order is the order that you will find words in a dictionary.) It will be 0 is the two strings are equal, a negative number if the object string precedes the argument, and a positive value if the object follows the argument:

```
int compResult = littleMary1.compareTo( littleMary2 );
```

In this case, compResult will be 0. But let's look at a few more cases – a few United States Presidents:

```
String Washington = "Washington, George";
String Jefferson = "Jefferson, Thomas";
String Lincoln = "Lincoln, Abraham";
String RooseveltT = "Roosevelt, Theodore";
String RooseveltFD = "Roosevelt, Franklin D";
int compResult1 = Washington.compareTo( Jefferson );
int compResult2 = Jefferson.compareTo( Lincoln );
int compResult3 = RooseveltT.compareTo( RooseveltFD );
```

Notice that we are comparing the names only, not their order in the presidency. The results would be as follows: compResult1 is positive, compResult2 is negative, compResult3 is positive. The value of compResult3 shows that "Roosevelt, Theodore" follows "Roosevelt, Franklin D": even though Theodore Roosevelt preceded Franklin D. Roosevelt as President, their lexicographic order is reversed.

Concatenation

By now we know how to create strings, find their lengths and lexicographic relationships. But we haven't done anything useful with them yet. So let's start putting strings together, creating longer strings. This is called **concatenation**. We do it using the + operator.

```
String yodaSaid = "Named must your fear be " +
    "before banish it you can.";
```

Here the concatenation is used to enhance readability: if we used a single string for Yoda's words, it will be a very long line that might spill off the end of the page.

The concatenation operator is much more powerful, though. Almost all objects have (or should have) a toString() method, which converts the contents of the object to a string. When using the concatenation operator on a non-string object, this method is invoked to supply a string to be used in the concatenation:

```
int year = 1961;
String factoid = "The year "+ year + " can be read upside down.";
```

If you assign another number to year, such as 6009, you can change the factoid string (of course, there is no verification that the factoid is correct, so if you assign the value 1234 you'll just have a wrong factoid...). We do not have to use a single number; we can use an expression:

```
double pi = 3.14159265358;
double e =  2.71828182845;
String aMathFact = "pi/e=" + ( pi / e) + ".";
```

The value assigned to aMathFact would be "pi/e=1.1557273497911649.".

We have used this type of concatenation extensively in System.out.println() statements because it allowed us to build an output string from different pieces of different types.

Another way to concatenate strings is by using the concat() method:

```
String gollumSaidFirst = "Very nice friends";
gollumSaid = gollumSaidFirst.concat( ", O yes my precious..." );
```

The value of gollumSaid would be "Very nice friends, O yes my precious...". This form is used much less frequently.

Substrings

Let's try to look inside a string. We know that it is a series of individual characters. Each one has an index in the string, which describes its position relative to the beginning. Assuming we have:

```
String darthVaderFamousWords = "Luke, I am your father.";
```

we can picture the string `darthVaderFamousWords` as follows:

0	1	2	3	4	5	6	7	8	9	10	11	12	13	14	15	16	17	18	19	20	21	22
L	u	k	e	,		I		a	m		y	o	u	r		f	a	t	h	e	r	.

The method `charAt()` returns the character at the specified index. The value is of type `char`, not `String`. Thus, `darthVaderFamousWords.charAt(6)` is 'I' and `darthVaderFamousWords.charAt(22)` is '.'. Note that positions start at 0, *not* 1.

(By the way, the correct quote from the movie is "No, I am your father".)

We can also look at a sequence of characters using the method `substring()`. This method takes two arguments, a beginning index and an ending index, and return the `String` that begins at the specified beginning index and extends to the character at the ending index minus 1. So the value of `darthVaderFamousWords.substring(16,22)` is `"father"` and `darthVaderFamousWords.substring(6,11)` is `"I am "`.

Lookup

The `substring()` and `charAt()` methods look into a string based on known indices. There are other ways, based on contents. The `indexOf()` method returns the index in the object string of the first occurrence of the argument string (or -1 if there is none). If you pass an integer as the second argument to the method, it will start the lookup at that index. The `lastIndexOf()` finds the last occurrence; optional second argument tells it where to start, but since it is searching backwards it means the "furthest" in the string where the search begins. Let's look at some examples:

```
int indexIAm1 = darthVaderFamousWords.indexOf( "I am" );
int indexIAm2 = darthVaderFamousWords.indexOf( "I am", 4 );
int indexu1 = darthVaderFamousWords.indexOf( "u" );
int indexu2 = darthVaderFamousWords.indexOf( "u", 5 );
int indexu3 = darthVaderFamousWords.lastIndexOf( "u" );
```

The values of `indexIAm1` and `indexIAm2` are the same – 6; it does not matter if we start the lookup at the beginning of the string or at position 4 – the string `"I am"` is at a position beyond that, at position 6. There is a difference, however, between the values of `indexu1` and `indexu2`, 1 and 13 respectively, because the starting position of the second one is beyond the first occurrence of the single-character string `"u"`. The value of `indexu3`, 13, is as expected, because we asked for the search to go backwards from the end.

There is yet another way of lookup, which just asks if a string contains another string: the methods `contains()`, `startsWith()` and `endsWith()`. The first takes one argument, a string, and returns a Boolean value of `true` or `false` depending if the argument string shows up anywhere in the object string. The two others return a Boolean value indicating whether the object string starts or ends with the argument string, respectively:

```
boolean startsWithLuke = darthVaderFamousWords.startsWith( "Luke" );
boolean endsWithFather = darthVaderFamousWords.endsWith( "father" );
```

`startsWithLuke` will be `true`, but `endsWithFather` will be `false` because the object string has a period at the end so it ends with `"father."`, not `"father"`.

Replacement

So far we have looked into strings, and looked again and again... But the only thing we really did with them was string them together (pun intended...). So here's how we can change their contents: we can convert a string to lower case or upper case, we can trim spaces off the end of a string, *and* (drum roll…) we can replace individual characters or substrings within a string. Let's take these one at a time (or may be two…).

The methods `toUpperCase()` and `toLowerCase()`, which take no arguments, do what you might expect: return a new string with the upper-case or lower-case representation of the object string:

```
String allUpper = darthVaderFamousWords.toUpperCase();
String allLower = darthVaderFamousWords.toLowerCase();
```

`allUpper` will be `"LUKE, I AM YOUR FATHER."` and `allLower` will be `"luke, i am your father."`. No big deal…

It happens quite often that we have a string with spaces at the beginning or (more frequently) at the end, and we want to get rid of them. To our help comes the `trim()` method, which does just that. Darth Vader's words cannot help us here (he has no spaces…), so let's look at another string for an example:

```
String spacedOutPigs = "  Pigs in space     ";
String trimmedPigs = spacedOutPigs.trim();
```

The `trimmedPigs` string will have the same text as `spacedOutPigs`, but without the two spaces at the beginning and the five at the end.

The `replace()` method takes two arguments: the first is a "search" string or character, and the second is a "replace" string or character. It replace all occurrences of the "search" string or character by the "replace" string or character and return the new string. (Both arguments must be of the same type, `String` or `char`.). Let's "mangle" our favorite string:

```
String replaceAmbyAre =
   darthVaderFamousWords.replace( "am", "are" );
String replaceEbyX = darthVaderFamousWords.replace( 'e', 'x' );
```

`replaceAmbyAre` will be the bad-English sentence `"Luke, I are your father."` while `replaceEbyW` will be the typed-by-a-bad-bad-typist sentence `"Lukw, I am your fathwr."`.

Example

Example 38 includes most of the code snippets we used above in the explanations of the various methods, so we will not replicate it here. Let's put together an example that will demonstrate most of what we learned about strings.

First. Let's define the problem. I am almost certain that your parents are not as advanced as you are in text messaging… One of the problems they probably face (beside the pathetically low texting speed at which they are capable of) is that they often do not understand all the abbreviations you use in your messages (such as "omg" or "brb".) In order to make your life (and your parents' lives) easier, wouldn't it be wonderful if you could install on your parents' phones a tiny utility that will translate the abbreviation into more "English-like" words? I'm sure it will remove a lot of aggravation from your relationship…

So what we need is a class that can translate text from abbreviations to English. It will take a line of text that may contain abbreviations and return it with the abbreviation replaced by their full English meaning. Let's call it `Translator`. In order to perform the translation of each abbreviation, we need another class which will apply the translation rules. An appropriate name for it is `Dictionary`. We also need a class that can break down each line of text into individual words or symbol, which are known in the vocabulary of programming as **tokens**. Naturally, this class is called `Tokenizer`.

`Dictionary` (lines 7-81) has two main methods: a method to load the translation rules from a file (`load()`), and a method to look up an abbreviation to find its translation (`lookUp()`). It also keeps statistics on the number of rules and number of look-ups and translations. The constructor (lines 15-20) creates two arrays, one for abbreviations and one for their translations. The `load()` method (lines 31-50) takes one argument: the name of the file containing the rules. The "guts" of this method is lines 42-47, where each line of rules is "decomposed". A rule is specified as an abbreviation, followed by a colon (':'), followed by its translation. For example:

```
brb: be right back
```

Note the use of the `indexOf` and `substring` methods of the `String` class in order to interpret the rules and store them in the arrays.

The loading of the dictionary assumes that the rules are sorted in alphabetical order. This is important for the `lookUp()` method, which accepts a word and tries to find its translation (if there is one). The search for an abbreviation's translation is performed using an algorithm called "Binary Search". The idea of a binary search is to always divide the world into two halves, and focus our search in the half where we are likely to find what we are looking for. So we first determine if our word (which may be an abbreviation) is in the first or second half of the dictionary by comparing it to the one in the middle: if it is smaller, it would most likely be in the lower half; if it is larger, the upper half is more likely. Then we look at the half we chose, and divide it into two halves (which are actually quarters of the whole dictionary, but we don't care – we narrowed down our universe to one half only). And so we go on until we find the abbreviation, or realize that it is not in the dictionary. It we find it, we return the corresponding translation; if we do not, we return the original word. The Binary Search algorithm can be described as follows:

1. Let L be the original array.

2. Check the middle element of the array L

3. If this element is what we are looking for, we are done.

4. Otherwise, compare this element with the value we are looking for. If that value is larger then the middle element, then let L be the portion of the array to the right of the middle element, otherwise let L be the portion of the array to the left of the middle element.

5. Go t o step 2

This algorithm is implemented in lines 57-77 in the `lookup()` method.

The `Tokenizer` class (lines 83-147) is based on the standard Java class `StringTokenizer`. It was made simpler for the purpose of this example. The class is used in the following steps:

❑ First, an instance is constructed for a line of tokens by calling the class' constructor (lines 95-103) and passing two strings: the line to be tokenized, and the characters (delimiters) that terminate a token; this method sets up all the necessary attributes for the "tokenization" of the string.

❑ Then, the method nextToken() is called repeatedly, each time returning the next token (which may be a single delimiter character). In order to ensure that we don't "fall off" the end of the string, we must call the method hasMoreTokens() before each call to nextToken(). Once hasMoreTokens() returns false, we know that we have fully tokenized the input line.

The last class in our example is `Translator` (lines 149-195). Its only public method is `translate()` (lines 174-194). This method accepts an input string to be translated (a line from the dialog), and the `Dictionary` to be used for the translation. The method goes into a `while` loop, getting all tokens from the input string (line 180-182), translating them (lines 187-190) and adding them to the output string (line 191).

The main program (lines 199-224), which as usual in our examples does not really belong within the class and is just placed there for convenience, is rather straightforward. It first instantiates and initializes objects of the various classes (`Dictionary` on lines 204-205, `Translator` on line 209, input and output file objects on lines 211-214). Then, in a short `while` loop (lines 216-221), it reads a line, translates it and writes it out; it's that simple!

```
01 // Example 39, file 'TextPlain.java'
02 // This file defines the class 'TextPlain'
03
04 import java.io.*;
```

```
05 import java.util.StringTokenizer;
06
07 class Dictionary
08 {
09    private String[] shortCut;
10    private String[] meaning;
11    private int countLooked;
12    private int countFound;
13    private int size;
14
15    public Dictionary( int maxEntriesArg )
16    {
17       shortCut = new String[ maxEntriesArg ];
18       meaning = new String[ maxEntriesArg ];
19       countLooked = countFound = 0;
20    }
21
22    public int getSize()
23    { return ( size ); }
24
25    public int getCountLooked()
26    { return ( countLooked ); }
27
28    public int getCountFound()
29    { return ( countFound ); }
30
31    public void load( String fileNameArg )
32       throws FileNotFoundException, IOException
33    {
34       BufferedReader fileDict = new BufferedReader(
35          new FileReader( fileNameArg ) );
36       String line;
37       size = 0;
38       // read in the dictionary
39       while ( fileDict.ready() )
40       {
41          line = fileDict.readLine();
42          int indexColon = line.indexOf( ':' );
43          shortCut[ size ] =
44             line.substring( 0, indexColon ).toLowerCase();
45          meaning[ size ] =
46             line.substring( indexColon + 1, line.length() ).
47                trim().toLowerCase();
48          size++;
49       }
50    }
51
52    public String lookUp( String shortCutArg )
53    {
54       int first = 0;
55       int upto = size;
56       countLooked++;
57       while ( first < upto )
58       {
59          // compute mid point
60          int mid = ( first + upto ) / 2;
61          // compare shortcut at mid-point to the one we need
62          int compared = shortCutArg.
63             compareTo( shortCut[ mid ] );
64          if ( compared < 0 )
65          { // search in bottom half
66             upto = mid;
67          }
68          else if ( compared > 0 )
69          { // search in top half
70             first = mid + 1;
71          }
72          else
```

```
 73                  {  // found it, return meaning
 74                  countFound++;
 75                     return ( meaning[ mid ] );
 76                  }
 77              }
 78          // failed to find shortcut, return original word
 79          return ( shortCutArg );
 80      }
 81 } // Dictionary
 82
 83 class Tokenizer
 84 {
 85      private int currentPosition;
 86      private int newPosition;
 87      private int maxPosition;
 88      private String str;
 89      private String delimiters;
 90      private boolean delimsChanged;
 91
 92      // Constructs a string tokenizer for the specified string.
 93      // All characters in the 'delim' argument are the delimiters
 94      // for separating tokens.
 95      public Tokenizer( String str, String delim )
 96      {
 97          currentPosition = 0;
 98          newPosition = -1;
 99          delimsChanged = false;
100          this.str = str;
101          maxPosition = str.length();
102          delimiters = delim;
103      }
104
105      // Skips ahead from startPos and returns the index
106      // of the next delimiter character encountered,
107      // or maxPosition if no such delimiter is found.
108      private int scanToken( int startPos )
109      {
110          int position = startPos;
111          while ( position < maxPosition )
112          {
113              char c = str.charAt( position) ;
114              if ( delimiters.indexOf( c ) >= 0)
115                  break;
116              position++;
117          }
118          if ( startPos == position )
119          {
120              char c = str.charAt( position );
121              if ( delimiters.indexOf( c ) >= 0 )
122                  position++;
123          }
124          return ( position );
125      }
126
127      // Tests if there are more tokens available from
128      // this tokenizer's string. If this method returns
129      // 'true', then a subsequent call to nextToken()
130      // will successfully return a token.
131      public boolean hasMoreTokens() {
132          return ( currentPosition < maxPosition );
133      }
134
135      // Returns the next token from this string tokenizer
136      public String nextToken()
137      {
138          currentPosition = ( newPosition >= 0 && !delimsChanged
139              ? newPosition
140              : currentPosition );
```

```
141          delimsChanged = false;
142          newPosition = -1;
143          int start = currentPosition;
144          currentPosition = scanToken( currentPosition );
145          return ( str.substring( start, currentPosition ) );
146       }
147 }
148
149 class Translator
150 {
151    Tokenizer tokenizer;
152    public static String delim =
153       " \t\n\r\f!@#$%^&*()<>{}[]_-+=|:;,.?~`";
154
155    private boolean isDelim( String text )
156    {
157       return ( text.length() == 1  &&
158          delim.indexOf( text ) >= 0 );
159    }
160
161    private String addText( String token, String line )
162    {
163       if ( !isDelim( token )  &&
164          line.length() > 0 )
165       { // the token is not a delimiter -
166          // add a space before it (if not
167          // at the beginning of the line)
168          line = line + " ";
169       }
170       // add the token to the line
171       return ( line + token );
172    }
173
174    public String translate( String input, Dictionary dict )
175    {
176       tokenizer = new Tokenizer( input, delim );
177       String token = "";
178       String output = "";
179       // get all tokens from the line
180       while ( tokenizer.hasMoreTokens() )
181       { // get tokens, skipping those that are only spaces
182          token = tokenizer.nextToken().trim();
183          if ( token.length() == 0 )
184             continue;
185          // translate token to text (if not a delimite)
186          String text;
187          if ( isDelim( token ) )
188             text = token;
189          else
190             text = dict.lookUp( token.toLowerCase() );
191          output = addText( text, output );
192       }
193       return ( output );
194    }
195 } // Translator
196
197 public class TextPlain
198 {
199    public static void main(String[] args)
200       throws FileNotFoundException, IOException
201    {
202       // create the Dictionary object and
203       // load it with translation data
204       Dictionary dict = new Dictionary( 100 );
205       dict.load( "Dictionary.txt" );
206       System.out.println( dict.getSize() +
207          " entries in the dictionary." );
208       // create the Translator object
```

```
209        Translator trans = new Translator();
210        // create the input and output file objects
211        BufferedReader fileIn = new BufferedReader(
212          new FileReader( "Dialog.txt" ) );
213        PrintStream fileOut = new PrintStream(
214          "Transcript.txt" );
215
216        while ( fileIn.ready() )
217        {
218          String input = fileIn.readLine();
219          String output = trans.translate( input, dict );
220          fileOut.println( output );
221        }
222        System.out.println( "Looked up " + dict.getCountLooked() +
223          " words, found " + dict.getCountFound() );
224    }
225 }
```

It's amazing how useful this little program would be to parents… With the short dictionary below:

```
2nite: tonight
a3: anyplace, anywhere, anytime
b4: before
bb: bye bye
bbfn: bye bye for now
bc: because
bf: boyfriend
brb: be right back
btw: by the way
c: see
c/s: change of subject
fsr: for some reason
fyi: for your information
g2g: got to go
g2k: good to know
gtg: got to go
h4u: hot for you
idk: i don't know
j/k: just kidding
k: ok
kyfc: keep your fingers crossed
l8: late
lol: laugh out loud
mtf: more to follow
n: and
n2m: not too much
ne: any
nething: anything
nm: never mind
ns: not sure
ntim: not that it matters
omg: oh my god
pu: that stinks
r: are
rofl: rolling on the floor laughing
sol: sooner or later
sup: what's up
thx: thanks
ttyl: talk to you later
u: you
werd: yes
y: why
```

This program took the following parent-incomprehensible dialog:

```
Sup? R U home?
Werd. Sup?
N2M. did U C the new kid?
```

```
OMG! Yeah! Shes so cute! Y?
FSR I think she's H4U n wants to chat!
Tell her A3!
LOL. J/K. ROFL. but G2K!!
Does she have a bf?
NS, NTIM
C/S, U doing NEthing 2nite?
IDK Y?
BC I wanted to go to the mall.
BRB i'll ask my mom, KYFC.
K.

NM, I can't 2nite.
PU. I g2g tho. TTYL!
BBFN!
Bb
```

And generated the following parent-readable transcript:

```
what's up? are you home?
yes. what's up?
not too much. did you see the new kid?
oh my god! yeah! shes so cute! why?
for some reason i think she's hot for you and wants to chat!
tell her anyplace, anywhere, anytime!
laugh out loud. just kidding. rolling on the floor laughing. but good to know!!
does she have a boyfriend?
not sure, not that it matters
change of subject, you doing anything tonight?
i don't know why?
because i wanted to go to the mall.
be right back i'll ask my mom, keep your fingers crossed.
ok.

never mind, i can't tonight.
that stinks. i got to go tho. talk to you later!
bye bye for now!
bye bye
```

Note that the program does not correct bad English or wrong punctuation… May be you can improve it to do that too…

NUMERICS AND MATH

A major benefit of computers is their capability to perform calculations. To that end, there are a lot of mathematically-oriented classes and methods. We will examine a small set of those, mostly to demonstrate how to approach this type of classes.

Let us take a simple problem in Trigonometry. A triangle has six attributes: three angles and three sides. It is possible to define a triangle using only three of those, and calculate the other three using Trigonometric functions. If we take a generic triangle, it would look like this:

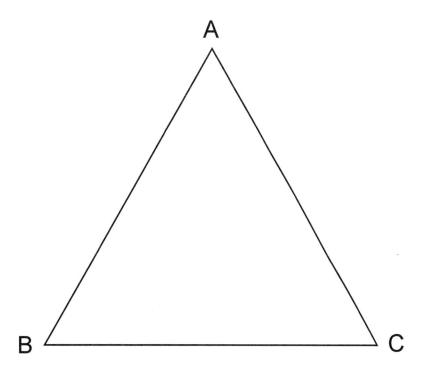

The formulae below allow us to describe any triangle using only three of its attributes.

Let's write a class to represent a triangle. Given three attributes of the triangle, it will calculate the other three and then allow us to inquire as to the values of all six.

$$(1)...\frac{\sin \angle ABC}{\overline{AC}} = \frac{\sin \angle ACB}{\overline{AB}} = \frac{\sin \angle BAC}{\overline{BC}}$$

$$(2)...\overline{AC}^2 = \overline{AB}^2 + \overline{BC}^2 - (2 \cdot \overline{AB} \cdot \overline{BC} \cdot \cos \angle ABC$$

$$(3)...\overline{AB}^2 = \overline{AC}^2 + \overline{BC}^2 - (2 \cdot \overline{AC} \cdot \overline{BC} \cdot \cos \angle ACB$$

$$(4)...\overline{BC}^2 = \overline{AB}^2 + \overline{AC}^2 - (2 \cdot \overline{AB} \cdot \overline{AC} \cdot \cos \angle BAC$$

First, some math… In order to solve this problem, we have to examine two possible sets of input:

1. We have two sides and the angle between them.
   For example, $\overline{AB}, \overline{BC}, \angle ABC$

2. We have two sides and the angle across from one of them.
   For example, $\overline{AB}, \overline{AC}, \angle ABC$

Each case require a different set of formulas to solve for the missing attributes. So here are the solutions:

1. If we have $\overline{AB}, \overline{BC}, \angle ABC$:

   1.1. Use formula (2) to calculate $\overline{AC} = \sqrt{\overline{AB}^2 + \overline{BC}^2 - 2 \cdot \overline{AB} \cdot \overline{BC} \cdot \cos \angle ABC}$

   1.2. Use formula (1) to calculate $\angle ACB = \sin^{-1}\left(\sin \angle ABC \, \dfrac{\overline{AB}}{\overline{AC}} \right)$

   1.3. Use formula (1) to calculate $\angle BAC = \sin^{-1}\left(\sin \angle ABC \, \dfrac{\overline{BC}}{\overline{AC}} \right)$

2. If we have: $\overline{AB}, \overline{AC}, \angle ABC$:

   2.1. Use formula (1) to calculate $\angle ACB = \sin^{-1}\left(\sin \angle ABC \, \dfrac{\overline{AB}}{\overline{AC}} \right)$

   2.2. Use the fact that the sum of all angles in a triangle is 180^0: $\angle BAC = 180^0 - \angle ABC - \angle ACB$

   2.3. Use formula (2) to calculate $\overline{BC} = \sqrt{\overline{AB}^2 + \overline{AC}^2 - 2 \cdot \overline{AB} \cdot \overline{AC} \cdot \cos \angle BAC}$

So now we are ready to look at the class `Triangle`. It is a quite simple class, but we are using some interesting features. It would have been nice to have two versions of the constructor to accommodate the two parameters cases we discussed, but unfortunately all the parameters we want to pass are of type `double` so we cannot create an overloaded constructor. So what we do is pass the "case" as an argument; in order to avoid the opacity of a `true`/`false`, (namely: what do these values mean) we define constant values with meaningful names on line 10. We also define constants on lines 11 and 12 for the indexes of the sides and angles in the arrays defined on lines 13 and 14. This is cleaner than having six separate variables named for the six attributes.

It is worth noting how we actually accomplish the effect of declaring a constant. Two keywords are involved: `static` and `final`. A Variable we define as `static` is not dependent on a specific object of the class, but will be part of all instances of the class. In other words, while a non-static variable can have a different value in each instance of the class (in our case, the length of the sides or the angles are such variables), a **static** variable is "shared" by all instances and belong to all of them; all instances see the same value, and if one instance changes the value all other instances see the new value. This is good for our AB, BC, AB variables – we want all instances to use the *same* values. But it is not enough – we want to ensure that no one can *change* these values. That's why we add the keyword `final`; this ensure that the value we assign to the variables is **final**; no one can change it after it was assigned. This is how we get a class-wide constant.

Lines 21-50 are the actual calculations for the two cases. The methods in lines 52-70 are the getters and display methods supporting the class. On lines 75-94 we create five triangles of different kinds.

```
01 // Example 40, file 'Triangle.java'
02 // This file defines the class 'Triangle'
03
04 import java.io.*;
05 import java.lang.Math;
06
07 public class Triangle
08 {
09     // Attributes
10     public final static boolean INSIDE = true, ACROSS = false;
11     public final static int AB = 0, AC = 1, BC = 2;
12     public final static int ABC = 0, ACB = 1, BAC = 2;
13     private double[] side = new double [ 3 ];
14     private double[] angle = new double [ 3 ];
15     // Constructors
16     public Triangle( double side1Arg,
```

```
17          double side2Arg,
18          double angleArg,
19          boolean angleLocArg )
20     {
21        if ( angleLocArg )
22        {
23           side[ AB ] = side1Arg;
24           side[ BC ] = side2Arg;
25           angle[ ABC ] = Math.toRadians( angleArg );
26           side[ AC ] = Math.sqrt(
27              Math.pow( side[ AB ], 2 ) +
28              Math.pow( side[ BC ], 2 ) -
29              2 * side[ AB ] * side[ BC ]
30              * Math.cos( angle[ ABC ] ) );
31           angle[ ACB ] = Math.asin( Math.sin( angle[ ABC ] )
32              * side[ AB ] / side[ AC ] );
33           angle[ BAC ] = Math.asin( Math.sin( angle[ ABC ] )
34              * side[ BC ] / side[ AC ] );
35        }
36        else
37        {
38           side[ AB ] = side1Arg;
39           side[ AC ] = side2Arg;
40           angle[ ABC ] = Math.toRadians( angleArg );
41           angle[ ACB ] = Math.asin( Math.sin( angle[ ABC ] )
42              * side[ AB ] / side[ AC ] );
43           angle[ BAC ] = Math.PI
44              - angle[ ABC ] - angle[ ACB ];
45           side[ BC ] = Math.sqrt(
46              Math.pow( side[ AB ], 2 ) +
47              Math.pow( side[ AC ], 2 ) -
48              2 * side[ AB ] * side[ AC ]
49              * Math.cos( angle[ BAC ] ) );
50        }
51     }
52     public double getAngle( int indexArg )
53     {
54        return( Math.toDegrees( angle[ indexArg ] ) );
55     }
56     public double getSide( int indexArg )
57     {
58        return( side[ indexArg ] );
59     }
60     public void display()
61     {
62        System.out.println(
63           "AB=" + side[ AB ] + ", " +
64           "BC=" + side[ BC ] + ", " +
65           "AC=" + side[ AC ] );
66        System.out.println(
67           "ABC=" + Math.toDegrees( angle[ ABC ] ) + ", " +
68           "ACB=" + Math.toDegrees( angle[ ACB ] ) + ", " +
69           "BAC=" + Math.toDegrees( angle[ BAC ] ) );
70     }
71
72     public static void main( String[] args )
73        throws FileNotFoundException, IOException
74     {
75        Triangle t1 =
76           new Triangle( 3.0, 4.0, 90.0, Triangle.INSIDE );
77        System.out.print( "\nt1: " );
78        t1.display();
79        Triangle t2 =
80           new Triangle( 10.0, 10.0, 60.0, Triangle.INSIDE );
81        System.out.print( "\nt2: " );
82        t2.display();
83        Triangle t3 =
84           new Triangle( 10.0, 10.0, 30.0, Triangle.INSIDE );
```

```
85        System.out.print( "\nt3: " );
86        t3.display();
87        Triangle t4 =
88           new Triangle( 3.0, 5.0, 90.0, Triangle.ACROSS );
89        System.out.print( "\nt4: " );
90        t4.display();
91        Triangle t5 =
92           new Triangle( 10.0, 10.0, 75.0, Triangle.ACROSS );
93        System.out.print( "\nt5: " );
94        t5.display();
95     }
96 }
```

This is the output from this program:

```
t1: AB=3.0, BC=4.0, AC=5.0
ABC=90.0, ACB=36.86989764584402, BAC=53.13010235415598

t2: AB=10.0, BC=10.0, AC=9.999999999999998
ABC=59.99999999999999, ACB=60.00000000000001, BAC=60.00000000000001

t3: AB=10.0, BC=10.0, AC=5.176380902050413
ABC=29.999999999999996, ACB=75.00000000000006, BAC=75.00000000000006

t4: AB=3.0, BC=3.9999999999999996, AC=5.0
ABC=90.0, ACB=36.86989764584402, BAC=53.13010235415598

t5: AB=10.0, BC=5.176380902050413, AC=10.0
ABC=75.00000000000001, ACB=75.00000000000001, BAC=29.99999999999998
```

Note that t1 is the classic 3-4-5 right triangle, t2 is an equilateral triangle and t3 is a isosceles one; they are all described by two sides and the angle between them. t4 is identical to t1 and t5 is the same as t3, but described using two sides and the angle across from one of them.

Note also the inaccuracy of the final results. This is due to the way that floating-point number are being stored internally: they not always represent exact whole integer numbers precisely.

DATE AND TIME

Date and time are very important aspects of computing, both in scientific and commercial applications. Java provides several classes to help with manipulating, acquiring and displaying dates and times.

First, some basic rules (copied from the Java API definition): In all methods that accept or return year, month, date, hours, minutes, and seconds values, the following representations are used:

- A year y is represented by the integer value y - 1900.
- A month is represented by an integer from 0 to 11; 0 is January, 1 is February, and so forth; thus 11 is December.
- A date (day of month) is represented by an integer from 1 to 31 in the usual manner.
- An hour is represented by an integer from 0 to 23. Thus, the hour from midnight to 1 a.m. is hour 0, and the hour from noon to 1 p.m. is hour 12.
- A minute is represented by an integer from 0 to 59 in the usual manner.
- A second is represented by an integer from 0 to 61; the values 60 and 61 occur only for leap seconds and even then only in Java implementations that actually track leap seconds correctly. We will not discuss here leap seconds, as they are not relevant to the understanding of the date and time handling capabilities of Java.

In all cases, arguments given to methods for these purposes need not fall within the indicated ranges; for example, a date may be specified as January 32 and is interpreted as meaning February 1.

There are three main concrete classes supporting date and time:

❑   Class `Date` – represents a specific instant in time, with millisecond precision.
❑   Class `SimpleDateFormat` – provides date and time formatting methods for both input and output.
❑   Class `GregorianCalendar` – provides date and time arithmetic methods.

These classes contain many methods, and we will not cover all of them here. We will use one example to cover the basics of all three classes. Our example revolves around the Apollo Lunar Landing missions, in particular Apollo 11 (the first ever human moon landing) and Apollo 12 (the second landing).

But first, let's see what these classes can do for us in our example.

The `Date` class is used to hold the dates we deal with. It is a very simple class, and its only useful method (in addition to its constructor, which we are not using here), is `getTime()`. This method returns the number of milliseconds since January 1, 1970, 00:00:00 GMT, also known as "The Epoch". Legend has it that this is the time the Unix operating system was invented, but it is hard to believe that this brainstorm occurred at exactly midnight on a new-year's eve…

`SimpleDateFormat` is the primary tool for conversion of dates from and to strings. Each instance of `SimpleDateFormat` has a pattern associated with it, which describes what the string looks like (on conversion from string to date – called parsing), and what the screen should look like (on conversion from date to string – called formatting). The pattern is composed of letters, indicating what component of the date is expected in the string at the position corresponding to the letters' position in the pattern. The letters and their meanings are as follow (copied from the Java API documentation):

Letter	Date or Time Component	Presentation	Examples
G	Era designator	Text	AD
Y	Year	Year	1996; 96
M	Month in year	Month	July; Jul; 07
w	Week in year	Number	27
W	Week in month	Number	2
D	Day in year	Number	189
d	Day in month	Number	10
F	Day of week in month	Number	2
E	Day in week	Text	Tuesday; Tue
a	Am/pm marker	Text	PM
H	Hour in day (0-23)	Number	0
k	Hour in day (1-24)	Number	24
K	Hour in am/pm (0-11)	Number	0
h	Hour in am/pm (1-12)	Number	12
m	Minute in hour	Number	30
s	Second in minute	Number	55
S	Millisecond	Number	978
z	Time zone	General time zone	Pacific Standard Time; PST; GMT-08:00
Z	Time zone	RFC 822 time zone	-0800

Pattern letters are usually repeated, as their number determines the exact presentation:

❑ *Text*: For formatting, if the number of pattern letters is 4 or more, the full form is used; otherwise a short or abbreviated form is used if available. For parsing, both forms are accepted, independent of the number of pattern letters.

❑ *Number*: For formatting, the number of pattern letters is the minimum number of digits, and shorter numbers are zero-padded to this amount. For parsing, the number of pattern letters is ignored unless it's needed to separate two adjacent fields.

❑ *Year*: If the formatter's Calendar is the Gregorian Calendar (which is what we use in this example), the following rules are applied:

○ For formatting, if the number of pattern letters is 2, the year is truncated to 2 digits; otherwise it is interpreted as a number.

○ For parsing, if the number of pattern letters is more than 2, the year is interpreted literally, regardless of the number of digits. So using the pattern "MM/dd/yyyy", "01/11/12" parses to Jan 11, 12 A.D.

○ For parsing with the abbreviated year pattern ("y" or "yy"), SimpleDateFormat must interpret the abbreviated year relative to some century. It does this by adjusting dates to be within 80 years before and 20 years after the time the SimpleDateFormat instance is created. For example, using a pattern of "MM/dd/yy" and a SimpleDateFormat instance created on Jan 1, 1997, the string "01/11/12" would be interpreted as Jan 11, 2012 while the string "05/04/64" would be interpreted as May 4, 1964. During parsing, only strings consisting of exactly two digits, as defined by Character.isDigit(char), will be parsed into the default century. Any other numeric string, such as a one digit string, a three or more digit string, or a two digit string that isn't all digits (for example, "-1"), is interpreted literally. So "01/02/3" or "01/02/003" are parsed, using the same pattern, as Jan 2, 3 AD. Likewise, "01/02/-3" is parsed as Jan 2, 4 BC.

❑ *Month*: If the number of pattern letters is 3 or more, the month is interpreted as text; otherwise, it is interpreted as a number.

Sounds complicated? Not really... Let's look at how we use patterns in our example. On line 112 we define the pattern "yyyy-MM-dd HH:mm:ss z". This patterns means that the date is represented as 4 digits for the year. Then a '-', then two digits for the month, another '-', two digit for the day, a space, two digits for the hour, a ':', two digits for the minutes, another ':', two digits for the seconds, another space, and finally the time-zone. Quite a mouthful... Obviously a pattern is a more concise way... Line 114 defines another pattern, but we will not try to describe it verbally.

We use two methods of the SimpleDateFormat class: parse() and format(). The first (lines 26-27) takes as arguments a date String and an object of class ParsePosition, which allows us to parse multiple dates from the same string (we will not discuss this class here); it returns an object of type Date, which represents the date we extracted from the string. The second method (line 40) formats a date into a string, and takes three arguments: the Date object to format, an object of type StringBuffer into which the formatting will be done, and an object of type FieldPosition, which allows us to put more than one formatted item into the buffer (we will not discuss the two classes here); the String can be retrieved from the buffer using the toString() method (line 41).

Lastly, the GregorianCalendar class is the main tool for date arithmetic. It allows us access to each individual component of a date (called fields), from the milliseconds to the era. Each field has a unique "name", used by prefixing it with GregorianCalendar., for example GregorianCalendar.YEAR. Lines 76-101 demonstrate how we access some of these fields in order to print them. One of its methods is getTime(), which returns a Date object representing the time held by the calendar. On lines 66 and 67 we use the getTime() methods of the returned Date objects to get an easy-to-manipulate representation of the date. Another useful method is the add() method, which is used to add value to any field in a GregorianCalendar and adjust all the other fields accordingly. On lines 200-201 we add seconds to the date in a calendar, and we get a date several month in the future.

It is time now to dive into our example. The class DateTimeCalc takes care of the operations we want to perform. Since this class has no life of its own (namely, we do not intend for it to represent any specific data, so we will never instantiate it), all the methods we define are static. The meaning of static here is similar to that of the keyword when used in the definition of a variable: non-static methods cannot be called unless the object to which they belong has been instantiated; they are referenced via the variable that points to the object's instance: on line 21 we call the method parse using dateFormatObj.parse(dateArg, parsePos), where dateFormatObj has been instantiated in line 23. Static methods, on the other hand, are accessible even if no instance of the class has been created, and are referenced via the name of the class: on line 205 we are calling calendarPrint using

`DateTimeCalc.calendarPrint( moonLanding12Calendar )` where `DateTimeCalc` is the name of the class, and no instance of this class has been created.

Lines 12-15 define a couple of "book-keeping" objects necessary for most of the methods in this class.

The method `dateParse()` (lines 19-29) will convert a string into a `Date` object based on a specified pattern. `dateFormat()` (lines 33-42) will format a Date object into a string, and `calendarFormat()` (lines 46-57) will do the same for a `GregorianCalendar` object. `secsBetween()` (lines 61-70), calculate the number of seconds between the times of two calendar objects. The last method, `calendarPrint()` (lines 74-103) prints some of the fields in a calendar object.

We start by defining two patterns, one for input and one for output (lines 110-114). We then define the first date we want to work with (lines 119-120). Following that, we parse that date `String` using the input pattern to create a `Date` object (lines 124-135) and then, using the output pattern, we display the date in a different format (lines 137-142). We continue with the creation of a `GregorianCalendar` object to hold the same date and follow by displaying its fields (lines 144-149). We do the same with the second date (lines 151-183).

Perhaps out of curiosity, we calculate and display the number of days between the two dates (lines 185-193). We use this calculation to re-calculate and print the second date (lines 195-206).

```
01  // Example 41, file 'DateTimeCalc.java'
02  // This file defines the class 'DateTimeCalc'
03
04  import java.io.*;
05  import java.util.Date;
06  import java.util.GregorianCalendar;
07  import java.util.Calendar;
08  import java.text.*;
09
10  public class DateTimeCalc
11  {
12      static public ParsePosition parsePos =
13          new ParsePosition( 0 );
14      static public FieldPosition fieldPos =
15          new FieldPosition( 0 );
16
17      // parse a date from input
18
19      static public Date dateParse(
20          String patternArg,
21          String dateArg )
22      {
23          SimpleDateFormat dateFormatObj =
24              new SimpleDateFormat( patternArg );
25          parsePos.setIndex( 0 );
26          Date dateObj =
27              dateFormatObj.parse( dateArg, parsePos );
28          return ( dateObj );
29      }
30
31      // format a date for output
32
33      static public String dateFormat(
34          String patternArg,
35          Date dateArg )
36      {
37          SimpleDateFormat dateFormatObj =
38              new SimpleDateFormat( patternArg );
39          StringBuffer dateBuff = new StringBuffer();
40          dateFormatObj.format( dateArg, dateBuff, fieldPos );
41          return ( dateBuff.toString() );
42      }
43
44      // format a calendar for output
```

```
45
46     static public String calendarFormat(
47        String patternArg,
48        GregorianCalendar calendarArg )
49     {
50        SimpleDateFormat dateFormatObj =
51           new SimpleDateFormat( patternArg );
52        StringBuffer dateBuff = new StringBuffer();
53        long timeInMillis = calendarArg.getTimeInMillis();
54        Date dateObj = new Date( timeInMillis );
55        dateFormatObj.format( dateObj, dateBuff, fieldPos );
56        return ( dateBuff.toString() );
57     }
58
59     // calculate number of seconds between two dates
60
61     static public long secsBetween(
62        GregorianCalendar cal1,
63        GregorianCalendar cal2 )
64     {
65        long milliSecs = Math.abs(
66           cal1.getTime().getTime()
67           - cal2.getTime().getTime() );
68        long secs = Math.round( milliSecs / 1000.0 + 0.5 );
69        return ( secs );
70     }
71
72     // print the contents of a calendar object
73
74     static private void calendarPrint( GregorianCalendar cal )
75     {
76        System.out.println("YEAR: " + cal.get(
77           GregorianCalendar.YEAR ));
78        System.out.println("MONTH: " + cal.get(
79           GregorianCalendar.MONTH ));
80        System.out.println("DATE: " + cal.get(
81           GregorianCalendar.DATE ));
82        System.out.println("WEEK_OF_YEAR: " + cal.get(
83           GregorianCalendar.WEEK_OF_YEAR ));
84        System.out.println("WEEK_OF_MONTH: " + cal.get(
85           GregorianCalendar.WEEK_OF_MONTH ));
86        System.out.println("DAY_OF_MONTH: " + cal.get(
87           GregorianCalendar.DAY_OF_MONTH ));
88        System.out.println("DAY_OF_YEAR: " + cal.get(
89           GregorianCalendar.DAY_OF_YEAR ));
90        System.out.println("DAY_OF_WEEK: " + cal.get(
91           GregorianCalendar.DAY_OF_WEEK ));
92        System.out.println("HOUR: " + cal.get(
93           GregorianCalendar.HOUR ));
94        System.out.println("AM_PM: " + cal.get(
95           GregorianCalendar.AM_PM ));
96        System.out.println("HOUR_OF_DAY: " + cal.get(
97           GregorianCalendar.HOUR_OF_DAY ));
98        System.out.println("MINUTE: " + cal.get(
99           GregorianCalendar.MINUTE ));
100       System.out.println("SECOND: " + cal.get(
101          GregorianCalendar.SECOND ));
102       System.out.println();
103    }
104
105    // main
106
107    public static void main( String[] args )
108       throws IOException, NullPointerException
109    {
110       // define the input and output patterns (formats)
111       String patternIn =
112          new String( "yyyy-MM-dd HH:mm:ss z" );
```

```
113      String patternOut =
114        new String( "EEEE, MMMM d, yyyy (G), h:m:s a z" );
115
116      // define the date we want to work with:
117      // Apollo 11's moon landing time
118
119      String moonLanding11Str =
120        new String( "1969-07-20 20:17:40 UTC" );
121
122      // load the date
123
124      Date moonLanding11Date =
125        DateTimeCalc.dateParse( patternIn, moonLanding11Str );
126      if ( moonLanding11Date == null )
127      {
128        System.out.println( "Invalid date '"
129          + moonLanding11Str + "' (position "
130          + parsePos.getErrorIndex() + ", character '"
131          + moonLanding11Str.charAt(
132            parsePos.getErrorIndex() )
133          + "')" );
134        return;
135      }
136
137      // display the date
138
139      String moonLanding11Out = dateFormat( patternOut,
140        moonLanding11Date );
141      System.out.println( "Apollo 11 landed on the moon on \n"
142        + moonLanding11Out + "\n" );
143
144      // create a calendar object
145
146      GregorianCalendar moonLanding11Calendar =
147        new GregorianCalendar();
148      moonLanding11Calendar.setTime( moonLanding11Date );
149      DateTimeCalc.calendarPrint( moonLanding11Calendar );
150
151      // define another date we want to work with:
152      // Apollo 12's moon landing time
153
154      String moonLanding12Str =
155        new String( "1969-11-19 06:55:35 UTC" );
156
157      // load the date
158
159      Date moonLanding12Date =
160        DateTimeCalc.dateParse( patternIn, moonLanding12Str );
161      if ( moonLanding12Date == null )
162      {
163        System.out.println( "Invalid date '"
164          + moonLanding12Str + "' (position "
165          + parsePos.getErrorIndex() + ", character '"
166          + moonLanding12Str.charAt( parsePos.getErrorIndex() )
167          + "')" );
168        return;
169      }
170
171      // display the date
172
173      String moonLanding12Out = dateFormat( patternOut,
174        moonLanding12Date );
175      System.out.println( "Apollo 12 landed on the moon on \n"
176        + moonLanding12Out + "\n" );
177
178      // create a calendar object
179
180      GregorianCalendar moonLanding12Calendar =
```

```
181              new GregorianCalendar();
182         moonLanding12Calendar.setTime( moonLanding12Date );
183         DateTimeCalc.calendarPrint( moonLanding12Calendar );
184
185         // calculate the number of days between the two landings
186
187         final double SECS_IN_DAY = 24.0 * 60.0 * 60.0;
188         int numOfSecs = (int)DateTimeCalc.secsBetween(
189             moonLanding11Calendar, moonLanding12Calendar );
190         int numOfDays =
191            (int)Math.round( numOfSecs / SECS_IN_DAY + 0.5 );
192         System.out.println("Days between missions: "
193            + numOfDays + "\n");
194
195         // re-calculate Apollo 12's landing time based on
196         // the number of seconds since Apollo 11's landing
197
198         moonLanding12Calendar =
199            (GregorianCalendar)moonLanding11Calendar.clone();
200         moonLanding12Calendar.add(
201            GregorianCalendar.SECOND, numOfSecs );
202         moonLanding12Out = DateTimeCalc.calendarFormat( patternOut,
203            moonLanding12Calendar );
204         System.out.println( "Apollo 12 landed on the moon on \n"
205            + moonLanding12Out + "\n" );
206         DateTimeCalc.calendarPrint( moonLanding12Calendar );
207     }
208 }
```

The output of this program is below:

```
Apollo 11 landed on the moon on
Sunday, July 20, 1969 (AD), 4:17:40 PM EDT

YEAR: 1969
MONTH: 6
DATE: 20
WEEK_OF_YEAR: 30
WEEK_OF_MONTH: 4
DAY_OF_MONTH: 20
DAY_OF_YEAR: 201
DAY_OF_WEEK: 1
HOUR: 4
AM_PM: 1
HOUR_OF_DAY: 16
MINUTE: 17
SECOND: 40

Apollo 12 landed on the moon on
Wednesday, November 19, 1969 (AD), 1:55:35 AM EST

YEAR: 1969
MONTH: 10
DATE: 19
WEEK_OF_YEAR: 47
WEEK_OF_MONTH: 4
DAY_OF_MONTH: 19
DAY_OF_YEAR: 323
DAY_OF_WEEK: 4
HOUR: 1
AM_PM: 0
HOUR_OF_DAY: 1
MINUTE: 55
SECOND: 35

Days between missions: 122

Apollo 12 landed on the moon on
```

```
Wednesday, November 19, 1969 (AD), 1:55:36 AM EST

YEAR: 1969
MONTH: 10
DATE: 19
WEEK_OF_YEAR: 47
WEEK_OF_MONTH: 4
DAY_OF_MONTH: 19
DAY_OF_YEAR: 323
DAY_OF_WEEK: 4
HOUR: 1
AM_PM: 0
HOUR_OF_DAY: 1
MINUTE: 55
SECOND: 36
```

Note that we somehow "gained" one second in the re-calculation of the second date… This was probably caused by a rounding error while calculating the new date after the addition of the seconds to the first one. Another thing to observe is that we specified the dates in the GMT time zone, but they were printed in the EST time zone. This is because the formatting is done in the local time zone of the computer unless forced to use another time zone.

STREAMS

Programs don't operate in a vacuum. They are expected to produce some output, and usually require some input to work with. The mechanisms used for this are files. You have encountered files in the past, as `.mp3` files for music, `.jpg` files for pictures, `.doc` files for Microsoft Word documents, and `.java` files for the source code of Java programs. (By the way, the 3- or 4-letter file extensions are only a convention, helping programs know what type of file to expect. All files are stored in the computer, whether on a hard drive or USB flash drives, the same way.) Files are the ultimate source or destination of data; lines types on the keyboard are treated as a file, and the printer is considered a file as well.

In essence, a file is a collection of bytes. In order to access them, we treat them as **streams**.

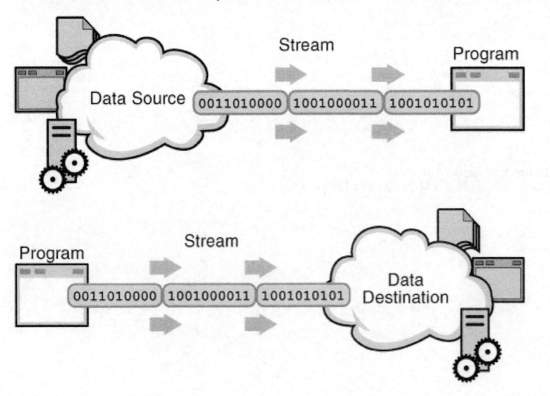

An input stream (the one at the top) is used by the program to read data from a source, and an output stream (the bottom one) is used to write data to its destination. (Graphics © Sun Microsystems.) The sources or destinations can be disk files, input/output devices (such as keyboards or printers), or even other programs.

Even though a stream is just a sequence of data, the structure of the data is of course important to the program. There are different types of streams, each one capable of different level of understanding of the data that moves through it.

The program below demonstrates one of the simples streams – character streams. There is an even more primitive type of stream, a byte stream, but it is very similar to character stream and is used less often.

The program is extremely simple. It opens two streams (lines 16-17), associating them with two disk files. It then dives into a loop (lines 20-21) where it gets characters one at a time from the input stream and puts it into the output stream. As Sherlock Holmes would say, "Elementary, my dear Watson." But let us take the opportunity to explore some interesting issues exposed by this trivial program.

First, why are we using and `int` rather than a `char`? After all, a character is just that – a character… There are two reasons. One is that it allows us to use -1 as an indication of the end of the stream (which is the end of the data in the file). The second reason is that a character can be represented by more than 8 bits in case of foreign languages (such as many Asian languages), and we need more than 8 bits.

Second notice the use of try-finally blocks. It is a good habit to enclosed input/out operations in a try-block in order to make sure we catch exceptions. The finally-block is used to ensure that we close the files, no matter if we succeeded in the copy or not. If you add a `System.out.println()` of some message in the finally-block, it will be printed no matter what! You can then experiment by changing the name of the input file, so that the `new FileReader` will fail and throw an exception.

```
01 // Example 42, file 'CopyChars.java'
02 // This file defines the class 'CopyChars'
03
04 import java.io.*;
05
06 public class CopyChars
07 {
08   public static void main( String[] args )
09    throws IOException
10    {
11      FileReader inputStream = null;
12      FileWriter outputStream = null;
13
14      try
15      {
16        inputStream = new FileReader( "Lincoln.txt" );
17        outputStream = new FileWriter( "Gettysburg.txt" );
18
19        int oneChar;
20        while ( ( oneChar = inputStream.read() ) != -1 )
21            outputStream.write( oneChar );
22      }
23      finally
24      {
25        if (inputStream != null)
26            inputStream.close();
27        if (outputStream != null)
28            outputStream.close();
29      }
30   }
31 }
```

So far, so good… But in many cases, we'd rather get the whole line rather than pick up the characters one at a time. That's what buffered streams were invented for. When using a buffered stream, we can get a whole line (not including the line's terminating characters) in one call, instead of having to get the characters one by one and watch out for those that mark the end of the line.

In the program below you can see how buffered streams are used. Note that we are using `PrintWriter` for output, because it is smarter than the `BufferedWriter` you would expect to use – it has the method `println()` which knows how to write line terminating characters. Note also that is the end of the file has been reached, the returned string will be `null`.

```java
01 // Example 43, file 'CopyLines.java'
02 // This file defines the class 'CopyLines'
03
04 import java.io.*;
05
06 public class CopyLines
07 {
08    public static void main( String[] args )
09     throws IOException
10    {
11      BufferedReader inputStream = null;
12      PrintWriter outputStream = null;
13
14      try
15      {
16        inputStream = new BufferedReader(
17           new FileReader( "Lincoln.txt" ) );
18        outputStream = new PrintWriter(
19           new FileWriter( "Gettysburg.txt" ) );
20
21        String line;
22        while ( ( line = inputStream.readLine()) != null )
23          outputStream.println( line );
24      }
25      finally
26      {
27        if (inputStream != null)
28            inputStream.close();
29        if (outputStream != null)
30            outputStream.close();
31      }
32    }
33 }
```

What is this buffering all about? A **buffer** is an area used to store data temporarily. An input buffer is used to store data, read into the computer's memory, until it is needed. When we used the `readLine()` method of a buffered input stream, a large amount of data is read from the disk into memory, and we get it line by line without having to go to the disk for each line (thus saving time by reducing the number of disk access operations); when all the buffer's contents has been delivered to the program, another chunk of data is read from the disk into the buffer. An output buffer is used in a similar way: when we call `println()`, the line is stored in the buffer; only when a buffer is full will its contents be written out to the disk, once again making fewer disk access requests. This is why it is important to close streams, particularly output streams: when we close the stream the buffer is cleared (in the case of an output stream, it is written out to the disk even if it not full); if we do not close the stream, we run the risk that the last few lines we wrote into the buffer will never make it out to the disk and will be lost.

What you learned in this chapter:

- ⋏ *Definitions of external classes can be* imported *into your program*
- ⋏ *Java already includes many* standard *classes that you can import*
- ⋏ String *standard classes provide method for manipulating strings of characters*
- ⋏ *Methods for many mathematical functions are included in the* numeric *standard classes*
- ⋏ *There are standard methods for handling calculations involving* dates *and* times
- ⋏ *The* streams *standard classes provide a wide variety of methods to perform input and output operations*

Head of the Class – Some Sample Classes

> *Armed with all that new knowledge, let's define some classes. These classes could be useful as part of a larger project, and will demonstrate the advantages of object-oriented programming.*
>
> *What you will learn in this chapter:*
> - *How to write a self-sufficient class*
> - *How to extend a class*

In this section we will try to build some general-purpose classes that may be helpful in your programming in the future. Some of them we will even use in the program examples in some of the following sections. Please note that the discussion of various programming techniques and data structures are limited and sometime over-simplified. A more thorough discussion of data structures and related algorithms can be found in a series of books which is considered the foundation of computer science: "The Art of Computer Programming" by Donald E. Knuth. Volumes 1 and 3 in particular are the authoritative text on data structures and algorithms, and you would be well advised to study these books. (It is a seven-volume series with the first volume published in 1968, but only the first three were published so far…).

LISTS, LISTS, LISTS

Lists are a very common programming data structure. It is often necessary to keep a list of object that the program is working with. The obvious choice would be to put them in an array, which is know as a **sequential allocation**: each item is placed sequentially in the array after the previous one. Graphically, the array would looks like the diagram on the left below.

Item 1
Item 2
Item 3
…
…
Item n
Spare
…
…
Spare

I can get to each element directly, using the array index operation ([]).Quite convenient, but with some challenges… For example, unless the number of elements is known in advance, I wouldn't know how many elements to allocate for the array and would need to guess. And if I need to add an item between items 2 and 3 (which might happen if the items are names and I want them sorted in alphabetical order), I'll have to move all the items from item 3 to item n to free up the slot for the new item, as you can see in the diagram on the right. The same difficulty applies if I want to remove an element – all the those beyond it have to squeeze back to fill its space.

An alternative which solves these issues (although perhaps not the in the best way) is called a **linked list**. In a list, each element points to the *next* element. So a list would look like this:

Item 1
Item 2
New Item
Item 3
…
…
Item n
Spare
…
Spare

To get from one element to the next, I follow the links, called **pointers**. The last element in the list has a special pointer that says "Stop!". Each time I need a new element, I can create a new object; no longer do I have to pre-allocate the number of object I guess I will need. In addition, If I need to **insert** an element between two others, I just change the links.

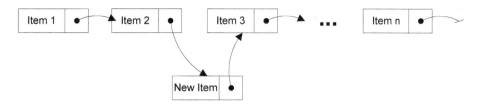

Similarly, to delete an element, changing the pointers is all that is required.

There are two weaknesses to this allocation mode: first, in order to get to a specific element, I have to walk the list from the beginning; I cannot get to any element directly by its ordinal number in the list. Second, I can only walk forward; if I am at element 14 and want to get back to element 10, I must start from element 1 again – no walking back.

It is usually advisable to keep two more pieces of information about a list: its **head** and its **tail**, which are also called **sentinel** elements. So the complete picture for a list would look like this:

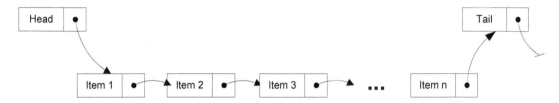

In order to overcome the problem of "forward only" walks, the doubly-linked list was invented. The improvement is in the form of another pointer in each list element, a pointer to the previous element:

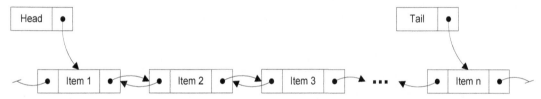

Just like with a singly-linked list, I can walk from one element to the next. But I can also go backwards, from one element to the previous one. Insertion and deletion work the same way, with one difference: two pointers need to be updated instead of just one.

The example below defines and implements classes for items and lists. These classes can be used in other programs, and as a matter of fact *will* be used in later examples. We define an `Item` class and a `List` class, both abstract – they cannot be instantiated as defined, and can be used only as base classes. Then we define derived classes `Person` and `Club`, derived from `Item` and `List` respectively. The derived classes have additional attributes that their base classes do not, but each shares the list-management attributes of its base class.

The abstract classes define two particularly interesting methods: `toString()` and `print()`. `toString()` is used automatically whenever an object appears in a context that requires a string representation, such as in string concatenation operation ('+'); it returns a string that provides the string representation for the object. We can see its use in the `print()` method, which just uses `this` to designate the object for a `println()` call. Note that the `toString()` method of the `List` class is referring to the list items directly in a concatenation operation when it needs their string representation to build the string representation of the list.

Another interesting method is the `dump()` method of the `List` class. Its purpose was to aid in the debugging of the class operations, but it was left as part of the class to help you see what the list actually looks like.

We also define an exception class, `ListException`, which allows us to report problematic activities.

We will not review this example line-by-line. By now, you should be able to understand all that the we are doing without that. Pay attention to the algorithms in the methods that manipulate the list: addAtBegin(), addAtEnd(), addBefore() and addAfter(). You may find it interesting to modify main() to experiment with various sequence of calls to the List class methods, adding calls to dump() to observe how lists grow and shrink as well as to try out triggering exceptions.

```
01  // Example 45, file 'Lists.java'
02  // This file defines the class 'Lists'
03
04  import java.io.*;
05
06  // class ListException - List exception
07
08  class ListException extends Exception
09  {
10    public ListException( Item itemArg, String messageArg )
11    {
12      super( messageArg + ": " + itemArg.toString() );
13    }
14  }
15
16  // class Item - an abstract class
17  // representing an item on a list
18
19  abstract class Item
20  {
21    private Item prev;
22    private Item next;
23
24    // constructor
25    public Item()
26    {
27      prev = null;
28      next = null;
29    }
30
31    // getters
32    public Item getPrev()
33    {
34      return ( prev );
35    }
36    public Item getNext()
37    {
38      return ( next );
39    }
40
41    // setters
42    public void setPrev( Item itemArg )
43    {
44      prev = itemArg;
45    }
46    public void setNext( Item itemArg )
47    {
48      next = itemArg;
49    }
50    public void setPrevNull()
51    {
52      prev = null;
53    }
54    public void setNextNull()
55    {
56      next = null;
57    }
58
59    // print the contents of the item
60    public void print()
```

```
61     {
62        System.out.println( this );
63     }
64
65     // convert this item to string
66     public abstract String toString();
67  } // Item
68
69  // class List - an abstract representing a
70  // list of items
71
72  abstract class List
73  {
74     private Item head;
75     private Item tail;
76
77     // constructor
78     public List( Item headArg, Item tailArg )
79     {
80        head = headArg;
81        tail = tailArg;
82        head.setNext( tail );
83        head.setPrevNull();
84        tail.setPrev( head );
85        tail.setNextNull();
86     }
87
88     // getters
89     public Item getHead()
90     {
91        return ( head );
92     }
93     public Item getTail()
94     {
95        return ( tail );
96     }
97
98     // add an item to the beginningn of the list
99     public void addAtBegin( Item itemArg )
100       throws ListException
101    {
102       addAfter( itemArg, head );
103    }
104
105    // add an item to the end of the list
106    public void addAtEnd( Item itemArg )
107       throws ListException
108    {
109       addBefore( itemArg, tail );
110    }
111
112    // add an item to the list after
113    // another item passed as argument
114    public void addAfter( Item newItemArg, Item oldItemArg )
115       throws ListException
116    {
117       if ( newItemArg.getPrev() != null  ||
118         newItemArg.getNext() != null )
119         throw new ListException( newItemArg, "Item is not free" );
120       if ( oldItemArg.getPrev() == null  &&
121         oldItemArg.getNext() == null )
122         throw new ListException( oldItemArg,
123           "Item is not in list" );
124       newItemArg.setPrev( oldItemArg );
125       if ( oldItemArg.getNext() == null )
126       {
127          newItemArg.setNextNull();
128       }
```

```
129      else
130      {
131        newItemArg.setNext( oldItemArg.getNext() );
132        oldItemArg.getNext().setPrev( newItemArg );
133      }
134      oldItemArg.setNext( newItemArg );
135    }
136
137    // add an item to the list before
138    // another item passed as argument
139    public void addBefore( Item newItemArg, Item oldItemArg )
140      throws ListException
141    {
142      if ( newItemArg.getPrev() != null  ||
143        newItemArg.getNext() != null )
144        throw new ListException( newItemArg, "Item is not free" );
145      if ( oldItemArg.getPrev() == null  &&
146        oldItemArg.getNext() == null )
147        throw new ListException( oldItemArg,
148          "Item is not in list" );
149      newItemArg.setNext( oldItemArg );
150      if ( oldItemArg.getPrev() == null )
151      {
152        newItemArg.setPrevNull();
153      }
154      else
155      {
156        newItemArg.setPrev( oldItemArg.getPrev() );
157        oldItemArg.getPrev().setNext( newItemArg );
158      }
159      oldItemArg.setPrev( newItemArg );
160    }
161
162    // delete an item
163    public void del( Item itemArg )
164    {
165      if ( itemArg.getNext() == null )
166        itemArg.getPrev().setNextNull();
167      else
168        itemArg.getPrev().setNext( itemArg.getNext() );
169      if ( itemArg.getPrev() == null )
170        itemArg.getNext().setPrevNull();
171      else
172        itemArg.getNext().setPrev( itemArg.getPrev() );
173    }
174
175    // print the contents of this list
176    public void print()
177    {
178      System.out.println( this );
179    }
180
181    // convert this list to a string
182    public String toString()
183    {
184      String thisString = "";
185      Item item = head.getNext();
186      if ( item == null )
187        return( "<None>" );
188      while ( item != tail )
189      {
190        if ( thisString.length() > 0 )
191          thisString += " / ";
192        //thisString += item.toString();
193        thisString += item;
194        item = item.getNext();
195      }
196      return ( thisString );
```

```
197      }
198
199      // dump the contents of this list
200      public void dump()
201      {
202        Item item = head.getNext();
203        if ( item == null )
204        {
205          System.out.println( "<None>" );
206          return;
207        }
208        while ( item != tail )
209        {
210          System.out.println(
211            "[ " +
212            item.getPrev().toString() + " : " +
213            item.toString() + " : " +
214            item.getNext().toString() +
215            " ]" );
216          item = item.getNext();
217        }
218      }
219    } // List
220
221    // class Person - represents a Person
222
223    class Person extends Item
224    {
225      private String nameLast, nameFirst;
226
227      // constructor
228      public Person( String nameLastArg, String nameFirstArg )
229      {
230        super();
231        nameLast = nameLastArg;
232        nameFirst = nameFirstArg;
233      }
234
235      // getters
236      public String getNameLast()
237      {
238        return ( nameLast );
239      }
240      public String getNameFirst()
241      {
242        return ( nameFirst );
243      }
244
245      // convert the contents of this item to string
246      public String toString()
247      {
248        if ( nameLast.length() == 0  &&  nameFirst.length() == 0 )
249          return ( "<None>" );
250        else
251          return ( nameLast + ", " + nameFirst );
252      }
253    } // Person
254
255    // class Club - represents a group of Persons
256
257    class Club extends List
258    {
259      private String name;
260
261      // constructor
262      public Club( String nameArg )
263      {
264        super( new Person( "", "" ), new Person( "", "" ) );
```

```
265        name = nameArg;
266    }
267
268    // getters
269    public String getName()
270    {
271       return ( name );
272    }
273
274    // convert the contents of this list to string
275    public String toString()
276    {
277       return( name + ": " + super.toString() );
278    }
279 } // Club
280
281 public class Lists
282 {
283    public static void main( String[] args )
284       throws IOException, ListException
285    {
286        Person al = new Person( "Lincoln", "Abraham" );
287        Person gw = new Person( "Washington", "George" );
288        Person rr = new Person( "Reagan", "Ronald" );
289        Person fr = new Person( "Roosevelt", "Franklin" );
290        Person ug = new Person( "Grant", "Ulysses" );
291        Club presidents = new Club( "Presidents" );
292
293        presidents.addAtEnd( al );
294
295        try
296        {
297          presidents.addAfter( rr, gw );
298        }
299        catch ( ListException ex )
300        {
301          System.out.println( "ListException: " +
302            ex.getMessage() );
303        }
304
305        presidents.addAtBegin( gw );
306        presidents.addAtEnd( ug );
307
308        try
309        {
310          presidents.addAtBegin( al );
311        }
312        catch ( ListException ex )
313        {
314          System.out.println( "ListException: " +
315            ex.getMessage() );
316        }
317
318        presidents.addAfter( rr, gw );
319        presidents.addBefore( fr, al );
320        presidents.del( ug );
321
322        presidents.dump();
323
324        System.out.println( presidents );
325    }
326 } // Lists
```

The results of this program are these:

```
ListException: Item is not in list: Washington, George
ListException: Item is not free: Lincoln, Abraham
[ <None> : Washington, George : Reagan, Ronald ]
```

```
[ Washington, George : Reagan, Ronald : Roosevelt, Franklin ]
[ Reagan, Ronald : Roosevelt, Franklin : Lincoln, Abraham ]
[ Roosevelt, Franklin : Lincoln, Abraham : <None> ]
Presidents: Washington, George / Reagan, Ronald / Roosevelt, Franklin / Lincoln,
Abraham
```

SUGGESTIOS, PLEASE

One of the common problems we run into in computer applications is the need for dictionaries. A dictionary in its most basic form is a list of words that can be quickly accessed; sometimes it is also required that new words can be added quickly, but most often the contents of a dictionary is relatively static. A good example for the use of a dictionary is the implementation of the Google "query suggestions" in the search box: when you start typing a word you want to search for, Google will display a drop-down list of suggestions, which are the most common search terms used in the past beginning with the letters you already typed. Although the implementation of the Google suggestion is tremendously more complex than can be covered in a book like this one, we will make an attempt to build a simple mechanism for "look ahead" – namely, when someone types a few characters of a word, we will look in a dictionary and display a few words that start with the characters already typed.

The best data structure for this application is called a **trie** (it is pronounced "try", even though some pronounce it "tree"). A trie is composed of nodes, each one pointing to other nodes. At each level, there can be up to 26 nodes, one for each letter of the alphabet. You walk down the tree and "pick up" the letters as you go to construct a word. For example, the trie below represents the words "in", "inn", "tea", "ted", "ten" and 'to' (we ignore single-letter words, and it is possible that some words don't really exist, such as "te"; we also assume all words are in lower case). At the top level we usually have a single empty node, called the **root**. In the case of this trie, at the second level we have only two options: the letters "i" and "t".

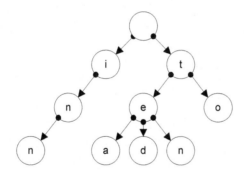

A non-graphic representation (which may be more useful for programming purposes) will look like this:

```
!
.i
..N
...N
.t
..e
...A
...D
...N
..O
```

This representation marks the last letter of a valid work by changing it to upper-case, Note the "e" remains in lower-case, because the word "te" does not exist. (It is the symbol for the element Tellurium, but it's not a real word).

As a string, this would look like this: !|.i|..N|...N|.t|..e|...A|...D|...N|..O|
(where | marks a new line).

A possible implementation of a trie is to have a each level an array of 26 pointers, each one pointing to all the sub-tries at the lower level. If there is no trie for a particular letter, the corresponding pointer will be empty. Graphically, it

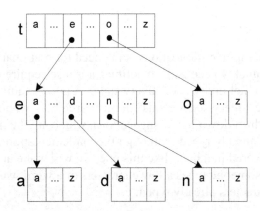

will look as below:

This graph shows only a part of the trie, starting with the "t" node. The "e" and "o" entries point to other nodes. The node for the "o" entry has no nodes to point to, but the one for the "e" entry has three pointers: to "a", "d", and "n". (Please note that this is *not* the most efficient implementation; it was chosen because it demonstrates the concept of a trie implementation in a straightforward way.) In order to handle the case of a word that is included within another word, such as "in" being part of "inn".), we put a special mark in each entry for a letter that can be the last on in a word. So the entry for "o" will be marked, as will be the entries for "a", "d", and "n".

So here's the program:

```
01  // Example 46, file 'AutoComplete.java'
02  // This file defines the class 'AutoComplete'
03
04  import java.io.*;
05
06  // class Trie - a Trie node
07
08  class Trie
09  {
10     public final static int MAX_LETTRS = 26;
11     public final static char CHAR_FILLER = '.';
12     public final static char CHAR_NEWLINE = '|';
13     public final static char CHAR_ROOT = '!';
14     private Trie[] nodes;
15     private String word;
16     private char letter;
17     private int count;
18     private int wordIndex;
19     private int wordIndexMax;
20     private boolean terminator;
21
22     // constructor
23     public Trie()
24     {
25        this( CHAR_ROOT, "" );
26     } // Trie
27     public Trie( char letterArg, String wordArg )
28     {
29        nodes = new Trie[ MAX_LETTRS ];
30        terminator = false;
31        count = 0;
32        letter = letterArg;
33        if ( letterArg != CHAR_ROOT )
34          word = wordArg + letterArg;
```

```
35       else
36         word = wordArg;
37     } // Trie
38
39     // setters
40     void setTerminator( boolean terminatorArg )
41     {
42       terminator = terminatorArg;
43     } // setTerminator
44
45     // add a string
46     public void add( String strArg )
47     {
48       char letterNext =
49         Character.toLowerCase( strArg.charAt( 0 ) );
50       int charIndex = letterNext - 'a';
51       if ( nodes[ charIndex ] == null )
52       {
53         nodes[ charIndex ] = new Trie( letterNext, word );
54         count++;
55       }
56       if ( strArg.length() > 1 )
57       {
58         nodes[ charIndex ].add( strArg.substring( 1 ) );
59       }
60       if ( strArg.length() == 1 )
61       {
62         nodes[ charIndex ].setTerminator( true );
63       }
64     } // add
65
66     // convert a Trie to a String
67     public String toString()
68     {
69       return ( flatten( 0 ) );
70     } // toString
71
72     // flatten a Trie node
73     private String flatten( int levelArg )
74     {
75       String str = "";
76       for ( int charIndex = 0;
77         charIndex < MAX_LETTRS;
78         charIndex ++ )
79       {
80         if ( nodes[ charIndex ] != null )
81         {
82           str += nodes[ charIndex ].flatten( levelArg + 1 );
83         }
84       }
85       String filler = "";
86       for ( int count = 0; count < levelArg; count++ )
87         filler += CHAR_FILLER;
88       return ( filler + CHAR_NEWLINE + str );
89     } // flatten
90
91     // get a list of all words
92     public int getWords( String[] wordsArg )
93     {
94       wordIndexMax = wordsArg.length;
95       wordIndex = 0;
96       return ( doGetWords( wordsArg, this ) );
97     } // getWords
98
99     // perform 'get a list of all words'
100    private int doGetWords( String[] wordsArg , Trie nodeArg )
101    {
102      for ( int charIndex = 0;
```

```
103        charIndex < MAX_LETTRS;
104        charIndex ++ )
105      {
106        Trie nodeCur = nodeArg.nodes[ charIndex ];
107        if ( nodeCur != null  &&
108           wordIndex < wordIndexMax )
109        {
110          if ( nodeCur.terminator )
111          {
112              wordsArg[ wordIndex ] = nodeCur.word;
113              wordIndex++;
114          }
115          if ( nodeCur.count > 0 )
116            doGetWords( wordsArg, nodeCur );
117        }
118      }
119      return ( wordIndex );
120    } // doGetWords
121
122    // get a list of words starting with a string
123    public int getWordsStartWith(
124      String[] wordsArg, String startWithArg )
125    {
126      wordIndexMax = wordsArg.length;
127      wordIndex = 0;
128      if ( startWithArg.length() > 0 )
129        return ( doGetWordsStartWith(
130          wordsArg, this, startWithArg ) );
131      else
132        return ( doGetWords( wordsArg, this ) );
133    } // getWords
134
135    // perform 'get a list of words starting with a string'
136    private int doGetWordsStartWith(
137      String[] wordsArg , Trie nodeArg, String startWithArg )
138    {
139      int charIndex = startWithArg.charAt( 0 ) - 'a';
140      Trie nodeCur = nodeArg.nodes[ charIndex ];
141      if ( nodeCur != null  &&
142         wordIndex < wordIndexMax )
143      {
144        if ( nodeCur.terminator   &&  startWithArg.length() <= 1 )
145        {
146            wordsArg[ wordIndex ] = nodeCur.word;
147            wordIndex++;
148        }
149        if ( nodeCur.count > 0  )
150        {
151          if ( startWithArg.length() > 1 )
152            doGetWordsStartWith(
153              wordsArg, nodeCur, startWithArg.substring( 1 ) );
154          else
155            doGetWords( wordsArg, nodeCur );
156        }
157      }
158      return ( wordIndex );
159    } // doGetWordsStartWith
160
161    // print a list of  words in the Trie
162    public void print( int wordCountArg, String startWithArg )
163    {
164      String[] words = new String[ wordCountArg ];
165      int numWords = getWordsStartWith( words, startWithArg );
166      for ( int wordIndex = 0;
167        wordIndex < words.length;
168        wordIndex++ )
169      {
170        if ( words[ wordIndex ] != null )
```

```
171              System.out.println( words[ wordIndex ] );
172        }
173    } // print
174 } // class Trie
175
176 public class AutoComplete
177 {
178    public static void main( String[] args )
179     throws IOException
180    {
181       // read in the dictionary
182
183       BufferedReader inputStream = new BufferedReader(
184          new FileReader( "words.txt" ) );
185       Trie trie = new Trie();
186       int wordCount = 0;
187       while ( inputStream.ready() )
188       {
189          String word = inputStream.readLine().toLowerCase();
190          wordCount++;
191          if ( word.length() == 1
192             ||  word.charAt( 0 ) == '#' )
193             continue;
194          trie.add( word.trim() );
195       }
196
197       // offer completion options
198
199       BufferedReader inputReader = new BufferedReader(
200          new InputStreamReader(System.in));
201       String line;
202
203       while ( true )
204       {
205          System.out.print(
206           "Enter the first few letters of a word: " );
207          line = inputReader.readLine();
208          if ( line.length() == 0 )
209             break;
210          trie.print( 1100, line.trim() );
211       }
212    } // main
213 } // class AutoComplete
```

The main ingredient is the class Trie, whose definition begins on line 8. The first few lines define some constants, and then a few private attributes. The nodes attribute is where the pointers to subordinate trie nodes will be stored. The constructor allocates these subordinate nodes (on line 29). The terminator attribute is used to indicate that this node is the last in a valid word. There could be other words that start with the same letters, so the count attributes tells us how many subordinate nodes actually exist (are not empty). We also keep the sequence of letters that this node is at the end of, in the word attribute (this could be a full word or only a part of a word).

Let's review some of the methods in this class.

add() (lines 45–64) is a recursive method that adds a string to the trie. It works by adding to the current node (which at the beginning is the top level node) a node for the first letter of the string, and then calling itself with the new node and the rest of the string. The second-level call doesn't know it's not the first one, and performs the same actions – adds a node for the first letter of the string it got (which is actually the second letter of the string), and calling itself again. At each level, if a node already exists for the letter, a new one is *not* created, but used in the call to the next level down.

toString() (lines 66–70) is a standard method recommended for any object that one may wish to print. It is using the private method flatten() to accomplish this, because flatten() is also a recursive method and needs an argument to start with, and toString() cannot have any arguments.

`flatten()` (lines 72–89) returns a string representation of the trie, convenient for debugging but not useful otherwise. It uses the same methodology of `add()`, by calling itself recursively and passing the level at which it has to word (level 0 is the top). At each level, it concatenates to the result string the flattened string of the lower levels (line 82). For each level, it calculate the number of "filler" characters to add to create the "indentation" necessary to reflect the hierarchy as we showed above (lines 85–87), and then adds the letter at that level (line 88).

The two pairs `getWords()` / `doGetWords()` (lines 91–120) and `getWordsStartWith()` / `doGetWordsStartWith()` (lines 122–159) are used to get lists of words from the trie. The first pair gets all the words, while the second pair gets only words that start with the specified string. They come in pairs for the same reason that `toString()` needs `flatten()`: the do…() methods are recursive and need to be called with top-level parameters. Both are relatively simple: they assemble a word by going down the trie, and every time they have a full word they add it to the array (lines 112 and 146). They both avoid going below the bottom of the trie by checking the `count` attribute (lines 115 and 149) to ensure there are more nodes below the current one.

`print()` (lines 161–173) is the "workhorse" method: it gets and displays a list of suggestions for completion of a word whose first few letters are passed as a parameter.

`main()` ties it all together. It first reads in a list of words for our "dictionary" (lines 181–195). The file in the example, `words.txt`, contains 1000 words that were found (unscientifically…) to be the most popular on the internet. The method then enters into a dialog with the user, asking for a "hint" and providing auto-complete options (lines 197–211). A simple example of a dialog is this:

```
Enter the first few letters of a word: he
he
head
health
heart
help
her
here
Enter the first few letters of a word: incl
include
includes
including
Enter the first few letters of a word: goo
good
google
```

What you learned in this chapter:

⋏ *Data structures are an important part of your programming arsenal*

⋏ *Well-behaved classes should include all the expected methods, including constructors, getter and setters, presentation and exception handling*

Objectively Speaking – Your First Object-Oriented Programs

> *And now, it's time to write complete object-oriented programs. We will take you through the steps of building programs with several classes that work with each other, and you will be able to finally see how all the pieces of the puzzle come together.*
>
> *What you will learn in this chapter:*
> - *How to design an object-oriented program*
> - *How to assemble a program out of several classes*

NEEDLES IN HAYSTACKS

Find a needle in a haystack – a colloquial expression meaning an almost impossible job. But isn't that what Google or Bing are doing? The needle is any word you want to find; the haystack is the internet. And the search engines find it. The technologies used by these search engines are very complex, and parts of them are trade secrets. But it may be interesting to create a "starter" search engine as an example of a real application. We call our application DocLook.

Instead of "crawling" all over the internet to find documents, we feed our application a set of document we selected for this example. Any text file can be used as a source, and you are encouraged to find other documents and experiment with them.

The application reads the documents and indexes them: it notes the location of each word (the document, line number and position in the line), and saves it in a searchable structure. Our structure is very primitive and extremely inefficient – we store them in a list, sorted alphabetically. That means the on the average we have to look through half the list in order to find a word, which is denoted mathematically as $O(n)$, which mean it's on the order of n (directly proportional to n) where n is the number of items in the list. There are several better methods to accomplish, cutting it down to at least $O(\log n)$, but we did not want to make the example too complex. (One of this methods is called "a balanced binary tree" – you should look it up!)

The application uses several classes of objects:

1. Documents (`Document`) – Our "library": the texts which we are indexing, storing and searching in. A `Document` object has a list of all the lines that belong to it. The object's constructor reads the document and adds the words in it to the word list of the library.

2. Lines (`Line`) – the individual lines of the documents. A group of lines makes up a document.

3. Words (`Word`) – the individual words in the library. Each `Word` object has a list of all the locations where it appears in the various documents.

4. Location (`Location`) – a specific place where a word appears. It is a triplet, containing the document, line and position in the line.

5. Location List (`LocList`) – a list of locations. Each `Word` object has a `LocList` object.

6. Line List (`LineList`) – a list of lines. Each `Document` object has a `LineList` object.

7. Word List (`WordList`) – a list of all the words in the library. A word can appear only once in the list. The list is sorted alphabetically.

8. Document List (`DocList`) – a list of all the documents in our "library".

The main class, DocLook, is the one which "glues" everything together. It is quite simple. It first goes through all the text files it can find, constructing Document objects for them and adding each to the library's DocList. This also creates the WordList of the library. It then goes into "interactive" mode, asking the user for a word and returning the list of locations where it can be found in the library.

For the various lists, we borrowed code we wrote for a previous example, and just modified it a little to fit our needs. In order to reduce clutter in the program, we kept it in a separate file and imported it, just like other standard Java import files. When you look at the actual files in the examples folder, you will find a peculiar folder hierarchy. This hierarchy is required by Java in order to support the package structure. To use the application, just run the 'look.cmd' file in the top folder.

At this time, you should be able to understand a program without detail notes. So here it is, starting with the list management package, and followed by the document management package.

```
01  // Example 47, file 'Lists.java'
02  // This file defines the list management classes
03
04  package doclook.lists;
05
06  public class Lists
07  {
08    // class ListException - List exception
09
10    public static class ListException extends Exception
11    {
12      public ListException( Item itemArg, String messageArg )
13      {
14        super( messageArg + ": " + itemArg.toString() );
15      }
16    }
17
18    // class Item - an abstract class
19    // representing an item on a list
20
21    public static abstract class Item
22    {
23      private Item prev;
24      private Item next;
25
26      // constructor
27      public Item()
28      {
29        prev = null;
30        next = null;
31      }
32
33      // getters
34      public Item getPrev()
35      {
36        return ( prev );
37      }
38      public Item getNext()
39      {
40        return ( next );
41      }
42
43      // setters
44      public void setPrev( Item itemArg )
45      {
46        prev = itemArg;
47      }
48      public void setNext( Item itemArg )
49      {
50        next = itemArg;
51      }
```

```
52         public void setPrevNull()
53         {
54            prev = null;
55         }
56         public void setNextNull()
57         {
58            next = null;
59         }
60
61         // print the contents of the item
62         public void print()
63         {
64            System.out.println( this );
65         }
66
67         // convert this item to string
68         public abstract String toString();
69      } // Item
70
71      // class List - an abstract class representing a
72      // list of items
73
74      public static abstract class List
75      {
76         private Item head;
77         private Item tail;
78
79         // constructor
80         public List( Item headArg, Item tailArg )
81         {
82            head = headArg;
83            tail = tailArg;
84            head.setNext( tail );
85            head.setPrevNull();
86            tail.setPrev( head );
87            tail.setNextNull();
88         }
89
90         // getters
91         public Item getHead()
92         {
93            return ( head );
94         }
95         public Item getTail()
96         {
97            return ( tail );
98         }
99
100        // add an item to the beginning of the list
101        public void addAtBegin( Item itemArg )
102           throws ListException
103        {
104           addAfter( itemArg, head );
105        }
106
107        // add an item to the end of the list
108        public void addAtEnd( Item itemArg )
109           throws ListException
110        {
111           addBefore( itemArg, tail );
112        }
113
114        // add an item to the list after
115        // another item passed as argument
116        public void addAfter( Item newItemArg, Item oldItemArg )
117           throws ListException
118        {
119           if ( newItemArg.getPrev() != null  ||
```

```
120            newItemArg.getNext() != null )
121            throw new ListException( newItemArg,
122              "Item is not free" );
123        if ( oldItemArg.getPrev() == null  &&
124          oldItemArg.getNext() == null )
125          throw new ListException( oldItemArg,
126            "Item is not in list" );
127        newItemArg.setPrev( oldItemArg );
128        if ( oldItemArg.getNext() == null )
129        {
130          newItemArg.setNextNull();
131        }
132        else
133        {
134          newItemArg.setNext( oldItemArg.getNext() );
135          oldItemArg.getNext().setPrev( newItemArg );
136        }
137        oldItemArg.setNext( newItemArg );
138      }
139
140      // add an item to the list before
141      // another item passed as argument
142      public void addBefore( Item newItemArg, Item oldItemArg )
143        throws ListException
144      {
145        if ( newItemArg.getPrev() != null  ||
146          newItemArg.getNext() != null )
147          throw new ListException( newItemArg,
148              "Item is not free" );
149        if ( oldItemArg.getPrev() == null  &&
150          oldItemArg.getNext() == null )
151          throw new ListException( oldItemArg,
152            "Item is not in list" );
153        newItemArg.setNext( oldItemArg );
154        if ( oldItemArg.getPrev() == null )
155        {
156          newItemArg.setPrevNull();
157        }
158        else
159        {
160          newItemArg.setPrev( oldItemArg.getPrev() );
161          oldItemArg.getPrev().setNext( newItemArg );
162        }
163        oldItemArg.setPrev( newItemArg );
164      }
165
166      // delete an item
167      public void del( Item itemArg )
168      {
169        if ( itemArg.getNext() == null )
170          itemArg.getPrev().setNextNull();
171        else
172          itemArg.getPrev().setNext( itemArg.getNext() );
173        if ( itemArg.getPrev() == null )
174          itemArg.getNext().setPrevNull();
175        else
176          itemArg.getNext().setPrev( itemArg.getPrev() );
177        itemArg.setNext( null );
178        itemArg.setPrev( null );
179      }
180
181      // print the contents of this list
182      public void print()
183      {
184        System.out.println( this );
185      }
186
187      // convert this list to a string
```

```
188      public String toString()
189      {
190        String thisString = "";
191        Item item = head.getNext();
192        if ( item == null )
193          return( "<None>" );
194        while ( item != tail )
195        {
196          if ( thisString.length() > 0 )
197            thisString += "\n";
198          thisString += item;
199          item = item.getNext();
200        }
201        return ( thisString );
202      }
203
204      // dump the contents of this list
205      public void dump()
206      {
207        Item item = head.getNext();
208        if ( item == null )
209        {
210          System.out.println( "<None>" );
211          return;
212        }
213        while ( item != tail )
214        {
215          System.out.println(
216            "[ " +
217            item.getPrev().toString() + " : " +
218            item.toString() + " : " +
219            item.getNext().toString() +
220            " ]" );
221          item = item.getNext();
222        }
223      }
224    } // List
225
226 } // Lists


01 // Example 47, file 'DocLook.java'
02 // This file defines the class 'DocLook'
03
04 package doclook.doclook;
05
06 import java.io.*;
07 import doclook.lists.Lists;
08
09 // class Word - represents a word in documents' collection
10
11 class Word extends Lists.Item
12 {
13   // attributes
14   private String word;
15   private LocList locList;
16
17   // constructors
18   // construct a null word
19   public Word()
20   {
21     super();
22     word = null;
23     locList = null;
24   }
25   // construct a word
26   public Word( String wordArg )
27   {
```

```
28        super();
29        word = wordArg;
30        locList = new LocList();
31        if ( wordArg.compareTo( "seven" ) == 0 )
32          System.out.println( wordArg );
33      }
34
35      // getters
36      public String getWord()
37      {
38        return ( word );
39      }
40      public LocList getLocList()
41      {
42        return ( locList );
43      }
44
45      // convert the contents of this item to string
46      public String toString()
47      {
48        return( "'" + word + "':" + locList );
49      }
50    } // Word
51
52    // class Location - represents a
53    // location within the documents' collection
54
55    class Location extends Lists.Item
56    {
57      private Document doc;
58      private int line;
59      private int pos;
60
61      // constructors
62      // construct a null location
63      public Location()
64      {
65        super();
66        doc = null;
67        line = 0;
68        pos = 0;
69      }
70      // construct an item for (doc,line, position)
71      public Location(
72        Document docArg, int lineArg, int posArg )
73      {
74        super();
75        doc = docArg;
76        line = lineArg;
77        pos = posArg;
78      }
79
80      // getters
81      public Document getDoc()
82      {
83        return ( doc );
84      }
85      public int getLine()
86      {
87        return ( line );
88      }
89      public int getPos()
90      {
91        return ( pos );
92      }
93
94      // convert the contents of this item to string
95      public String toString()
```

```
 96      {
 97          return( "(" + doc + "," + line + "," + pos + ")" );
 98      }
 99  } // Location
100
101  // class Line - represents a line in a document
102
103  class Line extends Lists.Item
104  {
105      private int line;
106      private String text;
107
108      // constructors
109      // construct a null line
110      public Line()
111      {
112          super();
113          line = 0;
114          text = null;
115      }
116      // construct a line item for (line,text)
117      public Line( int lineArg, String textArg )
118      {
119          super();
120          line = lineArg;
121          text = textArg;
122      }
123
124      // getters
125      public String getText()
126      {
127          return ( text );
128      }
129      public int getLine()
130      {
131          return ( line );
132      }
133
134      // convert the contents of this item to string
135      public String toString()
136      {
137          return( line + ":'" + text + "'" );
138      }
139  } // Line
140
141  // class Document - represents a document
142  // within the documents' collection
143
144  class Document extends Lists.Item
145  {
146      // attributes
147      private String fileName;
148      private LineList lineList;
149
150      // constructors
151      // construct a null document
152      public Document()
153      {
154          super();
155          fileName = "";
156          lineList = null;
157      }
158      // construct a document item for (file, wordlist)
159      public Document( String fileNameArg, WordList wordListArg )
160          throws IOException, Lists.ListException
161      {
162          super();
163
```

```
164        BufferedReader inputStream = null;
165
166        fileName = fileNameArg;
167        lineList = new LineList();
168        try
169        {
170          inputStream = new BufferedReader(
171            new FileReader( fileNameArg ) );
172
173          System.out.println( "Reading '" + fileNameArg + "!" );
174          int lineNum = 0;
175          while ( inputStream.ready() )
176          {
177            // read a line
178            String line = inputStream.readLine().toLowerCase();
179            lineNum++;
180            // construct a line item and add it to the line list
181            Line Line = new Line( lineNum, line );
182            lineList.addAtEnd( Line );
183            // split the line into words
184            String[] words = line.split( "[\\s\\p{Punct}]+" );
185            int wordPos = 0;
186            for ( int wordNum = 0;
187              wordNum < words.length;
188              wordNum++ )
189            {
190              // ignore very short words
191              if ( words[ wordNum ].length() <= 2 )
192                continue;
193              String wordStr = words[ wordNum ];
194              // find the word's position in the line
195              wordPos = line.indexOf( wordStr, wordPos );
196              // check if we already encountered this word
197              boolean[] isEqual = new boolean[ 1 ];
198              Word word = wordListArg.findWord( wordStr, isEqual );
199              Word wordNew;
200              if ( word == null )
201              {
202                // construct the word
203                wordNew = new Word( wordStr );
204                // add this word to the word list
205                wordListArg.addAtEnd( wordNew );
206              }
207              else if ( !isEqual[ 0 ] )
208              {
209                // construct the word
210                wordNew = new Word( wordStr );
211                wordListArg.addBefore( wordNew, word );
212              }
213              else
214                wordNew = word;
215              Location location =
216                new Location( this, lineNum, wordPos );
217              wordNew.getLocList().addAtEnd( location );
218            }
219          }
220        }
221        finally
222        {
223          if ( inputStream != null )
224            inputStream.close();
225        }
226      } // Document
227
228      // getters
229      public String getFileName()
230      {
231        return ( fileName );
```

```
232      }
233      public LineList getLines()
234      {
235        return ( lineList );
236      }
237
238      // convert the contents of this item to string
239      public String toString()
240      {
241          return( "'" + fileName + "'" );
242      }
243  } // Document
244
245  // class LocList - represents a list of items
246
247  class LocList extends Lists.List
248  {   // constructor
249    LocList()
250    {
251        super( new Location(), new Location() );
252    }
253  } // LocList
254
255  // class LineList - represents a list of lines
256
257  class LineList extends Lists.List
258  {   // constructor
259    public LineList()
260    {
261        super( new Line(), new Line() );
262    }
263  } // LineList
264
265  // class WordList - represents a list of words
266
267  class WordList extends Lists.List
268  {   // constructor
269    public WordList()
270    {
271        super( new Word(), new Word() );
272    }
273
274    // find a word in the list
275    public Word findWord( String wordStrArg,
276      boolean isEqualArg[] )
277    {
278      for ( Word word = (Word)getHead().getNext();
279        word != (Word)getTail();
280        word = (Word)word.getNext() )
281      {
282        int compare = word.getWord().compareTo( wordStrArg );
283        if ( compare < 0 )
284          continue;
285        if ( compare == 0 )
286          isEqualArg[ 0 ] = true;
287        else if ( compare > 0 )
288          isEqualArg[ 0 ] = false;
289        return( word );
290      }
291      return( null );
292    } // findWord
293  } // WordList
294
295  // class DocList - represents a list of documents
296
297  class DocList extends Lists.List
298  {   // constructor
299    public DocList()
```

```
300    {
301        super( new Document(), new Document() );
302    }
303 } // DocList
304
305 public class DocLook
306 {
307    public static final String pathName = ".";
308
309    public static void main( String[] args )
310        throws IOException, Lists.ListException
311    {
312        DocList docList = new DocList();
313        WordList wordList = new WordList();
314
315        // create a filter to get all files in current directory
316        File filter = new File( pathName );
317
318        // get a list of the files
319        String files[] = filter.list();
320        if ( files.length == 0 )
321        {
322            System.out.println( "No doucvments were found." );
323            return;
324        }
325
326        // go through the list and process all text files
327        for ( int fileNum = 0; fileNum < files.length; fileNum++ )
328        {
329            if ( files[ fileNum ].endsWith( ".txt" ) )
330            {
331                // add to the word list all words from the document
332                Document doc = new Document(
333                    pathName + "\\" + files[ fileNum ],
334                    wordList );
335                docList.addAtEnd( doc );
336            }
337        }
338
339        // turn on the search engine...
340        BufferedReader inputReader = new BufferedReader(
341            new InputStreamReader( System.in) );
342
343        // loop as long the user enters non-empty words to look for
344        while ( true )
345        {
346            // ask the user for a word to search
347            String wordStr;
348            System.out.print( "Enter word: " );
349            // we assume only a single word was entered
350            // and convert it to lower case
351            wordStr = inputReader.readLine().trim().toLowerCase();
352            if ( wordStr.length() == 0 )
353                break;
354            System.out.println( "Looking for '" + wordStr + "'." );
355            boolean[] isEqual = new boolean[ 1 ];
356            Word word = wordList.findWord( wordStr, isEqual );
357            if ( !isEqual[ 0 ] )
358            {
359                // word is not in any of the documents
360                System.out.println( "The word '" + wordStr
361                    + "' was not found." );
362            }
363            else
364            {
365                // word was found
366                System.out.println( "The word '" + wordStr +
367                    "' was found at the following location(s):" );
```

```
368              LocList locList = word.getLocList();
369              // loop over all locations
370              for ( Location location =
371                    (Location)locList.getHead().getNext();
372                  location != (Location)locList.getTail();
373                  location = (Location)location.getNext() )
374              {
375                 // get document information
376                 Document doc = location.getDoc();
377                 String docName = doc.getFileName();
378                 // get line/position in document
379                 int lineNum = location.getLine();
380                 int pos = location.getPos();
381                 // get the specific line
382                 LineList lineList = doc.getLines();
383                 int lineCount;
384                 Line line;
385                 for ( line = (Line)lineList.getHead().getNext(),
386                       lineCount = 1;
387                     line != (Line)lineList.getTail()  &&
388                       lineCount < lineNum;
389                     line = (Line)line.getNext(), lineCount++ )
390                 {}
391                 System.out.println( docName +
392                   "(" + lineNum + ":" + pos + "): " +
393                   line.getText() );
394              }
395           }
396        }
397     } // main
398  } // DocLook
```

UP AND DOWN IN AN ELEVETOR

Here's the mission: we were asked to program a system to simulate the operation of a bank of elevators in a building. The project sponsor wants to know if the number of elevators he's proposing to the landlord is sufficient to handle the traffic in the building, but wants to make sure that there aren't more elevators than necessary.

First, we have to make some assumptions.

1. The unit of time to use is one second. Everything happens in one second intervals.

2. At the beginning of each simulation, all the elevators start at the ground floor.

3. All elevators are identical and service all floors.

4. The elevators move at a constant speed (in tall buildings, elevators adjust their speed to the distance they have to travel before the next floor. But we want to simplify our lives.). We use this assumption to determine how many seconds it takes for an elevator to move from one floor to the next.

5. It does not take any time for passengers to get on or off an elevator. When an elevator shows up at a floor, all passengers that are getting off are doing it at the same time that new passengers are getting on, all within the same second. Quite amazing…

6. Passengers show up at the various floor at random times. We will use a uniform random function (which means all possibilities of when a passenger shows up have the same probability) rather than one that is statistically more correct (such as normal distribution, also known as bell-distribution).

7. In determining the capacity and occupancy of an elevator, we will not take into account the weight of passengers, but only the number of passengers.

8. We will need to experiment with different configuration of the elevator bank. We will want to vary the number of elevators, the number of floors, and the capacity and speed of an elevator.

The reason we have to make all these assumptions is that they will have an impact on how we are going to solve the problem. To a large extent, they will decide how complex the program is going to be. Even with that in mind, I might as well warn you up-front: the program in the example is far from being the best. It may do some silly things, such as sending several elevators to pick up the same passenger, or passing without stopping by a floor where a passenger is waiting. You are encouraged to fix these shortcomings, but the goal of the example is to demonstrate how to build a complete program, and having additional special logic to deal with these issue would have made the program just too big and complex. It is already significantly longer than any program you've seen so far in this book.

In designing this application, we begin by looking at which real objects we have to deal with:

1.   An Elevator Bank (`ElevatorBank`) – houses the elevators. This is just a "container".

2.   Elevators (`Elevator`) – which move up and down and ferry passengers.

3.   Floors (`Floor`) – where passenger get on and off elevators.

4.   Passengers (`Passenger`) – which use the elevators to move between floors.

5.   Passenger Lists (`PassengerList`) – which bunch a group of passengers together either travelling on an elevator or waiting for one on a floor.

Naturally, each one of these will be represented by a class. Other entities we have to represent are:

1.   Event (`Event`) – when a passenger shows up for an elevator.

2.   Configuration Options (`ConfigOption`) – describing the parameters of the simulation (such as the number of elevators and floors, the capacity of an elevator, the speed at which elevators move, etc.).

The final class we need is the one that actually runs the simulation, which we call `SimElevator`. We will put the necessary `main()` function in that class.

Before we present the complete example, let's go over some additional notes.

For the various lists, we once again borrowed the code we wrote in a previous example and structured the folders as required by Java.

We decide to use a configuration file in order to specify the parameters of the simulation, The use of a configuration file allows us to change those parameters without changing the program – just edit the parameters and re-run the program. The configuration file is composed of several lines, each one in a format called **name/value pair**. What it means is that each configuration line includes the name of a parameter and its value. So the file may look like this:

```
FLOORS=3
ELEVATORS=2
CAPACITY=4
SPEED=5
PASSENGERS=10
HORIZON=120
```

The parameters are quite self-explanatory. The only parameter that you should be wondering about is `horizon`. This parameter specify the time-horizon of the simulation (in seconds), 120 seconds (or 2 minutes) in the example above. The simulation will run for that number of seconds and then stop; we may actually have passengers stranded in an elevator or on a floor, but all we can do is feel sorry for them… By the way, the separator between the name and the value does not have to be an equal sign; it could be anything that is not expected to be part of the name or of the value, as you will see later when we discuss the `toString()` method.

Also notice that we defined the names of the parameters in a new type called **enum** (which is a shortcut for **enumeration**). Each `enum` behaves like a constant class: it has a constructor, which initializes each item. In our case, the values are a string and a number. The number is used as an index into an array where the values of the configuration options are stored. The method `getOptions()` in `SimElevator` takes care of reading the configuration file and storing the values. This gives us the possibility of easily changing the names or even adding new parameters. By working off of an array, that method does not depend on the actual names of the parameters, and if a name is changed or a new parameter is added, the method does not have to be changed. When the value of a parameter is required, the method findIndex() is called, as you can see in the constructor of the Elevator class. That method is also independent of the specific names, as the name of the parameter (which must be known it its value is required!) is passed to it.

Since this is a simulation, we need to keep track of all the activities. So each object reports on what it is doing. Whenever an elevator changes direction, it reports; when a passenger gets off an elevator, it is reported by the elevator; etc.

In order to get the random times at which passengers show up, as well as the random floors on which each arrive and the random floors which is each passenger's destination, we use the Random class. We create an object of this class at the beginning of SimElevator, giving it a seed. Without going into the theory of pseudo-random numbers, the seed is the "launch pad" for the series of numbers. As long as the seed is the same, each run of the program will have exactly the same series of random numbers (as you can see, they are not real random, but look like random – that's why they are called pseudo-random…). In real applications, it is common to use the current time as a seed, which almost guarantees that we will get different series every run; but here we picked a constant seed because it lets us run the program multiple times and get predictable numbers, so we can test in a stable environment.

All classes have a toString() method. This is a very good practice, as it makes it easy to get the contents of an object printed – just put the object as a parameter to a println() call. The result of the toString() method does not have to be fancy, but you want to make all of them return the representation of their object in a consistent manner. We chose to have a one-letter type of the object followed by the number of the instance between square brackets at the beginning of each returned string, followed by a comma-separated list of name/value pairs of the object's attributes.

Each class has the expected getters and setters, but also has a collection of small methods to do special tasks. For example, the method Elevator.goToFloor() takes care of setting the elevator on its way to the specified floor and also reports that change. The method Floor.add() puts a new passenger on the floor by adding him/her to the floor's passenger list, taking care of the necessary bookkeeping (how many passengers are on the floor and in which directions they are going), and of course reports that action.

In order to simplify the program, we generate all the events at the beginning, and keep them in a list. Then we start the clock, and each second go through the following steps (in SimElevator.run()):

1. Check if there is an event (a passenger arriving) at this time. If there is, process the arrival (add the passenger to the waiting list on the arrival floor).

2. Take care of all elevators' movements. If an elevator reached a floor, process that arrival (have passengers get off and on the elevator). If an elevator is idle, send it to a floor where a passenger is waiting (if there is one).

Of course, most of the complexity is hiding behind the deceptively simple word 'process'…

So here is the program. First is the list management package, followed by the elevator simulation package.

```
01 // Example 48, file 'Lists.java'
02 // This file defines the list management classes
03
04 package SimElevator;
05
06 public class Lists
07 {
08    // class ListException - List exception
09
10    public static class ListException extends Exception
11    {
12      public ListException( Item itemArg, String messageArg )
13      {
```

```
14          super( messageArg + ": " + itemArg.toString() );
15      }
16  }
17
18  // class Item - an abstract class
19  // representing an item on a list
20
21  public static abstract class Item
22  {
23      private Item prev;
24      private Item next;
25
26      // constructor
27      public Item()
28      {
29          prev = null;
30          next = null;
31      }
32
33      // getters
34      public Item getPrev()
35      {
36          return ( prev );
37      }
38      public Item getNext()
39      {
40          return ( next );
41      }
42
43      // setters
44      public void setPrev( Item itemArg )
45      {
46          prev = itemArg;
47      }
48      public void setNext( Item itemArg )
49      {
50          next = itemArg;
51      }
52      public void setPrevNull()
53      {
54          prev = null;
55      }
56      public void setNextNull()
57      {
58          next = null;
59      }
60
61      // print the contents of the item
62      public void print()
63      {
64          System.out.println( this );
65      }
66
67      // convert this item to string
68      public abstract String toString();
69  } // Item
70
71  // class List - an abstract class representing a
72  // list of items
73
74  public static abstract class List
75  {
76      private Item head;
77      private Item tail;
78
79      // constructor
80      public List( Item headArg, Item tailArg )
81      {
```

```
82          head = headArg;
83          tail = tailArg;
84          head.setNext( tail );
85          head.setPrevNull();
86          tail.setPrev( head );
87          tail.setNextNull();
88       }
89
90       // getters
91       public Item getHead()
92       {
93          return ( head );
94       }
95       public Item getTail()
96       {
97          return ( tail );
98       }
99
100      // add an item to the beginning of the list
101      public void addAtBegin( Item itemArg )
102         throws ListException
103      {
104         addAfter( itemArg, head );
105      }
106
107      // add an item to the end of the list
108      public void addAtEnd( Item itemArg )
109         throws ListException
110      {
111         addBefore( itemArg, tail );
112      }
113
114      // add an item to the list after
115      // another item passed as argument
116      public void addAfter( Item newItemArg, Item oldItemArg )
117         throws ListException
118      {
119         if ( newItemArg.getPrev() != null  ||
120           newItemArg.getNext() != null )
121           throw new ListException( newItemArg,
122             "Item is not free" );
123         if ( oldItemArg.getPrev() == null  &&
124           oldItemArg.getNext() == null )
125           throw new ListException( oldItemArg,
126             "Item is not in list" );
127         newItemArg.setPrev( oldItemArg );
128         if ( oldItemArg.getNext() == null )
129         {
130            newItemArg.setNextNull();
131         }
132         else
133         {
134            newItemArg.setNext( oldItemArg.getNext() );
135            oldItemArg.getNext().setPrev( newItemArg );
136         }
137         oldItemArg.setNext( newItemArg );
138      }
139
140      // add an item to the list before
141      // another item passed as argument
142      public void addBefore( Item newItemArg, Item oldItemArg )
143         throws ListException
144      {
145         if ( newItemArg.getPrev() != null  ||
146           newItemArg.getNext() != null )
147           throw new ListException( newItemArg,
148             "Item is not free" );
149         if ( oldItemArg.getPrev() == null  &&
```

```
150            oldItemArg.getNext() == null )
151            throw new ListException( oldItemArg,
152              "Item is not in list" );
153          newItemArg.setNext( oldItemArg );
154          if ( oldItemArg.getPrev() == null )
155          {
156            newItemArg.setPrevNull();
157          }
158          else
159          {
160            newItemArg.setPrev( oldItemArg.getPrev() );
161            oldItemArg.getPrev().setNext( newItemArg );
162          }
163          oldItemArg.setPrev( newItemArg );
164        }
165
166        // delete an item
167        public void del( Item itemArg )
168        {
169          if ( itemArg.getNext() == null )
170            itemArg.getPrev().setNextNull();
171          else
172            itemArg.getPrev().setNext( itemArg.getNext() );
173          if ( itemArg.getPrev() == null )
174            itemArg.getNext().setPrevNull();
175          else
176            itemArg.getNext().setPrev( itemArg.getPrev() );
177          itemArg.setNext( null );
178          itemArg.setPrev( null );
179        }
180
181        // print the contents of this list
182        public void print()
183        {
184          System.out.println( this );
185        }
186
187        // convert this list to a string
188        public String toString()
189        {
190          String thisString = "";
191          Item item = head.getNext();
192          if ( item == null )
193            return( "<None>" );
194          while ( item != tail )
195          {
196            if ( thisString.length() > 0 )
197              thisString += "\n";
198            thisString += item;
199            item = item.getNext();
200          }
201          return ( thisString );
202        }
203
204        // dump the contents of this list
205        public void dump()
206        {
207          Item item = head.getNext();
208          if ( item == null )
209          {
210            System.out.println( "<None>" );
211            return;
212          }
213          while ( item != tail )
214          {
215            System.out.println(
216              "[ " +
217              item.getPrev().toString() + " : " +
```

```
218                item.toString() + " : " +
219                item.getNext().toString() +
220                " ]" );
221          item = item.getNext();
222        }
223      }
224    } // List
225
226 } // Lists
```

```
01 // Example 48, file 'SimElevator.java'
02 // This file defines the class 'SimElevator'
03
04 package SimElevator;
05
06 import java.io.*;
07 import java.util.Random;
08
09 enum ConfigOptions
10 {
11    ELEVATORS ( 0, "ELEVATORS" ),
12    FLOORS ( 1, "FLOORS" ),
13    CAPACITY( 2, "CAPACITY" ),
14    SPEES ( 3, "SPEED" ),
15    PASSENGERS ( 4, "PASSENGERS" ),
16    HORIZON( 5, "HORIZON" );
17    // *** The value below must correspond to  ***
18    // *** the number of options defined above ***
19    public final static int MAX_OPTIONS = 6;
20
21    private final int index;
22    private final String name;
23
24    // constructor
25    ConfigOptions( int indexArg, String nameArg )
26    {
27      index = indexArg;
28      name = nameArg;
29    } // ConfigOptions
30
31    // actions
32    // find the index of a name
33    static int findIndex( String nameArg )
34    {
35      for ( ConfigOptions option: ConfigOptions.values() )
36      {
37        if ( option.name.equals( nameArg ))
38          return( option.index );
39      }
40      return( -1 );
41    } // findIndex
42 }; // ConfigOptions
43
44 // class Elevator - represents an elevator
45
46 class Elevator
47 {
48    // constants
49    enum Direction { UP, IDLE, DOWN };
50
51    // attributes
52
53    // elevator number:
54    private int elevatorNum;
55    // maximum number of passenger per elevator:
56    private int maxPassengers;
57    // current number of passenger in elevator:
```

```
58     private int numPassengers;
59     // elevator speed (seconds from one floor to next):
60     private int speedElevator;
61     // number of floors
62     private int numFloors;
63     // floor number where elevator is:
64     private int floorOn;
65     // floor number where elevator is going to:
66     private int floorGoingTo;
67     // elevator's position between floors:
68     private int position;
69     // elevator's direction (true=up, false=down):
70     private Direction direction;
71     // elevator just arrived at a floor
72     private boolean justArrived;
73     // list of passengers in elevator
74     private PassengerList passengers;
75     // configuration options:
76     private int[] options;
77
78     // constructor
79     Elevator( int elevatorNumArg, int[] optionsArg )
80     {
81        options = optionsArg;
82        elevatorNum = elevatorNumArg;
83        maxPassengers =
84           options[ ConfigOptions.findIndex( "CAPACITY" ) ];
85        speedElevator =
86           options[ ConfigOptions.findIndex( "SPEED" ) ];
87        numFloors =
88           options[ ConfigOptions.findIndex( "FLOORS" ) ];
89        passengers = new PassengerList( optionsArg );
90        // all elevators start on the ground floor; we set them to
91        // arrive at the ground floor going up in the first step
92        floorOn = 0;
93        position = speedElevator - 1;
94        direction = Direction.UP;   // all elevator must go up initially
95        justArrived = false;
96     } // Elevator
97
98     // getters
99     public int getElevetorNum()
100    {
101       return( elevatorNum );
102    }
103    public int getMaxPassengers()
104    {
105       return( maxPassengers );
106    }
107    public int getSpeedElevator()
108    {
109       return( speedElevator );
110    }
111    public int getFloorOn()
112    {
113       return( floorOn );
114    }
115    public int getFloorGoingTo()
116    {
117       return( floorGoingTo );
118    }
119    public int getPosition()
120    {
121       return( position );
122    }
123    public boolean getJustArrived()
124    {
125       return( justArrived );
```

```
126     }
127     public Direction getDirection()
128     {
129        return( direction );
130     }
131
132     // create a string representation
133     public String toString()
134     {
135        return( "E[" + elevatorNum + "]: "
136          + "maxPassengers:" + maxPassengers
137          + ",numPassengers:" + numPassengers
138          + ",speedElevator:" + speedElevator
139          + ",floorOn:" + floorOn
140          + ",position:" + position
141          + ",floorGoingTo:" + floorGoingTo
142          + ",direction:" + direction
143          + ",justArrived:" + justArrived );
144     } // toString
145
146     // put a passenger on the elevator
147     public boolean add( Passenger passengerArg )
148     {
149        // check if there is room on the elevator
150        if ( numPassengers >= maxPassengers )
151          return( false );
152        // put the passenger on the elevator
153        try
154        {
155          passengers.addAtEnd( passengerArg );
156        }
157        catch( Lists.ListException ex )
158        {
159          System.out.println( "Internal error: "
160             + ex.getMessage() );
161          return( false );
162        }
163        numPassengers++;
164        return( true );
165     } // add
166
167     // process elevator's arrival at a floor
168     public void arrivedAt( int timeArg, Floor floorArg )
169     {
170        System.out.println( "[" + timeArg + "] Elevator "
171           + elevatorNum
172           + " arrived at floor "
173           + floorOn );
174        justArrived = false;
175        // look for passengers that have to get off
176        Passenger passenger =
177          (Passenger)passengers.getHead().getNext();
178        // go through the list of passenger on the elevator
179        while ( passenger != null  &&
180          passenger != (Passenger)passengers.getTail() )
181        {
182          // check if the passenger is going to this floor
183          if ( passenger.getFloorGoingTo()
184            == floorArg.getFloorNum() )
185          {
186            // get the passenger off the elevator
187            passengers.del( passenger );
188            numPassengers--;
189            System.out.println( "[" + timeArg + "] Passenger "
190                + passenger.getPassengerNum()
191                + " got off elevator "
192                + elevatorNum
193                + " on floor "
```

```
194                  + floorOn );
195        }
196      // move on to next passenger
197      passenger = (Passenger)passenger.getNext();
198    }
199
200    // check if this elevator has passengers
201    // it has to take to another floor
202    if ( numPassengers == 0 )
203    {
204      direction = Direction.IDLE;
205      floorGoingTo = 0;
206    }
207
208    // are there any passengers on this floor?
209    if ( floorArg.getNumPassengersUp() == 0  &&
210         floorArg.getNumPassengersDown() == 0 )
211      return;
212
213    // look for passengers that have to get on
214    passenger =
215      (Passenger)floorArg.getPassengers().getHead().getNext();
216    while ( passenger != null  &&
217         passenger != (Passenger)floorArg.
218           getPassengers().getTail() )
219    {
220      // check if there is still room on the elevator
221      if ( numPassengers == maxPassengers )
222        break;
223      // check if the passenger is going in
224      // the same direction as the elevator
225      int floorDiff =
226        passenger.getFloorGoingTo() - passenger.getFloorOn();
227      Passenger passengerNext = (Passenger)passenger.getNext();
228      boolean goingUpPassenger = ( floorDiff > 0 );
229      if ( direction == Direction.IDLE
230         || ( goingUpPassenger  &&
231           direction == Direction.UP )
232         || ( !goingUpPassenger  &&
233           direction == Direction.DOWN ) )
234      {
235        // get the passenger off the floor
236        floorArg.del( passenger );
237        // get the passenger onto the elevator
238        boolean gotOnElevator = add( passenger );
239        if ( !gotOnElevator )
240        {
241          // there was no more room on the elevator
242          // put the passenger back on the floor
243          floorArg.add( passenger );
244          break;
245        }
246        goToFloor( timeArg, passenger.getFloorGoingTo() );
247        System.out.println( "[" + timeArg + "] Passenger "
248             + passenger.getPassengerNum()
249             + " got on elevator "
250             + elevatorNum
251             + " on floor "
252             + passenger.getFloorOn()
253             + " going to floor "
254             + passenger.getFloorGoingTo() );
255      }
256      // move on to next passenger
257      passenger = passengerNext;
258    }
259  } // arrivedAt
260
261    // send the elevator to a floor
```

```
262    public void goToFloor( int timeArg, int numFloorArg )
263    {
264      // is the elevator being sent to the same floor it's on?
265      floorGoingTo = numFloorArg;
266      if ( numFloorArg == floorOn )
267        return;
268      if ( numFloorArg > floorOn )
269      { // going up
270        directionChange( Direction.UP );
271      }
272      else
273      { // going down
274        directionChange( Direction.DOWN );
275      }
276      System.out.println( "[" + timeArg + "] Elevator "
277          + elevatorNum + " is going to floor "
278          + numFloorArg );
279    } // goToFloor
280
281    void directionChange( Direction newDirectionArg )
282    {
283      direction = newDirectionArg;
284      switch ( newDirectionArg )
285      {
286        case UP:
287          position = 0;
288          break;
289        case DOWN:
290          position = speedElevator;
291          floorOn--;
292          break;
293        case IDLE:
294          break;
295      }
296    } // directionChange
297
298    // move the elevator one step
299    public void move( int timeArg )
300    {
301      // decide if we need to change direction
302      switch ( direction )
303      {
304        case UP:
305          // change direction if we are on the top floor
306          if ( floorOn == numFloors  &&  position == 0 )
307            directionChange( Direction.DOWN );
308          break;
309        case DOWN:
310          // change direction if are on the bottom floor
311          if ( floorOn == 1  &&  position == 0 )
312            directionChange( Direction.UP );
313          break;
314        case IDLE:
315          break;
316      }
317
318      // move the elevator
319      switch ( direction )
320      {
321        case UP:
322          position++;
323          // did we just reach a floor?
324          if ( position == speedElevator )
325          {
326            justArrived = true;
327            position = 0;
328            floorOn++;
329          }
```

```
330              break;
331          case DOWN:
332              // are we on a floor?
333              if ( position == 0 )
334              {
335                position = speedElevator - 1;
336                floorOn--;
337              }
338              else
339              {
340                position--;
341                // did we just reach a floor?
342                if ( position == 0 )
343                {
344                  justArrived = true;
345                }
346              }
347              break;
348          case IDLE:
349              justArrived = true;
350              break;
351        }
352        if ( justArrived && floorOn == floorGoingTo )
353          floorGoingTo = 0;
354        System.out.println( "[" + timeArg + "] elevator "
355              + getElevetorNum()
356              + ( direction == Direction.IDLE
357              ? " stayed on " + getFloorOn()
358              : " moved "
359              + ( direction == Direction.UP ? "up" : "down" )
360              + " to ("
361              + floorOn + "."
362              + position + ")"
363              )
364        );
365      } // move
366  } // Elevator
367
368  // class Floor - represents a Floor
369
370  class Floor
371  {
372      // attributes
373
374      // floor number:
375      int floorNum;
376      // number of passengers waiting to go up:
377      private int numPassengersUp;
378      // number of passengers waiting to go down:
379      private int numPassengersDown;
380      // list of passengers waiting for elevator:
381      private PassengerList passengers;
382      // configuration options:
383      private int[] options;
384
385      // constructor
386      Floor( int floorNumArg, int[] optionsArg )
387      {
388        options = optionsArg;
389        floorNum = floorNumArg;
390        passengers = new PassengerList( optionsArg );
391      } // Floor
392
393      // getters
394      public int getFloorNum()
395      {
396        return( floorNum );
397      }
```

```
398     public int getNumPassengersUp()
399     {
400        return( numPassengersUp );
401     }
402     public int getNumPassengersDown()
403     {
404        return( numPassengersDown );
405     }
406     public PassengerList getPassengers()
407     {
408        return( passengers );
409     }
410
411     // put a passenger on the floor
412     public boolean add( Passenger passengerArg )
413     {
414        try
415        {
416           // add the passenger to the floor
417           passengers.addAtEnd( passengerArg );
418           // determine if passenger is going up or down
419           int floorDiff =
420              passengerArg.getFloorGoingTo() -
421              passengerArg.getFloorOn();
422           if ( floorDiff > 0 )
423              numPassengersUp++;
424           else
425              numPassengersDown++;
426        }
427        catch( Lists.ListException ex )
428        {
429           System.out.println( "Internal error: "
430              + ex.getMessage() );
431           return( false );
432        }
433        return( true );
434     } // add
435
436     // get a passenger off a floor
437     public void del( Passenger passengerArg )
438     {
439        // add the passenger to the floor
440        passengers.del( passengerArg );
441        // determine if passenger is going up or down
442        int floorDiff =
443           passengerArg.getFloorGoingTo() -
444           passengerArg.getFloorOn();
445        if ( floorDiff > 0 )
446           numPassengersUp--;
447        else
448           numPassengersDown--;
449     } // del
450
451     // create a string representation
452     public String toString()
453     {
454        return( "F[" + floorNum + "]: " + passengers );
455     } // toString
456  } // Floor
457
458  // class ElevatorBank - represents an elevator bank
459
460  class ElevatorBank
461  {
462     // attributes
463
464     // number of floors:
465     private int numFloors;
```

```
466    // number of elevators:
467    private int numElevators;
468    // the elevators:
469    private Elevator[] elevators;
470    // the floors:
471    private Floor[] floors;
472    // configuration options:
473    private int[] options;
474
475    // constructor
476    ElevatorBank( int[] optionsArg )
477    {
478      options = optionsArg;
479      numFloors = options[ ConfigOptions.findIndex( "FLOORS" ) ];
480      numElevators = options[
481        ConfigOptions.findIndex( "ELEVATORS" ) ];
482      // create the elevators
483      elevators = new Elevator[ numElevators ];
484      for ( int elevatorNum = 1;
485        elevatorNum <= numElevators;
486        elevatorNum++ )
487      {
488        elevators[ elevatorNum - 1 ] =
489          new Elevator( elevatorNum, options );
490      }
491      // create the floors
492      floors = new Floor[ numFloors ];
493      for ( int floorNum = 0;
494        floorNum < numFloors;
495        floorNum++ )
496      {
497        floors[ floorNum ] =
498          new Floor( floorNum + 1, options  );
499      }
500    } // ElevatorBank
501
502    // getters
503    int getNumElevators()
504    {
505      return( numElevators );
506    }
507    Elevator[] getElevators()
508    {
509      return( elevators );
510    }
511    Floor[] getFloors()
512    {
513      return( floors );
514    }
515    Elevator getElevator( int elevatorNumArg )
516    {
517      return( elevators[ elevatorNumArg - 1 ] );
518    }
519    Floor getFloor( int floorNumArg )
520    {
521      return( floors[ floorNumArg - 1 ] );
522    }
523
524    // create a string representation
525    public String toString()
526    {
527      String bankStr = "[Bank] floors:" + numFloors
528        + ",elevators:" + numElevators;
529      for ( int floorNum = 0;
530        floorNum < numFloors;
531        floorNum++ )
532      {
533        bankStr += ( "\n" + floors[ floorNum ] );
```

```
534        }
535      for ( int elevatorNum = 1;
536         elevatorNum <= numElevators;
537         elevatorNum++ )
538      {
539         bankStr += ( "\n" + elevators[ elevatorNum - 1 ] );
540      }
541      return( bankStr );
542    } // toString
543 } // ElevatorBank
544
545 // class Passenger - represents a Passenger
546
547 class Passenger
548    extends Lists.Item
549 {
550    // attributes
551
552    // next passenger number
553    private static int passengerNumNext = 1;
554    // passenger number
555    private int passengerNum;
556    // floor on which the passenger is currently on:
557    private int floorOn;
558    // floor where the passenger wants to go:
559    private int floorGoingTo;
560    // configuration options:
561    private int[] options;
562
563    // constructor
564    Passenger(
565      int floorOnArg,
566      int floorGoingToArg,
567      int[] optionsArg )
568    {
569      super();
570      options = optionsArg;
571      floorOn = floorOnArg;
572      floorGoingTo = floorGoingToArg;
573      if ( floorOn > 0  &&  floorGoingTo > 0 )
574        passengerNum = passengerNumNext++;
575    } // Passenger
576
577    // getters
578    int getPassengerNum()
579    {
580      return( passengerNum );
581    }
582    int getFloorOn()
583    {
584      return( floorOn );
585    }
586    int getFloorGoingTo()
587    {
588      return( floorGoingTo );
589    }
590
591    // create a string representation
592    public String toString()
593    {
594      return( "P[" + passengerNum + "]: "
595          + "floorOn:" + floorOn
596          + ",floorGoingTo:" + floorGoingTo );
597    } // toString
598 } // Passenger
599
600 // class PassengerList - a list of passengers
601
```

```
602  class PassengerList
603    extends Lists.List
604  {
605    // attributes
606    // configuration options:
607    private int[] options;
608
609    // constructor
610    PassengerList( int[] optionsArg )
611    {
612      super(
613        new Passenger( 0, 0, optionsArg ),
614        new Passenger( 0, 0, optionsArg ) );
615      options = optionsArg;
616    } // PassengerList
617  }; // PassengerList
618
619  // class Event - represents the event of a
620  // passenger showing up for an elevator
621
622  class Event
623    extends Lists.Item
624  {
625    // attributes
626
627    // next event number:
628    private static int eventNumNext = 0;
629    // event number:
630    private int eventNum;
631    // event time:
632    private int time;
633    // floor where passenger shows up:
634    private int floorOn;
635    // floor to which passenger wants to go:
636    private int floorGoingTo;
637
638    // constructor
639    Event( int timeArg, int floorOnArg, int floorGoingToArg )
640    {
641      time = timeArg;
642      floorOn = floorOnArg;
643      floorGoingTo = floorGoingToArg;
644      if ( floorOn > 0  &&  floorGoingTo > 0 )
645        eventNum = eventNumNext++;
646    }
647
648    // getters
649    public int getTime()
650    {
651      return( time );
652    }
653    public int getFloorOn()
654    {
655      return( floorOn );
656    }
657    public int getFloorGoingTo()
658    {
659      return( floorGoingTo );
660    }
661
662    // create a string representation
663    public String toString()
664    {
665      return( "V[" + eventNum + "]: "
666          + "time:" + time
667          + ",floorOn:" + floorOn
668          + ",floorGoingTo:" + floorGoingTo );
669    } // toString
```

```
670  }; // Event
671
672  // class EventList - represents a list of events
673  // sorted in order of occurrence
674
675  class EventList
676    extends Lists.List
677  {
678    // constructor
679    EventList()
680    {
681      // initialize the list with a head at time 0
682      // and tail at maximum time possible
683      super(
684        new Event( 0, 0, 0 ),
685        new Event( Integer.MAX_VALUE, 0, 0 ) );
686    } // EventList
687
688    // add an event in time sequence
689    public void add( Event eventArg )
690    {
691      // look for the first event that is later than the new  one
692      for ( Event event = (Event)getHead();
693        event != null ;
694        event = (Event)event.getNext() )
695      {
696        // check if current event is later than the new one
697        if ( event.getTime() > eventArg.getTime() )
698        {
699          // get the new event on the list before the current one
700          try
701          {
702            addBefore( eventArg, event );
703          }
704          catch ( Lists.ListException ex )
705          {
706            System.out.println( "Internal error: "
707              + ex.getMessage() );
708          }
709          break;
710        }
711      }
712    } // add
713  } // EventList
714
715  // class SimElevator - an Elevator Bank simulator
716
717  public class SimElevator
718  {
719    // attributes
720    // configuration options:
721    private static int[] options =
722      new int[ ConfigOptions.MAX_OPTIONS ];
723    // the time horizon of the simulation:
724    private static int horizon;
725    // the number of events in the simulation:
726    private static int numEvents;
727    // number of floors:
728    private static int numFloors;
729    // a random number generator:
730    private static Random rand = new Random( 2009 );
731
732    // set up the elevator bank
733    private static void getOptions()
734      throws IOException
735    {
736      BufferedReader inputStream = new BufferedReader(
737        new FileReader( "setup.cfg" ) );
```

```
738        while ( inputStream.ready() )
739        {
740          String line = inputStream.readLine().toUpperCase();
741          if ( line.isEmpty() || line.charAt( 0 ) == '#' )
742            continue;
743          int posEqual = line.indexOf( "=" );
744          if ( posEqual < 0 )
745          {
746            System.out.println(
747              "Invalid configuration line: '" + line + "'.");
748            continue;
749          }
750          String name = line.substring( 0, posEqual );
751          int value;
752          String valueStr = line.substring( posEqual + 1 ).trim();
753          try
754          {
755            value = Integer.valueOf( valueStr ).intValue();
756          }
757          catch ( NumberFormatException ex )
758          {
759            System.out.println(
760              "Invalid configuration value: '" + line + "'.");
761            continue;
762          }
763          int index = ConfigOptions.findIndex( name );
764          if ( index < 0 )
765          {
766            System.out.println(
767              "Invalid configuration option: '" + line + "'.");
768            continue;
769          }
770          options[ index ] = value;
771        }
772        horizon = options[ ConfigOptions.findIndex( "HORIZON" ) ];
773        numEvents = options[
774          ConfigOptions.findIndex( "PASSENGERS" ) ];
775        numFloors = options[ ConfigOptions.findIndex( "FLOORS" ) ];
776      } // getOptions
777
778      // set up the elevator bank
779      private static ElevatorBank setupBank()
780        throws IOException
781      {
782        ElevatorBank elevatorBank = new ElevatorBank( options );
783        return( elevatorBank );
784      } // setupBank
785
786      // set up the initial event list
787      private static EventList setupEvents()
788      {
789        // the event list itself
790        EventList events = new EventList();
791
792        for ( int eventNum = 0;
793          eventNum < numEvents;
794          eventNum++ )
795        {
796          // determine the floor the passenger shows
797          // up on and the floor he/she is going to
798          int floorOn = rand.nextInt( numFloors ) + 1;
799          int floorGoingTo = rand.nextInt( numFloors ) + 1;
800          // if both floors are the same, try
801          // until you get two different floors
802          while ( floorOn == floorGoingTo )
803            floorGoingTo = rand.nextInt( numFloors ) + 1;
804          // create the event
805          Event event = new Event(
```

```
806              rand.nextInt( horizon ),
807              floorOn,
808              floorGoingTo );
809       // add the event to the list
810          events.add( event );
811       }
812       return ( events );
813    } // setupEvents
814
815    // run the simulation
816    private static void run(
817       ElevatorBank elevatorBankArg,
818       EventList eventsArg )
819    {
820       Event event = (Event)eventsArg.getHead().getNext();
821       for ( int time = 0; time < horizon; time++ )
822       {
823          // process all events for current time
824          while ( event.getTime() == time )
825          {
826             Passenger passenger = new Passenger(
827                  event.getFloorOn(),
828                  event.getFloorGoingTo(),
829                  options );
830             Floor floor =
831                elevatorBankArg.getFloor( event.getFloorOn() );
832             floor.add( passenger );
833             System.out.println( "[" + time + "] Passenger "
834                + passenger.getPassengerNum() + " Arrived on floor "
835                + passenger.getFloorOn() + " going to floor "
836                + passenger.getFloorGoingTo() );
837             event = (Event)event.getNext();
838          }
839          // process all elevators
840          for ( int elevatorNum = 1;
841             elevatorNum <= elevatorBankArg.getNumElevators();
842             elevatorNum++ )
843          {
844             Elevator elevator =
845                elevatorBankArg.getElevator( elevatorNum );
846             elevator.move( time );
847             // did elevator reach a floor?
848             if ( elevator.getJustArrived() )
849             { // process the arrival
850                elevator.arrivedAt( time,
851                   elevatorBankArg.getFloor(
852                      elevator.getFloorOn() ) );
853             }
854             // is the elevator idle?
855             if ( elevator.getDirection() ==
856                Elevator.Direction.IDLE )
857             { // find somewhere for it to go
858                // search for a floor with waiting passengers
859                for ( int floorNum = 1;
860                   floorNum <= numFloors;
861                   floorNum ++ )
862                {
863                   Floor floor = elevatorBankArg.getFloor( floorNum );
864                   // are there any passengers on the target floor?
865                   if ( floor.getNumPassengersUp() == 0  &&
866                      floor.getNumPassengersDown() == 0 )
867                      continue;
868                   // peek into all elevators and find out if another
869                   // elevator already going to the target floor?
870                   boolean isAnyElevator = false;
871                   for ( int elevatorNumPeek = 1;
872                      elevatorNumPeek <=
873                         elevatorBankArg.getNumElevators();
```

```
874                              elevatorNumPeek++ )
875                        {
876                          Elevator elevatorPeek =
877                            elevatorBankArg.getElevator( elevatorNumPeek );
878                          // is the elevator we are peeking
879                          // into going to the target floor?
880                          if ( elevatorPeek.getFloorGoingTo() == floorNum )
881                          {
882                            isAnyElevator = true;
883                            break;
884                          }
885                        }
886                        if ( !isAnyElevator )
887                          elevator.goToFloor( time, floorNum );
888                      break;
889                  }
890              }
891            }
892          }
893
894      } // run
895
896      // main
897      public static void main( String[] args )
898        throws IOException
899      {
900        getOptions();
901        ElevatorBank elevatorBank = setupBank();
902        System.out.println( elevatorBank );
903        EventList events = setupEvents();
904        System.out.println( events );
905        run( elevatorBank , events );
906        System.out.println( elevatorBank );
907      } // main
908
909  } // SimElevator
```

What you learned in this chapter:

⌄   *A program must take care of all aspects of its operation*

⌄   *It is a good practice to make configuration information specified when running the
    program rather than hard-code it in the program*

⌄   *A well-designed object-oriented program represents real-life objects with program
    objects as much as possible*

PART FOUR – THE NITTY-GRITTY DETAILS

> *This book has many examples of programs and program fragments. Hopefully you don't want to just be a spectator – you want to program. So this section will teach you what you need to do in order to run the examples, write your own programs and deal with potential errors.*
>
> *What you will learn in this section:*
>
> - *How to set up the software you need to run the examples*
> - *How to type in a program, compile and run it*
> - *How to interpret and fix errors*

How to Obtain and Install the Software You Need

> *In order to run any program, you need certain software. This chapter will tell you where to find it and how to set it up.*
>
> *What you will learn in this chapter:*
>
> - *What software you need in order to experiment with the examples*
> - *Where to find this software and how to get it*
> - *How to install it*

The software you need falls into two categories:

- ❑ A text editor.
- ❑ The Java environment.
- ❑ The examples in the book.

For the latest information about needed, recommended and suggested software, please go to http://www.kidscanprogramtoo.com/setup.htm.

TEXT EDITOR

The source code of a program is stored as a plain text file. Unlike documents prepared by a word processor, in such a file there is no information that tells how to print or show the text – only the text itself. Therefore, you cannot use a word processor (like WordPad, Microsoft Word, Word Perfect, etc.) to type in or edit your programs – you must use a text editor, one that does not get involved in formatting at all.

There are many text editors. The simplest (and most primitive one) is Notepad, which is part of any Microsoft Windows environment. On Windows XP, you can usually find it by clicking on Start, then selecting Programs, Accessories, Notepad. It may be in a slightly different place in other versions of Windows. Notepad's major shortcoming is that it is not a programming editor, and therefore does not know anything about the Java language (or any other programming language, for that matter).

You might ask, "Why do I want the editor to know about the language I program in?" I'm glad you asked... When the editor knows about the language, it can help you when you type in your program. For example, it uses different colors to show keywords or other words it recognizes, so it visually shows you if you typed them wrong; it shows comments in a different color too, so that you know what is code and what are comments; it can also indent the code automatically, helping you visualize the structure of your program by matching opening braces to closing ones by placing them in the appropriate position on the line; some editors may even help you by "completing your sentences," namely guessing what you want to code and typing for you the necessary structure (for example, if you type the word while, the editor will automatically supply () to enclose the condition.)

Two other editors (among many others) are smarter, and know a little about the language. They are UltraEdit (from http://www.ultraedit.com) and EditPlus (from http://www.editplus.com) . They both cost a little bit of money, but it's well worth it if you are serious about programming. You can download an evaluation version of each, so that you can find which one you really like.

There is one more editor which is worth mentioning – Everyone's Java Editor, or EJE. This editor is FREE (Hurray!) and also knows about the Java language (Hurray! Hurray!). Its only drawback is that it is not good for much else, but then again you don't need it for anything else… It can be downloaded from http://sourceforge.net/projects/eje.

Other options, which are more than editors, are Eclipse and NetBeans. They are full development environment, known as an IDE (Interactive Development Environment). They are both free and can be downloaded from http://www.eclipse.org/downloads (you need the "Eclipse IDE for Java Developers") or https://netbeans.org/features/index.html, but they are more complex than the other options. One of their advantages, though, is that you can not only edit your programs within these environments, but run them too, so you do not need to execute them from the command line. Be aware, though, that installation is a little bit more involved than any of the other options, but it's worth it. They are written in Java and are especially designed for Java programming. They know the language so well that will try to help you complete your code even as you type by offering (mostly) sensible suggestions.

THE JAVA ENVIRONMENT

This book uses Java as the programming language in which all rules, examples and samples are given. In order to be able to run the sample programs,. It is necessary to install the Java environment, which includes both the JRE (Java Runtime Environment) and the JDK (Java Development Kit). You can download the latest version from http://www.oracle.com/technetwork/java/javase/downloads/index.html (just select the latest version of the JDK; you do not need the EE version).

THE EXAMPLES

All the examples in the book are available for downloading at http://www.kidscanprogramtoo.com/examples.html.

How to Type, Compile and Run a Program

> *What you will learn in this chapter:*
> - *How to type in or edit a program in source code*
> - *How to compile a program*
> - *How to run a program*

The instructions below are for those who choose not to use one of the IDEs described in the previous section. If you do decide to use and IDE, you should follow the instructions that apply to that IDE.

TYPING AND EDITING SOURCE CODE

The first step in working with source code is creating a folder (directory) for your programs. It doesn't matter where on your hard drive you place this folder, as long as you remember where you put it… For example, you can create your program folder on your C: drive with the name MyJava, and then its full pathname will be C:\MyJava.

Typing in a new program is just that: using your text editor, you type in the source code of your program into a new file. You then need to save it in your program folder as a file with the extension `.java`; for example, `MyProgram.java`. It is important to remember that the name of the file is case-sensitive, so `MyProgram.java` is not the same file as `myprogram.java`.

If you want to edit an existing program, open it with the text editor, make your corrections and save it again. This way you can edit the sample programs that came with this book on the CD or in the accompanying ZIP file. (Note, however, that you cannot save programs back to the CD – it's read-only. You'll have to save the modified program to your programs folder on your hard drive.)

COMPILING A PROGRAM

In order to compile your program, you have to use the DOS Command Prompt. After you click on it and it comes up, go to your program directory by typing the following command:

```
CD <pathname>
```

where *<pathname>* stands for the full pathname to your program folder. For example:

```
CD C:\MyJava
```

In order to run the Java compiler, you should use the following command:

```
javac <progname>
```

where *<progname>* stands for the name of the file in which you saved your program (*with* the `.java` extension!). For example:

```
javac MyProgram.java
```

The compiler will perform the compilation and will inform you if there are any errors. If that happens (and believe me, it does…), you should go back to your text editor and correct the program, and then try to compile it again.

RUNNING A PROGRAM

Once your program compiles successfully, you can run it. This is done by using the following command:

```
java <progname>
```

where *<progname>* stands for the name your program (*without* the `.java` extension!). For example:

```
java MyProgram
```

The program will run and produce its output on the screen. If any errors are encountered, error messages will be produced as well.

How to Tackle Errors

When you write a program, it often happens that things do not work out the way you expect them to. In this chapter, we will explore why this may happen and how you can fix these mistakes and get your programs to run correctly.

What you will learn in this chapter:

➢ *The various types of errors you may encounter*
➢ *The difference between "typos" and "bugs"*
➢ *How to analyze and fix errors*

SYNTAX ERRORS

Syntax errors are the first type of errors you will encounter. In a human language, such as English, syntax is the set of rules that define how sentences are constructed. In a computer language, syntax is the set of rules for coding valid statements. What that means is that the compiler is analyzing your program code, based on the syntax of the programming language, and then generates the instructions in the language that the computer understands. (If you are not sure how this works, take another look at the description of this process in Part One.)

If the compiler cannot understand what you wrote, it cannot generate the instructions. The reasons for these misunderstandings are usually simple and even silly. For example, if you code the following program:

```
public class Syntax
{
  public static void main(String[] args)
  {
    int value = 1;
    System.out.println(Value);
  }
}
```

You will get an error message similar to this:

```
Syntax.java:6: cannot resolve symbol
symbol: variable Value
location: class Syntax
    System.out.println(Value);
                      ^
```

The first line of this error message shows the name of the file (`Syntax.java`), the line number where the error was found (10) and the error message (`cannot resolve symbol`). The next line provides the additional information that the symbol causing the problem is `Value`. The third, fourth and fifth lines provide more detailed information regarding the location of the error.

Can you figure out what the error is? Hint: variable names are case-sensitive (see *"Variables"*).

Most syntax errors will be similar. A missing semi-colon, unbalanced parentheses, etc. Unfortunately, in many cases the location at which the error is identified is not really where the problem is. Look at this program:

```
public class Syntax
{
  public static void main(String[] args)
  {
    int a[] = new int[10];
    for (int i = 0; i < 10; i++)
    {
```

```
      a[i] = i;
   }
}
```

The error message you'll get is:

```
Syntax.java:10: '}' expected
}
^
```

The line in trouble is the last line of the program, and if the ∧ points *after* the last brace of the program. At first glance, you might think the compiler is wrong because it appears obvious (because of the nice indentation we used) that the } on the last line matches the { on the second line – so where's the problem? But the compile does not care for indentation – it must balance all braces. Because we forgot to match the opening brace after the for (on the 7th line), the compiler matched it with the closing brace on the 9th line; therefore, the closing brace on the last line matches the opening one on the 4th line, and the opening brace on the first line has no match! Conclusion: the compiler points you to where it *encountered* the problem, not to where the problem *originated*.

As you get more practice in programming, so you'll get more practice in resolving these types of errors. Usually, they are simple to fix because they occur only when you break the rules of the language; there is not a lot of sophistication involved.

Syntax errors will always be identified by the compiler, at the compilation stage. A program will never get to the running (execution) stage if it has syntax errors.

LOGIC ERRORS

Syntax errors are just annoying. They happen because of carelessness, typing too fast, not paying attention, etc. Logic errors are much worse, and are the greatest challenge of a programmer. What are they? Unlike syntax errors, which occur because of failure to follow the language's rules, logic errors happen when the program's logic is flawed. For example, suppose you want to create an array with the numbers 1 to 10. Here's a program that tries to do it:

```
public class Syntax
{
   public static void main(String[] args)
   {
      int a[] = new int[10];
      for (int i = 1; i <= 10; i++)
         a[i] = i;
   }
}
```

It seems innocent enough: we run a for loop from 1 to 10, assigning the running number to the corresponding element of the array. What do you expect would happen? This is what you'll get:

```
java.lang.ArrayIndexOutOfBoundsException: 10
   at Syntax.main(Syntax.java:7)
Exception in thread "main"
```

We get an "array out of bound" error with the value 10. Why? Array indexes start at 0, so this array has valid index values of 0–9 (you can refresh your memory by looking at *"Arrays"*); 10 is beyond the end of the array, and we didn't assign any value to the first (index of 0) element. Logic error!

Logic errors happen when you run (execute) your program. Only then does the computer perform the instructions that make up the program, and if it "gets into trouble", it announces the error. Logic errors vary from the simple (like the one you just saw) to very complex. Sometimes they show up as error messages, other times they are discovered because of bad results from the program. They are an expected part of the life of a programmer. The trick is to make sure that you get all of them out of your program, so that the program works the way it's supposed to.

DEBUGGING

Most programs do not work the first time they are run. They frequently contain errors, known as **bugs**. Legend has it that the late Rear Admiral Grace Murray Hopper, who is considered the first programmer, coined this term in the late 1940's when she traced an error in the Mark II computer to a moth trapped in a relay; since then, whenever a computer has a problem, it's referred to as a bug.

The process of getting rid of all the errors (bugs) in your program is called **debugging**. There are many techniques for debugging programs, and they depend on the type of program and the tools available. It is beyond the scope of this book to discuss this subject. In fact, it is considered more an art than a science – as you dive deeper and deeper into programming, you will develop your own style and technique for debugging. However, remember this: all programs have bugs, but good programs have only a few and they are well hidden…

Glossary

A

Algorithm · *A step-by-step procedure for solving a problem in a finite number of steps.*
Allocate · *Reserve space for data.*
AND Operator · *An operator that calculates the Boolean* and *of its operands.*
Argument · *An actual value passed to a function for processing via a parameter. See **Parameter**..*
Array · *An ordered arrangement of data elements with identical data types.*
Array Index · *A number used to select an element of a list or an array.*
Assembler · *A program that converts assembly language into machine language.*
Assembly Language · *The programming language one step above machine language, where each statement corresponds to one machine language instruction.*
Assignment Conversion · *A conversion of a value prior to assigning it to a variable.*
Assignment Statement · *placing a value into a variable, giving the variable that value.*
Attribute · *A characteristic of an object.*

B

Bandwidth · *The transmission capacity of an electronic pathway such as a communications line, computer bus or computer channel. I*
Base Class · *A class which serves as a base for a derived class.*
Behavior · *The way in which an object responds to a specific set of conditions.*
Binary · *A number representation consisting of zeros and ones used by practically all computers because of its ease of implementation using digital electronics.*
Binary Decision · *A decision to choose from one of only two options.*
Binary Operator · *An operator that operates on two opernads.*
Binary Output · *Output in a binary form (internal to the computer) that is meant to be readable only by a computer.*
Binary Promotion · *A promotion involving two operands.*
Block · *A group of program statements that are treated as a unit., A group of disk or tape records that is stored and transferred as a single unit.*
Boolean · *Data that can have only one of two possible values: true or false.*
Buffer · *A region of memory used to temporarily hold data while it is being moved from one place to another.*
Bug · *An error in a program., An error in a program, named so after a moth that caused an error in the Mark II computer in the late 1940's.*
Bus · *A common pathway, or channel, between multiple devices.*
By Reference · *A reference to the argument is passed to the function, so that the original value is accessible.*
By Value · *A copy of the value of the argument is passed to the function, so that the original value is not accessible.*

C

Cache · *A temporary storage area for frequently-accessed or recently-accessed data, used to quickly move data between the memory and the CPU.*
Case-Sensitive · *Distinguishing lower case from upper case; characters must match exactly, including their case, for two strings to be equal.*
Cast · *The forced conversion of one data type into another.*
Chained Assignment · *A single statement containing a series of assignments.*
Character Output · *Output in the form of characters (letters, digits and other symbols) that is meant to be readable by humans.*
Class · *A construct that is used as a blueprint (or template) to create objects of that class.*

Comment · *A descriptive statement in a program that is used for documentation.*

Compiler · *A program that translates a program written in a high-level programming language into machine language.*

Complement · *The* opposite *value.*

Compound Assignment Operators · *An operator that performs a calculation and assigns its result to one of its operands.*

Concatenation · *The operation of joining two strings together., To join together two or more sets of data in a series or a chain to create one new big set.*

Conditional Operator · *An operator that tests for a condition and performs different operations depending on that condition.*

Consecutive · *Following one after another without interruption.*

Constant · *A value or a property that does not change., A fixed value, a value that cannot be changed.*

Constructor · *A method which is called when an object is created.*

Conversion · *Changing data from one format to another.*

CPU · *Central Processing Unit, the computing part of the computer; Also called the processor.*

Cross-Compiling · *Using a compiler on one platform to produce machine language code for another.*

Cylinder · *The set of tracks on a multi-headed disk that may be accessed without head movement. That is, the collection of disk tracks which are the same distance from the center about which the disks rotate.*

D

Data · *Information, raw facts.*

Data Type · *A category of data, a set of values from which a variable, constant, function, or other expression may take its value.*

Debugging · *The process of eliminating erros ("bugs") from a program.*

Declaration · *A statement that defines data (such as fields, variables, arrays or structures) and other resources, but does not create executable code.*

Decrement · *To subtract a number from another number; decrementing a counter means subtracting 1 (or some other number) from its current value.*

Default · *A setting or an action taken if the user has not specified otherwise.*

Default Constructor · *A constructor that is automatically generated in the absence of explicit constructors.*

Defensive Programming · *A programming style that anticipates and avoids errors by coding checks and responses to potential error situations.*

Derived Class · *See Subclass.*

Deterministic · *A system whose change over time can be predicted exactly.*

Device Driver · *A sub-program that links a peripheral device to the operating system.*

Dimension · *A measure of size, such as length, width or height.*

Directory · *A collection of files or other directories used to organize files by subjects or other common attributes.*

Disk Drive · *A peripheral storage device that holds, spins, reads and writes magnetic or optical disks.*

Dot Notation · *The syntax for connecting members to the objects to which they belong.*

Doubly-Linked List · 213

Dynamic · *An operation that is performed "on the fly," based on decisions made while the program is running rather than beforehand.*

E

Element · *A single item of data in an array or structure.*

Embedded Assignment · *An assignment that is included in another statement.*

Encapsulation · *The ability of an object to be a container (or capsule) for related properties (data variables) and methods (functions).*

Enum · *See Enumeration.*

Enumeration · *An exact listing of all the elements of a set.*

Escape Sequence · *A command that starts with an escape character.*

Evaluation · *Converting an expression into a value by applying the operators to the operands and performing the specified calculations.*

Exclusive OR Operator · *See **XOR Operator**.*

Executable Program · *A program in machine language which is ready to be executed*

Execute · *See **Run**.*

Expression · *A combination of operators and operands (literals and variables) which describes a caluclation and produces a value.*

F

File · *A collection of data or information which is available to a computer program and is usually based on some kind of durable storage., A collection of bytes stored as an individual entity.*

Final · *A variable which cannot have its value changed, a method which cannot be overridden, or a class which cannot be extended.*

Floating Point Number · *A number that can have its decimal point in any position.*

Folder · *Another name for a **directory**.*

For Loop · *A loop construct which executes one or more statements (the "loop body") repeatedly so long as some condition evaluates to true, and includes the loop set up and loop control.*

Formatted Output · *Output that has a user-controlled structure.*

Funcation Call · *A statement that requests services from another function or program by temporarily transferring to it control of execution.*

Function · *See Method., A self-contained software routine that performs a job for the program it is written in or for some other program.*

G

Getter · *A method whose name starts with "get", takes no parameters, and returns the value of an object's attributes.*

H

Head · *The first element in a list., A component of a hard disk drive that reads (senses) and writes (records) data on a magnetic disk or tape.*

I

Identifier · *A sequence of characters that identifies a programming entity (such as a variable, function, or structure).*

If Statement · *A statement performing a decision based on a condition.*

Immutable · *A variable or a value which cannot be changed.*

Import · *A statement which is used to reference classes and interfaces declared in other classes or packages.*

Increment · *To add a number to another number; incrementing a counter means adding 1 (or some other number) to its current value.*

Indent · *To align text some number of spaces to the right of the left margin.*

Inheritance · *The capability of a class to use the properties and methods of another class while adding its own functionality.*

Initializer · *An expression whose value is used as the initial value of a variable.*

Input/Output Services · *Sub-programs that manage the transfer of data between the CPU and peripheral devices.*

Insert · *Place an element between to other elements.*

Instantiation · *The creation of a real object as an instance of a class.*

Integer · *A whole number.*

Interactive Program · *A program whose input and output are interleaved, like a conversation, allowing the user's input to depend on earlier output from the same run.*

Interface · *A collection of methods exposed by an object, defining its interaction with other objects.*

Internet Service Provider · *An organization that provides access to the Internet.*

Interpreter · *A program which executes source code by reading it one line at a time and performing each instruction immediately.*

Invoke · *To activate a function. See also **Function Call**.*

ISP · *See **Internet Service Provider**.*

L

Leading Zeros · *Zeros to the left of a number used to fill a field and do not affect the numerical value of the data.*

Left-Associative Operator · *An operator whose operands are evaluated left-to-right.*

Linear · *Sequential allong a straight line.*

Linked List · *A method of allocating memory for multiple elements where each element points to the next element.*

Literal · *An explicit value that remain unchanged.*

Loop Index · *A variable that controls the number of times a loop is repeated.*

M

Machine Instruction · *An instruction in machine language.*

Machine Language · *The language which is actually read and understood by the computer, consisting of instructions written in binary code that a computer can execute directly.*

Member · *An attribute or a method that belongs to a class.*

Method · *A group of instructions that is given a name and can be called up at any point in a program simply by using that name.*

Multi-Tasking · *Providing concurrent execution of multiple tasks or programs.*

N

Name/Value Pair · *A data representation where each element specifies the name of the an attribute and its value.*

NOT Operator · *An operator that calculates the complement of its operand.*

Numeric · *Data in the form of numbers, specifically quantities used for calculation.*

O

Operand · *An entity on which an operation is performed, or data to be operated on.*

Operating System · *The main control program of a computer that schedules tasks, manages storage, and handles communication with peripherals.*

Operator · *A symbol used to perform an operation on some value or values.*

OR Operator · *An operator that calculates the Boolean or of its operands.*

Overflow · *An error condition that results when a numeric value is so large that the number cannot fit in the area allocated for it.*

Overloading · *The ability to define multiple methods with the same name. but with otherwise different signatures, in the same class., The ability to use the same name for more than one function with different number of parameters and types, requiring the compiler to differentiate them based on context.*

Override · *Replacement of a method in a superclass by a method in a subclass with the same signature (name, plus the number and the type of its parameters) and return type.*

P

Parallel · *Side by side, at the same time.*

Parameter · *A variable representing a value to be passed as an argument to a function for processing. See* **Argument**.

Parsing · *To analyze a set of data and break it into its individual components.*

Pattern · *A plan or a model to be followed in making things.*

Peripheral · *Any hardware device connected to a computer; any part of the computer outside the CPU and working memory*

Pointer · *A variable which contains a reference to a value (instead of the value itself)., See* **Reference**

Polymorphism · *The ability of one data type to appear as and be used like another data type.*

Portability · *The ease with which a program can be made to run on other platforms without modifications.*

Postfix · *To put or attach after or in at the end of.*

Precedence · *Priority in the order in which an expression is evaluated.*

Precision · *The number of digits used to express the fractional part of a number; the more digits, the more precision.*

Prefix · *To put or attach before or in front of.*

Primitive Data Type · *A fundemental data type that is built into the language.*

Private · *An access modifier, used before a method or other class member to indicate that the member can only be accessed from within the class, and not from any subclass.*

Program · *A sequences set of instructions that tell the computer what to do and how to do it.*

Promotion · *Automatically converting operands of an operator to a common type so that the operation can be performed.*

Property · *A characteristic of an object.*

Protected · *An access modifier, used before a method or other class member to indicate that the member can be accessed only by classes in the same package, or subclasses.*

Pseudo Code · *A language resembling a programming language but not intended for actual compilation.*

Public · *An access modifier, used before a method or other class member to indicate that the member can only be accessed any other class or subclass.*

R

Raw Data · *See* **Binary Output**.

Reference · *A value or a variable that is used to point to some other variable, value, element or object.*

Register · *A small component inside the CPU that holds values of internal operations, such as the address of the instruction being executed and the data being processed.*

Relational Operator · *An operator that compares two values.*

Remainder · *The number left over when one integer is divided by another.*

Reverse Engineering · *The process of analyzing an existing system to identify its components and their relationships.*

Right-Associative Operator · *An operator whose operands are evaluated right-to-left.*

Root · *The top-level node in a tree.*

Run · *To perform the instructions that make up a program.*

S

Scheduling · *Allocating CPU time to various tasks in an optimal and fair way.*

Scientific Notation · The display of numbers in floating point form. The number is always equal to or greater than one and less than 10, and the base is 10.

Scope · *The region of a program within which a variables is known.*

Sector · *The smallest unit of storage read or written on a disk.*

Seed · *A* number *used to initialize a pseudorandom number generator.*

Sentinel · *A mark of the beginning or end of an ordered collection of information., A value or an element that marks the end of a sequence of data.*

Sequential · *One after the other in some consecutive order, such as by name or number.*

Sequential Allocation · *A method of allocating memory for multiple elements where each element is allocated memory immediately following the previous one.*

Serial · *One after the other, one at a time.*

Setter · *A method whose name starts with "set", takes one parameter and sets the value of an object's attribute.*

Side-Effect · *Unexpected results of an action, which affect parts of the system other than the ones on which the action was performed.*

Signature · *The minimum information required to uniquely define a method, usually includes the method's name, and the number, order and types of its parameters.*

Sort · *To organize information in a desired order.*

Source Program · *A program in the original language as written by the programmer, which must be translated into a machine-language for the computer to run it.*

Statement · *An instruction written in a high-level programming language, directing the computer to perform specified actions.*

Static · *A variable which has one copy per class, not one for each object, no matter how many instance of a class might exist., Something that is fixed and unchanging.*

Stored Program · *The fundamental computer architecture in which the computer executes instructions stored in its memory.*

Stream · *A representation of an input source or an output destination.*

Structured Programming · *A techniques that impose rules of logical structure on the writing of a program.*

Subclass · *A class which extends a base class, to derive a new class with all the base's variables and methods, plus some of its own.*

Superclass · *A class which is extended by a sublass.*

T

Tail · *The last element in a list.*

Ternary Operator · *An operator that operates on three opernads.*

Text · *Data in the form of alphanumeric (letters and digits) characters as well as special symbols (such as punctuation).*

Throw · *Interrupt the execution flow of the current method and deliver an exception object to the caller.*

Token · *A portion of a string, such as a work or a number, separated from other portions of the string by a standard set of delimiters, such as spaces or punctuation marks., A string composed of a combination of characters, making a grammatically indivisible unit of a language (such as a keyword, an operator or a name).*

Trie · *An ordered tree data structure that is used to store an associative array where the keys are usually strings.*

Truncation · *To cut off leading or trailing digits from an item of data without regard to the accuracy of the remaining data.*

Try-Catch Block · *A statement which encloses code that can cause errors and code to handle those errors.*

U

Unary Operator · *An operator that operates on one operand.*

Unary Promotion · *A promotion involving only one operand.*

Unformatted Output · *Output that does not have a pre-defined or user-controlled structure.*

V

Value · *The result of a calculation or of an operation.*

Variable · *A location in memory referred by a name and contains a data value that can be changed.*

Video · *The visual display of information on a computer screen.*

Virtual Machine · *An abstract machine that is independent of the actual machine on which it is implemented.*

W

While Loop · *A loop construct which executes one or more statements (the "loop body") repeatedly so long as some condition evaluates to true.*

White Space · *A contiguous sequence of spaces, tabs, carriage returns, and line feeds.*

X

XML · *Extensible Markup Language.*

XOR Operator · *An operator that calculates the Boolean* exclusive or *of its operands.*

CPSIA information can be obtained
at www.ICGtesting.com
Printed in the USA
LVOW03s2341061215

465688LV00009B/37/P